BLACK SEA BATTLEGROUND
THE ROAD TO UKRAINE

Washington, DC
March 2023

THE JAMESTOWN FOUNDATION

1310 L Street NW
Suite 810
Washington, DC 20005
http://www.jamestown.org

Copyright © 2023 The Jamestown Foundation

All rights reserved. Printed in the United States of America. No part of this book may be reproduced in any manner whatsoever without written consent.

For copyright and permissions information, contact The Jamestown Foundation, 1310 L Street NW, Suite 810, Washington, DC 20005.

This publication is a compilation of reports completed for the project "Black Sea Battleground: Risks and Challenges in Europe's Threatened Frontier." The project was supported by the Smith Richardson Foundation and The Jamestown Foundation.

The views expressed in the book are those of the contributors and not necessarily those of The Jamestown Foundation or any other organization or government.

For more information on this book, email pubs@jamestown.org.

ISBN: 979-8-9874519-1-5

Cover art provided by Peggy Archambault of Peggy Archambault Design, archdesign1.com.

Jamestown's Mission

The Jamestown Foundation's mission is to inform and educate policymakers and the broader community about events and trends in those societies that are strategically or tactically important to the United States but that frequently restrict access to such information.

Using indigenous and primary sources, Jamestown's material is delivered without political bias, filter or agenda. It is often the only source of information that should be, but is not always, available through official or intelligence channels, especially in regards to Eurasia and terrorism.

Origins

Founded in 1984 by William Geimer, The Jamestown Foundation made a direct contribution to the downfall of Communism through its dissemination of information about the closed totalitarian societies of Eastern Europe and the Soviet Union.

William Geimer worked with Arkady Shevchenko, the highest-ranking Soviet official ever to defect when he left his position as undersecretary general of the United Nations. Shevchenko's memoir *Breaking With Moscow* revealed the details of Soviet superpower diplomacy, arms-control strategy and tactics in the Third World at the height of the Cold War. Through its work with Shevchenko, Jamestown rapidly became the leading source of information about the inner workings of the captive nations of the former Communist Bloc.

In addition to Shevchenko, Jamestown assisted former top Romanian intelligence officer Ion Pacepa in writing his memoirs. Jamestown ensured that both men published their insights and experience in what became bestselling books. Even today, several decades later, some credit Pacepa's revelations about Nicolae

ii | BLACK SEA BATTLEGROUND

Ceausescu's regime in his bestselling book *Red Horizons* with the fall of that government and the freeing of Romania.

The Jamestown Foundation has emerged as a leading provider of information about Eurasia. Our research and analysis on conflict and instability in Eurasia has enabled Jamestown to become one of the most reliable sources of information on the post-Soviet space, the Caucasus, Central Asia, as well as China. Furthermore, since 9/11, Jamestown has used its network of indigenous experts in more than 50 different countries to conduct research and analysis on terrorism and the growth of al-Qaeda and its offshoots throughout the globe.

By drawing on our ever-growing global network of experts, Jamestown has become a vital source of unfiltered, open-source information about major conflict zones around the world—from the Black Sea to Siberia, from the Persian Gulf to Latin America and the Pacific. Our core of intellectual talent includes former high-ranking government officials and military officers, political scientists, journalists, scholars and economists. Their insight contributes significantly to policymakers engaged in addressing today's newly emerging global threats in the post-9/11 world.

Table of Contents

Acknowledgments vii

Introduction. viii

1. Seven Years of Deadlock: Why Ukraine's Military Reforms Have Gone Nowhere, and How the US Should Respond
   Glen Grant. 1

2. Blind, Confuse and Demoralize: Russian Electronic Warfare Operations in Donbas
   Sergey Sukhankin. 49

3. Guardian of the Danube: Romania's Mixed Progress in Implementing a Black Sea Strategy
   George Visan 72

4. Bulgaria's Black Sea Dilemma: NATO Ally or Russian Gateway
   Valeri R. Ratchev, Todor Tagarev 107

5. Water Crises and the Looming Ecological Catastrophe in Occupied Crimea and Devastated Donbas
   Alla Hurska. 137

6. Vulnerable Arteries: Severe Challenges to the Security of Ukraine's Internal Waterways
   Andrii Ryzhenko. 170

7. Neutrality With No Guarantees: The Evolution of Moldova's Defense and Security Policies
   Dumitru Minzarari 190

iv | BLACK SEA BATTLEGROUND

8. Referee and Goalkeeper of the Turkish Straits: The Relevance and Strategic Implications of the Montreux Convention for Conflict in the Black Sea
John C. K. Daly 223

9. Arsenal of Empire: Russian Naval Construction in Crimea and Its Implications for Black Sea Security
Ihor Kabanenko. 260

10. Turkish Drone Strategy in the Black Sea Region and Beyond
Can Kasapoglu. 289

Author Biographies 308

Map 1. Black Sea Region

Acknowledgments

In preparing this collection of essays, there are numerous persons we would like to thank and acknowledge for their critical roles in this project. First of all, we would like to thank the 11 authors for writing the project's ten essays and for pulling together their in-depth research. All are experts on the Black Sea region and come from diverse backgrounds. And many are former senior policymakers in their respective countries who were intimately involved in national security decision-making.

Furthermore, the most challenging parts of any project involving various non-native English speakers are the editing process, procurement of each essay and organization of the respective topics to be the most effective. This involves constant correspondence in integrating the changes made throughout the publication process. None of this would be possible without the role played by superb editors. Luckily, Jamestown has always been blessed in this regard. Matt Czekaj, formerly of The Jamestown Foundation and his successor, Joseph Bebel, a Senior Program Associate for Europe and Eurasia, played a key role in this process. Both contributed to the editing, design layout and creation of this book. I am grateful for their assistance in this endeavor.

Special thanks are also extended to the Board of Directors of The Jamestown Foundation for providing us with the opportunity to focus on the Black Sea region and offer this important work as a reference tool to policymakers in the United States and around the world. As the Russian war against Ukraine continues, one can be sure that research material on the battleground unfolding in and around the Black Sea will be relevant for years to come.

Introduction

The Russian re-invasion of Ukraine on February 24, 2022, is a major turning point for the West in how it deals with a strategically important country straddling Europe and Asia, currently involved in Europe's largest land war since the end of World War II. More importantly, it underscores how critical Ukraine is to the strategy of the United States and its North Atlantic Treaty Organization (NATO) allies in the Black Sea region. For centuries, the Black Sea has been a cockpit of rivalry and confrontation between competing powers, mostly involving Ottoman Turkey and Imperial Russia, as the scales ebbed and flowed back and forth between these two regional rivals.

Geography often has a way of determining battlegrounds, and the Black Sea is no different. Ask almost any expert what part of the Black Sea is synonymous with the term "battleground" and they would say Crimea. Since the Crimean War (1855–1856) the focal point of grand strategy in the Black Sea has been all about controlling the strategic peninsula and its naval base at Sevastopol. The struggle for Crimea is no different than the contest for the other great peninsula that has dominated Mediterranean geopolitics since the rise of ancient Rome, commonly referred to as the "Italian boot."

The Crimean Peninsula traditionally has been viewed as a platform for projecting Tsarist power not only into the Black Sea but also into the Mediterranean, where Russian, and later Soviet, naval squadrons affected the naval balance of power during the Cold War. It was not until Catherine the Great's annexation of Crimea in 1783, ousting the Crimean Tatar Khanate from power, that Tsarist Russia turned Crimea into a naval base, beginning its efforts to dominate the Black Sea. One should bear in mind what the noted geopolitician Zbigniew Brzezinski once said: "Without Ukraine, Russia ceases to be a Eurasian empire." And taking this statement a step further, one can argue that Russia ceases to be a Black Sea power without Crimea. Except for Brzezinski, few

Introduction | ix

policymakers in the West really understood how pivotal Ukraine was to Russia's great-power ambitions.

In both World War I and World War II, the Black Sea largely served as a side theater to the Allied powers, as Western Europe dominated their attention. With the closure of the Turkish Straits during both wars, the Black Sea became a military theater where naval forces were used in auxiliary roles to land-based operations in a clash of titans between the Soviet Union and Nazi Germany. When German forces advanced into Eurasia and the Soviets later recovered the territory lost during Hitler's 1941 invasion, Crimea played a prominent role in both Soviet and German strategy. With the Nazi defeat and the start of the Cold War, the Black Sea became a "Soviet Lake" and largely vanished from Western strategic thinking until the collapse of the Soviet Union in 1991.

If one looks back at the history of modern conflict and warfare in the Black Sea, a common theme that is repeated again and again is that warfare was greatly affected by the opening and closure of the Turkish Straits. Once the Bosporus was closed, the continental powers of Nazi Germany and the Soviet Union fought a bitter contest for control in and around Crimea, competing over the land corridors adjoining the Crimean Peninsula as part of their tug of war over Ukraine. The geopolitical importance of this area was recognized as early as 1944 by the Dutch American geopolitcian Nicholas Spykman, who referred to this region as the "Eurasian Rimland."[1]

Spykman believed that control over this part of the Eurasian Rimland would serve as both a chokepoint and gateway that could affect world geopolitics. Today, this is evidenced by the war in Ukraine and the grain convoys exporting Ukrainian wheat,

---

[1] Nicholas John Spykman, *The Geography of the Peace*, edited by Helen R. Nicholl (New York: Harcourt, Brace, 1944), 43. Also see Spykman's classic work: *America's Strategy in World Politics: The United States and the Balance of Power* (New York: Institute of International Studies, Yale University, 1942). For a discussion of the Rimland thesis see: Robert D. Kaplan: *The Revenge of Geography* (New York: Random House, 2012), 88–102.

fertilizers and corn from the Black Sea to the hungry nations of Africa and Asia, particularly China, which consumed all of its exports of Ukrainian corn in 2022 via the grain convoys. And here, the Turkish Straits and Turkey's control over the waterway checkmate geography, limiting Russia's ability to use Crimea to project power beyond the Black Sea. Turkey's ability to block and even regulate Russian transit to and from the Bosporus has been an irritant to the Kremlin for centuries and affects the egress of regional and outside powers controlling the nature of land and naval warfare in the Black Sea and its surrounding areas.

Closure of the straits in World War I and Britain's inability to import grain from the Black Sea as a result led to the ill-fated Gallipoli expedition in 1916 and Allied efforts to knock Ottoman Turkey out of the war.[2] In the book, *Seapower: The History and Geopolitics of the World's Oceans*, retired US Admiral James G. Stavridis alluded to this when he wrote that, during the Cold War, the Black Sea was a no-go area for US naval operations and was referred to as the "sea of death" in US naval circles due to the risk of conflict with the Soviets there.[3] According to Stavridis, US naval forces avoided even entering the Black Sea because it was encircled by the Soviet Union and its Warsaw Pact allies, with Turkey being the lone NATO member in the region.

Fast forward to the present, and the strategic situation is vastly different. The Black Sea is now bordered by three NATO member states, while the Russian Federation is at a geopolitical disadvantage. Russia offsets this disadvantage in turn by courting Turkey. Due to the war between Russia and Ukraine, Turkey has sought to contain the conflict and limit access by enacting the 1936 Montreux Convention, closing the Turkish Straits to outside naval powers. By doing so, Ankara prevents Moscow from sending any new warships into the Black Sea, thus creating a naval stalemate that relegates the Russo-Ukrainian war to its two

---

[2] Paul G. Halpern, The Mediterranean Naval Situation: 1908–1914 (Harvard: MA: Harvard University Press, 1971), 1.
[3] Admiral James Stavridis, *Sea Power: The History and Geopolitics of the World's Oceans* (London: Penguin Books, June 2018), 133.

continental combatants. As before, the Black Sea remains a key battleground and a new frontline between Russia and the West. With this in mind, the specific aim of this collection of essays is to enhance readers understanding about the various dimensions of the Black Sea regional security environment prior to Russia's re-invasion of Ukraine on February 24, 2022. With this baseline in mind, the project began prior to the Russian re-invasion and offers policymakers the opportunity to familiarize themselves with the salient security issues affecting the Black Sea up to the outbreak of the war. Our book offers regional perspectives, assessments of military technology and regional geography issues, including how water and ecological issues are affecting Crimea. It also sheds light on the nature of Ukrainian military reforms prior to Russia's re-invasion and explains the electronic warfare lessons learned by Russia up to February 2022.

Crimea has historically played a central role in the history of Russian military technology and naval development as an arsenal of empire for Tsarist and Soviet Russia. One key issue of this collection in this respect is an assessment of Crimea's role as an arsenal of empire for Russian naval modernization and development, which has been largely ignored by Western experts since the Russian re-annexation of Crimea in 2014.

Turning to other issues, this volume also includes topics related to the regional issues and strategic concerns of Ukraine's Black Sea neighbors. Wedged between Ukraine and Romania, Moldova continues to deal with the lingering Russian military presence in Transnistria, and the breakaway region's hold over the vast arsenal of weapons and ammunition stored at the Cobasna arms depot should not be ignored. Through its Transnistrian proxy, Russia has the ability to menace the pro-Western government in Moldova and has done so since the country became independent in 1991. Moldova remains poorly understood in Western policy circle, and this volume contains a rare essay addressing the evolution, development and numerous weaknesses in Moldovan defense and security policies.

Security perspectives from Bulgaria and Romania are also represented in this collection. The importance of these two countries in Black Sea security has been poorly understood in the West due to the traditional American weakness in understanding the geography of Eastern Europe. Romania is and will remain the guardian of the Danube, and thus, it is crucial to understand Romania's historical role in securing this strategic waterway since World War I.

No discussion of Black Sea security is complete without an explanation of Turkish strategic perspectives in the region. Turkey remains both the referee and goalkeeper of the Turkish Straits, and no matter how much some might dislike Turkey's ability to regulate commercial and military traffic coming into the Black Sea, the 1936 Montreux Convention will continue to affect US and NATO strategy in the region for the foreseeable future, unless the agreement is modified to allow outside powers unhindered access to the Black Sea.

In light of Montreux's vast importance, this volume contains an assessment of the role that the Convention has played in the region up to and since the outbreak of the war in Ukraine. Aside from this, we also present an excellent essay on the role played by Turkish drone technology in reshaping the security of Ukraine through Turkish technology transfers. Turkish support for Ukraine will also continue to influence battlefield developments in the ongoing war as a key technological conduit to not only Ukraine but also several NATO member states, ranging from Norway and Poland to Latvia and Romania—all of which have become part of the Turkish drone nexus.

Finally, it is our hope that this volume of essays will serve as a useful policy tool for experts to consult and refer to as they watch the war in Ukraine evolve. As the conflict enters its second year, it remains abundantly clear that Russia's war against Ukraine will make the Black Sea a key battleground for years to come.

Glen E. Howard
President
The Jamestown Foundation

1.

Seven Years of Deadlock: Why Ukraine's Military Reforms Have Gone Nowhere, and How the US Should Respond

Glen Grant

July 16, 2021

It is remarkable and stretching credibility that, after seven years of war, neither the Ukrainian military nor the defense industry has undergone any substantial or lasting reforms. Historically, during the two world wars of the early 20th century, fear of losing created powerful motivations on all sides to adopt changes and innovations in every aspect of defense. These wars drove the creation of new forces, such as the Special Air Service; innovations, including the tank, long-range rockets and drones; and, of course, the nuclear bomb. But more than seven years since losing Crimea, as fighting has engulfed eastern Donbas, Ukraine has made virtually no more changes than would have occurred naturally by evolution over time or in reaction to Russian attacks. Moreover, even those incremental developments have totally and utterly failed to create a sensible military answer. This sounds inexplicable, but it is completely true.

The following chapter describes how and why this has happened, as well as the reasons this trend continues to this day. The survey and analysis consists of three main parts. First, the background

2 | BLACK SEA BATTLEGROUND

section covers the war and sets the scene for the huge external support and reform efforts that followed. Then, the chapter describes why little reform actually occurred, despite the willingness, high energy and resources of the United States and North Atlantic Treaty Organization (NATO) allies to help. Within Ukraine, there has been little or no political direction or support for change, rhetoric to the contrary notwithstanding. The bones and flesh of the military system remain steadfastly Soviet both in approach and methods, underpinned by a strong legacy of Soviet laws, rules and regulations. Secrecy is ubiquitous. The arguably broken system is strongly maintained by officers and staff averse to change and quick to punish. The procurement system remains steadfastly dysfunctional, though positive changes to the law were supposed to usher in competition and transparency.

Second, the paper examines why the "Gold Standard" support system of the US does not function as hoped. Especially in Ukraine, explanation is needed as to why this program is not creating the desired effects. This study, thus, highlights various factors, including insufficient understanding of the culture and organization as well as dysfunctionality stemming from a lack of conditionality for the aid.

Third, this review suggests how to take US support forward, including the recommendation to assign a single military commander to the process who will be focused on reform and spending, as well as putting a stronger emphasis on selection and training of personnel.

Throughout this chapter, it is important to keep in mind that the Ukrainian military, from the political leadership down to the basic soldier, functions as one of the last vestiges of the Communist and Soviet system. The pathologies run deep. It is not representative of the vast body of Ukrainian society but rather should be seen as a historic anomaly in a country that is slowly modernizing.

Background

Ukraine has one of the most complex post-Communist defense and security systems remaining in the former Soviet, Warsaw Pact and Yugoslav spaces. While the war and allied support has ensured that Ukrainian front-line soldiers have improved greatly, the defense system itself is clearly and publicly broken at the organizational level—perhaps beyond repair, according to many defense-supporting activists. Before 2014, Ukraine's defense forces were encouraged to be "friends" with their Russian allies, while the armed forces themselves were systematically destroyed and emasculated by politicians, including former president, Viktor Yanukovych. This occurred through the simple act of removing any parts of the system that could deter or fight Russia. Vast swathes of operational military equipment were sold off or stockpiled, and the most significant units were cut. Typical of these acts was the closing of the newly formed Joint Operations Command Headquarters, which had been created and developed over several years with strong US help and training. It has still not been recreated, despite the war.

Only about 50,000 soldiers could have deployed when the war in Crimea started in February 2014; but of those, "only about 6,000 were combat ready."[1] How many were ready and willing to fight remains an open question. They were never given fighting orders by the political leadership.[2] Political inaction and a strict military culture of waiting for orders meant the navy was largely lost by being bottled up in Sevastopol Bay. Many sailors committed treason and went over to work for Russia; some simply resigned. Their personal justifications included the fact that they had been born and raised in Crimea and so had no life elsewhere. Others simply despaired of the Kyiv government.

---

[1] Yuriy Rudenko, *War by the Book: War.RU* (Kyiv, Ukraine: DIPA, 2020), 21.

[2] Nazarov Victor, interview with Angelika Rudenko, Crimean News, 2014, https://ru.krymr.com/a/general-viktor-nazarov-krym-2014-intervyu/31153209.html?fbclid=IwAR1MHyrF8qfLeeCAbURVtGoXiwd UYrEO0A_8nhDDDuh--bVw1Uq6EiI1wLc.

4 | BLACK SEA BATTLEGROUND

The irony is that, since then, many of these sailors have been scattered to the four winds of Russia to serve, their ultimate loyalty to Moscow, of course, in doubt. Those who did stay loyal to Ukraine were ostracized by the General Staff in Kyiv and had to find their own accommodation in Kyiv and Odesa—and often new assignments. Many lived several years on ships in Odesa in appalling conditions. To this day, some have not been given accommodations for themselves or families, and many left the navy early in disgust and despair.

Russia's invasion of Donbas in April 2014 started slowly, with political agitation by Russian military infiltrators and in a highly confused fashion, all accompanied by a serious Russian international PR campaign suggesting that what was occurring was a civil war. The Ukrainian government with a caretaker president, Oleksandr Turchynov, was confused, frightened and slow to act because of its uncertainty over which authorities it possessed. Officials in Kyiv initially called the war an Anti-Terrorist Operation (to this day, the Donbas war area is still called the "ATO" by civil society) and gave the task of managing the situation to the security services.

The security services were quickly overwhelmed, however, as the war became hot with Russian tanks and other weapons appearing. The task then moved to the army, which was still too small and slow. Acting as taught, the Ukrainian army generals managed their forces centrally right down to platoon level, sometimes even from Kyiv. The weak army had to be quickly reinforced on the frontline by national guard and even military police units.

With a few exceptions, the troops were extremely brave but usually overwhelmed by numbers, better equipment and lack of clear orders. The so-called "humanitarian convoys" from Russia were resupplying Russian troops with ammunition and weapons. The day was saved by a civil society that mobilized. The Ukrainian Ministry of Defense and General Staff hastily created 33 small territorial defense battalions from May to August 2014. Many other volunteers from Ukraine, the diaspora and others, such as from Georgia, went to the frontline in small groups, sometimes with no uniform or weapons. They hoped to find these on arrival. This now national composite force suffered many serious losses of all units, including a transport aircraft full of reinforcement parachute soldiers shot down and a unit caught in the open by multi-barrel rocket launchers. Almost without exception, the defeats indicated that both the leadership and units were seriously unprepared for war.

Some public successes also occurred, however, such as the daring 400-kilometer raid behind enemy lines commanded by now–Lieutenant General Mykhailo Zabrodskyi, currently a member of parliament (MP).[3] The second battle of Donetsk airport saw nearly four months of public and heroic defense. The forces were eventually defeated, but the extreme bravery shown by the few Ukrainian troops there earned the soldiers a title of respect from their Russian enemy of "cyborgs."[4]

The Russian operation effectively ended with two savage defeats of the composite Ukrainian forces at Ilovaisk in August 2014 and again at Debaltseve in January 2015. In each battle, Ukrainian troops were surrounded by regular Russian forces. Many Ukrainians died and were captured. Those captured were later killed or tortured by the Russians. Because there are no records of the Ukrainian civilians who deployed, the exact numbers killed or missing will likely never be truly known. The two battles forced then-President Petro Poroshenko to sign the Minsk agreements to effectively halt the open warfare.

The second Minsk agreement, in 2015, saw the war stabilize to trench warfare. This has now dragged on for seven years, with steady and regular Ukrainian casualties. Yet, this stability should have been a chance to rebuild society and the armed forces. However, it did not work out like that. The national and senior military leadership never forgave the fact that the military failure was so obvious to all of Ukraine. The consequence was a steady attempt by the government to unravel the social gains made during the Maidan Revolution and to remove the added strength

---

[3] Rudenko, *War by the* Book, 110–117.
[4] Rudenko, *War by the Book*, 233–240.

6 | BLACK SEA BATTLEGROUND

that society had gained from fighting the war. This attack on society included trumped-up charges and prison. One political blogger summarized it thus: "Injustice became the basis of a new political order."[5]

Instead of cleaning out the failed officers from the armed forces, as the public expected, Poroshenko left the senior military intact. The response of the senior military leadership was to turn toward NATO in public pronouncements; but instead of engaging in reform, they looked backward and set out to recreate a mirror image of a "small Soviet Army,"[6] or a Russian copy. Admiral Ihor Kabanenko, a former deputy defense minister, noted that this should have been no surprise as they were "educated on [the] former Soviet System."[7] Colonel Serhii Sobko, Hero of Ukraine, recently supported this notion in a TV interview, arguing that the current Ukrainian forces are mentally and physically in a past era.[8] They talk about NATO but, in fact, try to recreate the past. The public face says one thing, but the internal workings are totally another. There has been some change, but Adm. Kabanenko has said often that much of the public face of the senior defense officials really shows skilled use of artifacts, not any desire for modernization. Most non-governmental organizations (NGO) and military observers agree with this idea totally.

---

[5] Bassarab Michaelo, "About Legitimacy," Facebook, April 3, 2021.

[6] Grant Glen, "How Ukraine Can Build an Army to Defeat Putin, *Kyiv Post*, January 31, 2018.

[7] Ihor Kabanenko, "Ukrainian Military Reform: Can the Armed Forces Escape Their Soviet Past?" (virtual, Jamestown Virtual Roundtable Discussion), comments at 18:30, March 25, 2021, https://jamestown.org/event/upcoming-virtual-roundtable-ukrainian-military-reform-can-the-armed-forces-escape-their-soviet-past/.

[8] Serhii Sobko (colonel, former brigade commander of 128th Brigade and hero of Ukraine), Interview with Tashaya Trofimova, 4Echo, https://www.facebook.com/4tv.ua/videos/2936457403257142.

Where Are We Today?

After seven years of war, defense forces remain unreformed and, in many cases, managerially dysfunctional. As recently as April 2021, public complaints have grown about poor army food,[9] even to the extent of having a special public Parliamentary Defense Committee meeting demanded by MP Solomiia Bobrovska. She had inspected the navy food and found it desperately wanting as well as a procurement monopoly.[10] Massive overpayments for defense housing projects and many other public exposures, such as poorly managed careers, continue today.[11] Medical support in the military remains dysfunctional, especially when dealing with COVID-19. Procurement is simply broken, both within the Ministry of Defense and in dealings with defense firms. Corruption and inefficiency are at the heart of all this.[12]

The mess surrounding new weapons and equipment is legion. None of these problems are new. They are repeated regularly, but despite loud pronouncements from the Ministry of Defense and sometimes sackings of staff, nothing seems to change. The usual mantra is that all is OK, we have completed thousands of NATO standards, and reform is going well.

---

[9] Lyudmila Zhukova, "Fighters of the Armed Forces of Ukraine Are Fed with Rot with Mold: A Scandal Erupted in the Network," Rbc.ua, March 26, 2021, https://www.rbc.ua/rus/styler/boytsov-vsu-kormyat-gnilem-plesenyu-seti-1616760374.html?fbclid=IwAR0rqFYIp4315sir96jdCwSS46fCe0Id3Yk h_f4-7DS89vr0KjiHmLIDUlo.

[10] Ukraine Defense and Security Committee, Verkhovna Rada, "Special Meeting on Military Food," April 14, 2021, https://www.facebook.com/watch/live/?v=1405565073111430&ref=watch_permalink.

[11] Serhii, interview. Officer talks about the Ukrainian Armed Forces (AFU) commander refusing to let him study in the US and broken promises about promotion and how the lack of proper career planning is commonplace in the AFU.

[12] Radetzky Ruslan (National Agency for the Prevention of Corruption), discussion with author, May 3, 2021.

8 | BLACK SEA BATTLEGROUND

In the military, the system is still full of "red commanders" at every level who punish those with NATO-leaning views.[13] It is, therefore, little surprise that 65 percent of soldiers are leaving after their first contract. And although the army is publicly declared to be 250,000 strong, the actual trained fighting force is closer to 130,000 and probably less. Many non-fighting soldiers are in the large Soviet legacy training and administrative structures alongside civilians and conscripts who do not deploy.

The Illusion of Defense Reform and Reaching NATO Standards

The hardest thing for outside observers to accept is that much of what they read and hear is an illusion created by the Ukrainian government and defense staffs, designed to convince their own countrymen, NATO allies and probably even Russia that reform is underway and that the armed forces are powerful and strong. Certain change is, of course, happening—there must be after more than half a decade of war. The front-line troops have improved immeasurably. Special Operations Forces (SOF) are considerably better. Some of this is because of war and the natural passage of time, but much is because of the energy and huge resources poured in by the US and NATO allies. And yet, this has not brought Ukraine the operational benefits one might have expected considering the level of the US effort. (For a more detailed description of how SOFs are reforming, see **Appendix A**.)

But at the same time, volunteer organizations are trying to stave off organizational disaster created by political and military decisions that severely degrade operational effectiveness.[14] For example, the latest naval doctrine to replace that of the US-supported Naval Doctrine 2035 is "harmful and impracticable because it is based on ambitions only and does not take into

---

[13] Joint Staff officer (name withheld), Facebook Messenger discussion with wuthor, April 26, 2021. The officer has been on many international exercises but has been punished 11 times for his pro-NATO views. He is now taking a commander to court for this.
[14] Marco Serg, Facebook post on the increasing deaths from Russian sniper fire and the lack of military support for the front line, May 3, 2021.

account the real resources of the state that can be directed to the Navy."[15] The reality is that any improvement is simply random.

Promotion to senior positions is dominated by loyalty to military and political leaders (personal, financial and material), or by bribe. Basic training concepts have changed little since Soviet times; and what the West calls "collective training," in which exercising doctrine, leadership and decision-making dominate, only exists when units deploy on NATO exercises. The system still does not recognize the need or value of this, likely as it has no basis in Soviet thinking and runs against the prevailing centralized culture.

Much of the evidence for this was collected by Come Back Alive,[16] the largest NGO supporting Ukraine's military forces in financial terms. Team members are mainly former service people who are on the frontlines weekly. They provide significant support to front-line troops, including weapons sights, drones and training, which is not provided by the armed forces themselves. They have also recently completed a survey of the army, trying to identify why volunteer (contract) soldiers are leaving in such large numbers. Other evidence comes from senior retired officers, activists and volunteers who work with units, active and reserve military in the system, and a wide range of US officials who have engaged with, or served, in Ukraine.

Before discussing the possible causes of failure to reform, one must understand how this failure manifests itself. Of the hundreds of such cases, two are especially salient: the failure of procurement by the Ministry of Defense and failed artillery reform. The first is causing operational shortages not only within the system itself but also leaving the defense industry with work but no funding.[17] The second failure by the General Staff has left a

---

[15] Ihor Kabanenko (admiral, former deputy minister), discussion with author, May 4, 2021.

[16] Save Life, website, https://savelife.in.ua/en/.

[17] Oleg Panfilovich, *Statewatch: A Number of Businesses Have Complained to the Government About the Lack of Funds to Fulfill a*

10 | BLACK SEA BATTLEGROUND

key part of the system outdated and totally unmodernized. The two, when combined, have ensured that Ukrainian artillery units are completely short of ammunition and front-line troops are at high risk of operational failure.

Procurement

The Ukrainian Ministry of Defense's procurement system is broken and has been since before the war. Historically, the defense budget was seen as a tool for supporting the party in power and enriching those in the system. This did not change after the war, and purchases were often clearly made at inflated prices. The process of purchase is archaic. The defense ministry's own website described it thus:

> Unregulated Ukrainian legislation in the sphere of public procurements, primarily paper-based document control and lack of transparent and fair tender procedures result in the inefficient use of public money and corruption. As a result, the level of logistical support of the army drops and poor-quality equipment and weapon systems are procured putting at risk [the] security of forces and the public.[18]

Even today, all the requirements are gathered on paper by the General Staff and Ministry of Defense and consolidated into one document called the "Defense Order." This secret document goes to the national legislature for authority to purchase during the year. It is valid for only one year, which makes the procurement of complex systems difficult. For cultural and historical reasons, no effective defense policy exists in Ukraine's Defense Ministry

---

Defense Order, Babel.ua, https://babel.ua/news/64643-statewatch-nizka-pidpriyemstv-poskarzhilisya-uryadu-na-vidsutnist-koshtiv-dlya-realizaciji-proyektiv-oboronnogo-zamovlennya?fbclid=IwAR0nVtXo_oYYO3KK8hsZoettJgKqWHLOOyDibmoxGY67LHIlxDwTRYc3RTY.

[18] Ministry of Defense of Ukraine, website, https://www.mil.gov.ua/en/, accessed April 18, 2021.

(despite there being a department with this name) so the listed requirements, instead of supporting the frontline, have been more to do with making money by corruption, or in propping up the moribund and Soviet-style, ministry-owned defense industry. Procurement is complicated further by excessive secrecy that does not allow anyone outside the system to see what is being put on the order—even in many cases what is being purchased.[19] In the past, many under-the-table deals occurred frequently supporting political friends of the government.[20] Parliamentary deputy Solomiia Bobrovska writes that the navy's food procurement was a monopoly in which "the state could have spared tens of millions of hryvnias, should other companies have won. ... The firm often supplies expired as well as rotten products at a price that is at least 10–20 percent higher than the market price."[21]

But it is not just basics, such as food and fuel, that are mismanaged; even technology and the modernization of equipment, management of housing and the purchase of replacement ammunition all appear dysfunctional.

The former Ministry of Defense Reform Office, a group of civilians working alongside (but *not inside*) the defense ministry since 2014, managed to persuade ministers to use the ProZorro IT-based procurement platform for competitive tendering. In a short time, 900 million hryvna (over $32 million) was saved, and the competition reduced some purchases by 40-percent below the anticipated price. Despite this, it has not stopped ministers from procuring without a competition.

The same group of civilians created a new procurement law for the parliament designed to streamline the system. This was accepted amid fanfare on July 17, 2020, as a great reform step

---

[19] Arturs Pereverziev, "Defense Secrets vs. Army Strength?: NATO's Advice to Ukraine," video interview with Bigus, April 12, 2021, https://www.youtube.com/watch?v=j7AFsSZjy6o.
[20] Pereverziev, "Defense Secrets vs. Army Strength?"
[21] Solomiia Bobrovska (member of Ukrainian Parliament and Defense Committee), notes to author, April 2021.

12 | BLACK SEA BATTLEGROUND

forward and would bring Ukraine closer to NATO.[22] But the law required that the government then tidy up the old legislation and implement the new processes. The authorities did nothing, so the new law cannot be used.

Worse, today, there is a "completely secret state defense order"[23] for 2021, the contents of which cannot even be mentioned by members of the Parliamentary Defense Committee for fear of prosecution. This order, signed five months late, has resulted in a complete paralysis of defense supply and a total unwillingness of officials to take procurement and logistical risks for fear of punishment, even with the possible approach of a wider war.

Failure to Modernize Artillery

The Ukrainian artillery came into the war with structures, equipment and manpower totally unsuited for battle. In some cases, units were expected to fight with fewer than one-quarter of the numbers of their Western counterparts. Little has changed. The staff answer has been to mothball the guns they cannot man, thus appearing to be more significant as a force than they really are.

The guns are also Soviet-produced weapons, reaching the end of their useful life. They are firing old and totally unreliable ammunition. They do not have technical support, such as modern meteorology systems or muzzle-velocity radars, to track firing speeds. Thus, ballistic accuracy is extremely limited. Worse still, the artillery processes are mainly paper-based. During the early stages of the war in 2014, a few new tablet and phone-based apps were produced. The latest of these are complex ballistic firing systems with maps, hard tested and world beating. But in seven years, the General Staff has not agreed they are militarily

---

[22] "Law on Defense Procurement Brings Ukraine Closer to NATO—Kuleba," *Ukrinform*, July 17, 2020, https://www.ukrinform.net/rubric-polytics/3065166-law-on-defense-procurement-brings-ukraine-closer-to-nato-kuleba.html.
[23] Mariana Bezuhla, Comments on the State Defense Order, Facebook, April 23, 2021.

acceptable. Nor has the military leadership delivered an alternative system. Civilian volunteers have purchased the phones and apps for the army but not in sufficient numbers to allow the units to try any modern dispersed-deployment methods. Thus, they remain easy targets for the enemy. In exercises, the staff demand the troops go back to slow 1960s-type paper calculations.[24]

The national ammunition stocks are low, causing some weapons to be withdrawn from the frontline.[25] As of April 2021, 18 explosions have occurred in ammunition and vehicle depots in Ukraine since 2014. These are likely linked to recent revelations that the Bulgarian and Czech arms depot explosions in previous years were caused by Russia.[26] Two hundred and ten thousand tons of ammunition have been lost in Ukraine, while 70,000 tons were actually fired in the war. Hardly any has been replenished. Serious shortages of 152-millimeter and rocket-launcher ammunition abound.[27] (More discussion of this issue can be found in **Appendix B**.)

The artillery commanders know what they need and want, but the General Staff and Ministry of Defense do not support them.

Lack of Political Will

The biggest factor in Ukraine inhibiting change is the lack of political will. How much of this is corruption and the influence of

---

[24] Senior Ukrainian artillery commander (name withheld), discussion with author, April 10, 2021.

[25] Roman Pagulich and Roman Rebriy, "Ammunition Famine of the Armed Forces: What Do Soldiers Have to Shoot in Economy Mode?," Zbroya Info, https://zbroya.info/uk/blog/16172_boiepripasnii-golod-zsu-chim-biitsiam-dovoditsia-striliati-v-rezhimi-ekonomiyi/.

[26] Gotev Georgi, "Bellingcat Connects the Dots Between Czech Explosion and Bulgarian Poisoning," Euractiv, https://www.euractiv.com/section/global-europe/news/bellingcat-connects-the-dots-between-czech-explosion-and-bulgaria-poisoning/.

[27] Ukrainian former Ministry of Defense advisor (name withheld), email to Glen Howard (president, Jamestown Foundation), April 10, 2021.

local oligarchs, how much is Russian influence and what can be attributed to a genuine lack of understanding of what to do is impossible to say. The first deputy chief of the Main Operations Directorate of the General Staff at the start of the war remarked, "We did not receive a single directive from the Commander-in-Chief [President Poroshenko] during 2014–2015,"[28] despite this being the height of hostilities. It appears that President Volodymyr Zelenskyy is acting in much the same way, having showed little interest in the military beyond PR opportunities. He leaves both political and military direction of the armed forces to his commander-in-chief, General Ruslan Khomchak.

The government's apparent public desire for NATO membership is not because the political elite want or like the North Atlantic Alliance (many senior officials do not, and they regularly display openly negative attitudes toward NATO values within their own commands). Rather, the objective stems from their inability to reform the security system themselves and their hopes that NATO—or the US—will bail them out. Zelenskyy, on April 6, 2021, arguably exposed his lack of confidence in his own forces when talking to NATO Secretary-General Jens Stoltenberg: "We are fully dedicated to reforms, but we cannot stop Russia just by reforming. NATO is the only way to stop the war."[29]

It is widely recognized in Ukraine that the domestic body politic and society have a weak understanding of the US and the West. Irakli Jhanashija, formerly a member of the Defense Ministry's Reform Office, suggests that the Ukrainian political leadership

---

[28] Nazarov Victor, "Threatened with Invasion: Was It Possible to Limit Russia's 'Appetites' in Crimea in 2014?," interview with Angelika Rudenko, Crimean News, 16 March 2021, https://ru.krymr.com/a/general-viktor-nazarov-krym-2014-intervyu/31153209.html?fbclid=IwAR1MHyrF8qfLeeCAbURVtGoXiwd UYrEO0A_8nhDDDuh--bVw1Uq6Eil1wLc.

[29] "The President Had a Telephone Call with the Secretary General of NATO," Official Website of the President of Ukraine, April 6, 2021, https://www.president.gov.ua/news/prezident-ukrayini-proviv-telefonnu-rozmovu-z-generalnim-sek-67813?fbclid=IwAR1mBHnF1XkrOCPZ6dizP7vE9IGMq-E_TYkkhg_cGcU6Gbepu5XmWiuzgBQ.

misinterprets NATO's true nature. As such, the politicians in Kyiv are growing increasingly intolerant of NATO delays in granting membership and what they see as added conditionalities. They think NATO owes them for fighting Russia.[30]

A Legacy of Post-Communist and Post-Soviet Culture

Ukraine's national military culture is best understood by utilizing Geert Hofstede's model as a guide. Hofstede views countries or organizations through six main cultural dimensions, four of which have strong influence in Ukraine. These four dimensions strongly influence the organization's working culture. Although the national culture today is not reflected exactly within the defense system, research shows Hofstede's findings to be remarkably fitting.[31]

The most significant for this organization is power distance, whereby workers "accept a hierarchical order in which everybody has a place and which needs no further justification." Ukraine scores an extremely high 92/100 in that category.[32] This can be compared to the low figure of 35/100 for the United Kingdom, where equality is more dominant and working life is based more on competence and results rather than power and loyalty. Observations of how people behave in the Ukrainian Ministry of Defense shows that power is everything and inequality is culturally accepted and apparently welcomed as a military right. The minister must be a strong officer, and civilians are weak. This makes the Western concept of civilian control of the military highly problematic culturally, even for the public.

---

[30] Irakly Jhanashija (advisor to Parliamentary Defense Committee and former Ministry of Defense Reform Office member), Facebook Messenger discussion with author, April 29, 2021.

[31] Glen Grant and Vladimir Milenski, "Identifying the Challenges to Defense Reform in Central and Eastern Europe: Observations from the Field," *Defense & Security Analysis* 34, no. 2 (June 2018): 191–209, https://www.tandfonline.com/doi/abs/10.1080/14751798.2018.147 8182?journalCode=cdan20.

[32] Scores can be found for most countries at: https://www.hofstede-insights.com/product/ compare-countries/.

16 | BLACK SEA BATTLEGROUND

Military commanders are lauded and revered as strong for their adherence to a culture of total discipline and control. The consequence is simple: No one will act without orders for fear of punishment. Decisions, even for the purchase of socks, are always made at the highest level. Unless an idea has the written sanction of senior leadership, it goes nowhere.

The second key dimension, "uncertainty avoidance," is even higher, at 95/100. Hofstede indicates this shows total anxiety of uncertainty and ambiguity and fear of acting in any way that might create uncertainty or ambiguity for others. Thinking and decision-making are dominated by laws, rules and regulations. Western ideas such as mission command, flexibility or proactivity are anathema. Speaking honestly can quickly result in punishment. Having to tell something unpleasant to a senior officer will cause extreme physical nervous reactions of sweating and shaking, even for generals. People simply go sick rather than deliver truth. What this means for US support is that good ideas passed on to anyone except the most senior Ukrainians are never passed on or implemented. Foreign advice is stillborn.

"Individualism" scores low, at 25/100. In sum, Ukraine is thus a collectivist culture, in which clans and group trust are seen as more important than individual performance and results. This dominates careers. Selecting loyal friends and family is always more important than performance. Status is given to seniority rather than youth and action. Adm. Kabanenko highlights four separate clans running within the Ministry of Defense, and each protects its own.[33] When linked to the previous two dimensions, it means that nothing can or will happen within a clan grouping that is contentious or could upset the apple cart. Failure to deliver results is simply overlooked.

"Masculinity" also scores low at 27/100. A high score is indicative of a competitive and results-driven country, such as the US. A low score indicates more "feminine" traits such as quality of life, being modest and not standing out from the crowd. Telling a

---

[33] Grant and Milenski, "Identifying the Challenges to Defense Reform in Central and Eastern Europe: Observations from the Field."

commander that something is not right, or worse that he might be wrong, would be seen as cultural heresy and simply unlikely to happen. Hofstede suggests that status symbols in this environment indicate power rather than masculinity—big offices, many bodyguards and fleets of colonels following you wherever you go are normal. The high uncertainty index, low individual score and the desire for harmony, taken together, suggest that whistleblowing about problems like corruption, is highly unlikely.

But one key attribute missing from Hofstede is that, during Communist and then Soviet times, Ukrainian officers were pushed aside for senior posts by their Russian counterparts, destroying serious chances of growing a national leadership culture. With a few rare exceptions since independence, that prevailing carry-over culture has shaped the officer class to act more as master sergeants than visionary strategic thinkers and leaders. When added to the national cultural drivers mentioned earlier, any change in the military becomes impossible without brutally strong top-down direction, with laws and regulations put in place first.

Defense Management: A Non Sequitur

Normally defense system management is a Ministry of Defense activity. But the Defense Ministry is not configured to do this. Historically, apart from its role as a money conduit for politics, it has worked primarily as a resource provider for the military's demands. It is more a shopping organization than a security arm of government. It has historically never made well-argued policy and still does not. Moreover, the centralized culture (and corruption) means that ministers keep all decision-making for themselves.

Today, the minister of defense *de facto* lacks real power over Commander-in-Chief Khomchak, who has a direct constitutional command line from and to the president, while the minister has neither. (Some suggest the minister of defense is even subservient to Khomchak.) Before Ukrainian independence, there was effectively no ministry, as anything of significance came by order

18 | BLACK SEA BATTLEGROUND

of Moscow. After independence, this continued, with Russians playing a major part *inside* the ministry. For example, during 2013 and right up to February 2014, then–Defense Minister Pavlo Lebedyev was a Russian passport holder. How many senior appointments inside the defense system are still of the "Russian World" (*Russkiy Mir*) is hard to judge, but a few are notable for talking a great game to NATO and allies while afterward ensuring that no reform of significance ever takes place.

Other critical problems are overbearing bureaucracy and a replication of competences. The defense system still works on paper, with brigades sending up to 40 paper returns and reports daily. The General Staff has developed a life of its own. In many functions, such as defense planning and housing, it duplicates the non-delivering Defense Ministry functions. This lack of a clear focus, responsibility and authority has further aggravated the inability to create positive change. The vertical power structure has been further reinforced by recently adopting the NATO J-code structure. Now, nine vertical power groups are run by senior generals who answer only to the commander-in-chief. They do not allow formal horizontal staffing without their orders and, usually, signed papers. Despite the war, staff activity of any kind moves with glacial slowness.

Both organizations—the Defense Ministry and the General Staff—follow two highly developed cultural habits. One is that the process is more important than the result. Hence, when a senior visitor or US adviser, such as Gen. Abizaid comes, the visit itself is seen as the work, not the outcome. Whatever is agreed on is likely to go no further than the door. Second, the complex and longwinded Soviet-style academic process of finding the right answer by "seeking the correct algorithm" dominates all thinking. This translates into further complicating everything in the system. Simplicity is not acceptable because it must be wrong. The staff turn planning documents into tortuous processes that are totally unworkable. The more complex the better. They do this because if they produced something simple and workable, they would not be considered clever. The latest complex Ukrainian doctrine on how to manage the lessons learned is a case in point.[34] Lessons can never be learned formally in the Ukraine military, because it is not acceptable to report failure. Even then, no one can work out who is responsible or will take responsibility.

It is also not clear whether the General Staff or Ministry of Defense ever really see a clear picture of what is happening on the ground.

> The Armed Force[s] of Ukraine [have] developed a culture of providing the leadership with reports that would not raise questions and blend with other paperwork. This encourages commanders to report not on the real situation—no matter how bad or good it is— but rather what the leadership expects to hear and what will not create any further hassle.[35]

This has resulted in even serious accident reports being falsified.[36]

To make matters worse, historically, the Ministry of Defense and General Staff have only communicated formally, through long-winded written papers with multiple signatures or necessarily signed by the minister or commander-in-chief himself. This has not changed despite seven years of war and often public exposure of the most ridiculous exchanges that cause national harm.

---

[34] Ukraine General Staff (2020), "Doctrine on the Study and Implementation of Experience in the Armed Forces of Ukraine," *VKP*, 7-00(01).01.

[35] "Why are Servicemen Leaving the Armed Forces?" *Come Back Alive*, 15.

[36] Brigade commander (name withheld), discussion with author, Kyiv, 2017. The discussion centered around the fact that the Army commander had ordered the brigade commander to rewrite an accident report about a mortar accident in which solders had died. Reportedly, the minister (Stepan Poltorak) would not have liked the conclusions.

20 | BLACK SEA BATTLEGROUND

The Mirage of Civilian Control

After the EuroMaidan Revolution in 2014, there was a serious attempt to bring civilian control to the Ministry of Defense. The people did not object, as they knew it was desperately needed. Many civilian experts volunteered to work and created the Reform Office within the ministry. They tried to bring sense to ministry systems in supply and logistics areas including procurement, food, uniforms, military equipment, housing and fuel.

They additionally started projects to create logistics IT systems to replace the heavy bureaucratic paper monster. But the ministry's culture of secrecy in all things has persisted (to this day); and the Reform Office was never fully integrated, with staff workspaces remaining outside the main Ministry of Defense building. Also, the pre-Maidan organizations inside the ministry remained intact and did not change to reflect the new processes or ideas.

The Reform Office nevertheless did manage to register some successes, and its presence at meetings both in the Ministry of Defense and military committees started to force a stronger focus on modernization and doing things properly. Then–Defense Minister Septan Poltorak, however, visibly used the office more as a PR exercise for the reelection of President Poroshenko and Ukraine's NATO membership drive than for creating real change; moreover, he tended to simply ignore recommendations that did not suit his purpose. Ukraine briefly experimented with appointing a civilian defense minister, Andriy Zagorodnyuk (August 29, 2019–March 4, 2020), but his attempts to curb corruption quickly resulted in him being replaced.

When the next minister of defense, Gen. Andriy Taran, arrived, he immediately closed the Reform Office despite it having strong international backing. He also removed the Civilian Council, which had provided oversight and advice to the minister; and he illegally sacked the key reform advisor, Capt. Andrii Ryzhenko, the architect, with US support, of post-Maidan Ukraine's naval reform. All this happened without comment from the Presidential Office or the cabinet.

Finally, civilian control is severely distorted by the oligarchs. They manipulate the appointment of senior posts throughout government. The current commander-in-chief, Khomchak, is reputedly associated with billionaire Ihor Kolomoisky.[37] The oligarchs wish to run business opaquely, which allows them to continue stealing money from the Ministry of Defense budget. They do not want changes toward NATO, and this can be judged by how they distort procurement away from real operational requirements toward big-ticket items in which the oligarchs have financial interests.

Education and Training

Some military personnel now study and train toward NATO standards with assistance from the US and its allies. However, this occurs almost exclusively at the tactical level. At the strategic and operational levels, education and training are still predominantly Soviet, including the teaching of Soviet operational art. To become a defense lecturer at Ukraine's National Defense University (NDU) means devoting four years away from the mainstream military to gain a doctorate degree in military science—a field that does not exist in the West.

All PhD education for future NDU lecturers comes from the old school. Normal Western practice, in which an officer teaches straight after operations while those lessons are still fresh in the mind, does not happen in Ukraine. Thus, the Soviet cycle of education at NDU continues unbroken. After basic officer school, no effective operational courses exist, as these are classroom-based at NDU. This leaves a comprehensive knowledge gap of vital field work at company, battalion and brigade command levels. Proper staff training also does not happen. Some of the knowledge that might help brigade commanders is taught in a two-year course at NDU—but bizarrely not until after completing their command.

---

[37] On Ties, "Ruslan Khomchak—Known for the New Chief of the General Staff of Ukraine," *Strana.ua*, May 22, 2019, https://onties.com/ukraine/ruslan-khomchak-known-for-the-new-chief-of-the-general-staff-of-ukraine/.

A fundamental difference also exists conceptually between the mission command process taught by the US and allies and the orders thinking process of Ukrainian officers. But Ukrainians think it is the same, and allies think the Ukrainians understand Western thinking. But due to the cultural drivers, both sides could not be more wrong.

Defense Industry: Research and Development and Procurement Support

The best illustration of the government-controlled defense industry is that, after seven years of war, the tank factory is bankrupt. The second best is that it has taken this many years to create the first national ammunition factory, which, in fact, is still a long way from producing workable artillery ammunition. The publicly owned defense-industrial umbrella corporation, Ukroboronprom, is being reformed and is now officially profitable. But while the government supports this, it does nothing for the independent defense manufacturers who are producing world-class equipment such as modern hybrid-drive armored vehicles, attack drones, anti-sniper radars, command-and-control systems and technological advancements for both direct and indirect weapon sights. For their own private reasons, the Ukrainian Ministry of Defense and General Staff shun virtually all these advancements. Importantly, these firms are not corrupt.

The official Ukrainian military research and development institutions are still manned with Soviet "leaders" with no knowledge of NATO or English. They are confident in their positions not because they are creative but because first they prepare PhD dissertations for high-ranking Defense Ministry and General Staff officials (who do not write their own). And second, they form an incestuous grouping with the military staff and defense industry to unfairly set up and manipulate the technical requirements for new equipment and weaponry.[38] This also

---

[38] Private defense industry leaders (UARPA, ELEKS, Turingismus, Arey and others), discussions with author, 2017–2021.

ensures that they focus on what they already know and do not support possible advancements that might come from outside.

Reserves

If one takes the General Staff at its word, Ukraine has 25 territorial defense brigades, totaling 100,000 ordinary, private Ukrainian citizens. But how many people regularly go to reserve military training and education is a mystery to society. Even after changes to the Budget Code in 2018, which legally allowed spending on training, it is clear "the authorities lack the desire and understanding of how to finance [territorial] defense."[39] In reality, there is little, or no training, and the reserves make their dissatisfaction publicly clear. Territorial defense is a public wish. It has been given to the Ministry of Defense to organize but with no change in the defense budget.

Wrong Incentives at Every Level

Come Back Alive sums up the problem of incentives for the forces simply:

> In most cases the military is still using the negative motivation system... This legacy is based on an inappropriate attitude to individual servicemen and seeing the Armed Forces of Ukraine as a conscription-based army, despite the declared intentions to make it professional and join NATO.[40]

The NGO further comments, after its recent survey of the army:

> The respondents have repeatedly stated that the Armed Forces as an institution has a massive lack of such values as respect, justice, trust, efficiency and

---

[39] Eugene Rudenko and Eldar Sarakhman, "Guerrillas for Putin. Who and How Will Defend Kyiv in the Event of a Full-Scale Russian Invasion?" *Ukraine Pravda*, April 2, 2021, https://www.pravda.com.ua/articles/2021/04/2/7288704/.
[40] Come Back Alive, *Why are Servicemen Leaving the Armed Forces?*, 18.

rationality, and instead, indifference, humiliation, distrust, ostentation and arrogance are common.[41]

But the non-governmental group suggests change can happen as "such kind of behaviour is very rare for young officers, commanders with combat experience and older people who have experience in international missions and operations."[42] The problem is keeping these good people serving, because on top of the systemically poor value system, the pay scales also provide disincentives to perform: "The existing payroll system is not encouraging servicemen to grow professionally and get promoted and get a higher responsibility."[43]

Pay is loaded positively for soldiers on operations, but soldiers in barracks receive the same salary as a cashier at McDonalds. This has perverse effects, as married service people cannot possibly support families on the low pay when back in camp. Additionally, training instructors are deemed to be in barracks and, thus, are on the lowest pay for their rank.

The staff often must trawl for anyone to teach courses even if they have no knowledge of the subject. This severely limits the ability to conduct quality training. When no foreign instructors are present, the result is that courses can be run with limited military content. The students all too often know more than those teaching them.

Is Reform Possible?

Reform expert Vladimir Milenski from Bulgaria explains the challenge for Ukraine: The main problem with defense reform is that it is expected to be completed by the defense system itself. To work, the reform process must be separated from defense management because it is this same management that created the failures in the first place. The same top people are now assigned

---

[41] Ibid.

[42] Ibid., 21.

[43] Ibid., 20.

to make changes effectively to themselves. This is like asking them to confess they have been wrong and incompetent (or outright traitors) this whole time. Even if they do want to change, they still want to hold onto to the old system like a security blanket. But this produces "conceptual spaghetti" as new ideas and old ideas cannot coexist. One cannot take the best of each, because they are antithetical.

Defense reform could be assigned to the Defense Ministry only if there is a firm separation between military and civilian authority, with appropriate delegation and personalization of responsibilities in place. This is far from the case in Ukraine (or indeed any Central and East European country), where *de facto* there is almost total fusion between the political and military at the highest level. *De jure* everything is fine, until one looks at their laws and see how cunningly they are written to enable this.

Even the Cabinet of Ministers does not have effective power as the commander-in-chief can easily bypass both the government and the Defense Ministry more specifically by going directly to the president—the supreme commander. Or, he can just ignore everything he does not like. The ministry budgets and controls the money, but the president can spend it on his own political whims, or at the request of the commander-in-chief. In a presidential system run like this, there can be no unity of command, clarity of budget or coherence in management. Thus, to work, reform must be controlled and led by the legislature and implemented under strict parliamentarian supervision.

But this does assume that that a well-functioning democracy is in place with a good system of separation of powers and checks and balances between the legislative and executive. Of course, the parliament will not need to go into micro details. It needs to arrange, within law, the missions and key tasks and assign the responsibilities and authorities, so the defense system will deliver as ordered by law. The US (and NATO) hardly touches or supports this difficult legal challenge at all.

US Support

Ukraine is a country at war. Yet, US support for Ukraine is configured similarly to the support of any other peacetime country in Central and Eastern Europe and using the same tools. This does not work and is inappropriate in multiple ways. Arguably, support for Ukraine should be for a military operation. An unambiguous political and military focus would likely force Ukraine to become more serious as well. Support requires an operational military commander to assess, direct and guide all the disparate US actors and to be the spending focus. This is totally absent, and thus, the support itself is discordant and dissipated.

US support is often lauded by its adherents as the "Gold Standard." The trouble with this is that it is the Gold Standard for the US but not always for Ukraine or other countries. It could be likened to a guest arriving at a birthday party of vegetarians with a prime, two-pound Texas steak. The present is great for the giver but totally inappropriate for those receiving. The guests, of course, will be diplomatically profuse in their thanks but simultaneously mortified. The challenge the US must overcome with Ukraine is that both countries have extremely complex government and security systems, each with a cultural and conceptual base diametrically opposed and antithetical to each other. It could be likened to one being analogue and the other digital. Military expert Thomas Young highlights that there is nothing in common between the two.[44]

Today, the US and Ukrainian systems interact intermittently with each other and primarily at the extremities. Contact at the political and political-military level is rare, poorly briefed, often through interpreters and usually with limited positive results. The whole is insufficient for either side to teach the other anything other than superficially. The senior leadership of the Ukrainian Armed Forces is convinced that it has nothing to learn from the West, believing it only must make some slight

---

[44] Thomas-Durrell Young, *Anatomy of Post-Communist European Defense Institutions. The Mirage of Military Modernity* (London: Bloomsbury, 2017), 7, 40, 44, 52, 160, and 205.

adjustments to its current system to align it with NATO via adopting meaningless or nonexistent NATO standards. Leaders often speak to themselves about this but ignore incoming messages. Poor results are predictable.

The US support system, as it is configured today, is simply not designed to deal with this complexity at any level. The US staff may be deploying the Gold Standard for themselves, but the US's problems are systemic, and many, such as short tour lengths and limited pre-training, contain powerful built-in causes of failure. The result of support is all too often a failed task or a misunderstanding on both sides that not only does not help reform but in some cases also makes things worse, causing the US to lose the respect it deserves for its efforts.

Human Interfaces: Political Down to Tactical Military

The political interaction with Ukraine since 2014 has never really focused on defense reform but more on what support is available and can be easily provided by the US. Support has been wonderfully strong in parts. However, the discussions and interactions surrounding support of the Ukrainian defense system have usually been left at the non-political and tactical level, assuming that the US Gold Standard equipment and "best practice" tools would solve everything. Since the initial intense activity in 2014 and 2015, high-level discussions, including the Multinational Joint Commission, have also become routine, cursory and over-guided by the bounds of diplomatic nicety. Embassy contacts appear to be limited to the government and senior officials in power at any given time, and thus, US actions have primarily been in response to those interactions.

The Ukrainian government and senior officials are masters at telling people what they want to hear, however. Additionally, many Ukrainian NGOs that brief foreign embassies live off the grants from those same diplomatic missions and therefore are suspect in their offerings. The Ukrainian political mantra has been solidly, "We want to join NATO," and "We are meeting NATO standards." Yet, neither of those declarations holds up to scrutiny.

28 | BLACK SEA BATTLEGROUND

The challenge is that, at the political level, the US system has simply not dug deep enough or spent enough time trying to understand the beast. The US Embassy has been seriously disadvantaged by moving to "Fortress America" miles from Kyiv's city center and is now distanced from mainstream political interaction. Casual relations have effectively ended. Formal relations in Ukraine are made more difficult by a combination of the time needed to travel to and from meetings and a less-than-welcoming US Embassy mired in force protection policies, lack of trust and defense secrecy issues. It is no surprise that the embassy staffers are increasingly less noticeable around town. The US Defense Cooperation Office is nowhere near the Ukrainian Ministry of Defense's main building. The result is that in understanding defense reform, the US system barely comprehends the complexity already outlined, nor does there often appear an ability to separate PR nonsense from what is real.

The largest, most active financially and well-informed defense NGO in Ukraine is Come Back Alive. Its staff is on the frontlines and embedded with units constantly. When asked by the author, in March 2021, if the group ever had contact with the US Embassy or Defense Cooperation Office, its representative replied "never" and laughed. It was a serious question if the US Embassy even knew the NGO existed before a briefing to NATO attachés in the Latvian Embassy about their report on May 26, 2021.

At the political-military level, there appears to be no coherence to US support. No senior officer is focused solely on helping Ukraine reform. In logical terms, Congress should not grant money to defense if that money is not properly focused. The US commander of European Command, who now has added Africa responsibilities, is too busy, and his staff is too far geographically removed to be actively engaged other than in a formal bureaucratic way. The defense attaché team is composed of diplomats who have their own multiple roles to play; they are to a large extent formally controlled by the Ukrainians (probably except for the naval attaché) and are kept far away from the parts of the system the General staff and Ministry of Defense do not want them to see.

The challenge, therefore, is that defense reform is inherently a political problem; but without a strong political and military understanding of the problem and lacking the links to gain that understanding, both sides fail to cross the conceptual divide. Thus, the US agrees mostly with all it hears, and the Ukrainian side just asks for more weapons. When the Ukrainians do receive them, they "field" them arbitrarily and possess little understanding that these weapons systems will help them anyway.

But many on the US side—who have a poor grasp of the Ukrainian system—think that this will help. Furthermore, too many visiting senior officials and generals (not only from the United States) who are not familiar the stark reality, come and hand out medals and tell the Ukrainians what a great job they are doing on reform without ever having seen anything real. These contacts were described by one interpreter as meetings of gratitude and praise for two hours with zero recommendations or criticism.[45] These platitudes pander to the Ukrainians' belief that they *are* doing well, ensuring that true reform again takes a back seat.

Weapons and Equipment

Most of the money authorized by Congress is for weapons and equipment. Examples that expose the huge challenge of providing effective support are worth noting.

The first is Harris combat radios. These have been supplied to Ukraine in large numbers—as to other CEE militaries. The chief of communications of the Ukrainian Airborne Forces, the unit that has received the most Harris radios, told Come Back Alive[46] that, because of the low quality of soldiers, they could not be taught properly. The soldiers would also not take responsibility for the equipment because if they lost anything, they had to pay for it. A brigade staff officer deployed to Donbas in a line infantry brigade confirmed that "signal and communication is the weakest part in

---

[45] Adelfi Criseyde (pen name, retired sergeant, former Ukraine military interpreter and defense blogger), discussion with author, May 3, 2021.
[46] Come Back Alive, discussion with author, March 30, 2021.

30 | BLACK SEA BATTLEGROUND

battalions."[47] He continued, "For example we get Harris Radios—but only a few people know how they work. And in day-to-day communication we doesn't [sic] use them." The soldiers employ their cell phones because, for them, they work better than the radios, despite the fact that their phones are easily monitored and jammed by the Russians. The Ukrainian incentives for using the US equipment here are wrong, and thus, the US training does not stick. The soldiers would be happier with a cheap old radio that, if they lost or broke it, would not cost them so much.

The second is the supply of Javelin anti-tank weapons. This was more a political gift than a war-fighting weapon. The US government was concerned (quite rightly) that if delivered to the front line, the weapons might either be sold or lost to the Russians. They were, therefore, put into storage near Kyiv, 750 miles from the frontline. The Ukrainians advertised the weapon as their prime tank killer, both within the military and in PR campaign across the country. However, no attempt was made to understand how to use the Javelins if deployed. They would just be spread among the units in a tactical fashion. Amid considerable national fanfare, training was conducted for soldiers. If these were the soldiers who would fire them in wartime, it would be a lucky coincidence, not planning; the exercise was just a show. A check-in with a front-line brigade in a key battle zone on April 2021 showed that its solders had no Javelins and had never seen any.[48]

No attempt has been made to date by the Ukrainian staff (nor apparently the US) to think about strategic uses of the weapon, which could require changes to battle doctrines, structures, tactics or training of commanders at any level to deploy it effectively. Thus, the political and show value (and likely deterrence) was high, but the operational value was no better than that of the anti-tank weapons the Ukrainians already produce themselves. The lesson is that any equipment aid must be treated in the same way to how a complex capability is fielded

---

[47] Staff officer (name withheld, deployed on the Donbas front line), discussion with Author, April 25, 2021.
[48] Ibid.

in the US. It should cover all aspects of capability development—from leadership, doctrine and training to organization and logistics. This means rethinking the processes.

US analysts routinely suggest grand schemes for spending congressional money, such as revitalizing the Ukrainian Air Force with modern F-16 fighter jets.[49] Spending money on excess defense article programs, such as F-16s or Patriot missile defense batteries, is deeply alluring for policymakers and even more so for Ukrainians, but it takes no account of the culture, budget and skill sets within the Ukrainian system. Moreover, it does not account for the "willingness/ability of the Ukrainians to absorb the life-cycle sustainment costs from the get-go."[50] Strong arguments exist, echoed by the Ukrainian officers leading the fight, that rather than looking for big-ticket items requiring serious change, the US should spend money on supporting and improving the fighting systems Ukraine already has.

Yavoriv Infantry Training

The infantry training in Yavoriv really has been the Gold Standard, and most who attend love it. The tactical training, battle discipline and use of the Military Integrated Laser System (MILES), which assists tactical training, are all regularly spoken about by soldiers afterward. But the residual value of the training is heavily distorted by systemic problems on the Ukrainian side. The training is not part of the programmed system preparing units for operations. And no capacity exists for allied instructors to focus unit training, because the Ukrainians often do not know which part of the front they will hold next.

The Ukrainian military system is also predicated on brigades not battalions; as a result, battalions become subunits with no power

---

[49] Stephen Blank, "Upgrading Ukraine's Air Force Could Deter Russia," *UkraineAlert*, Atlantic Council, April 6, 2021, https://www.atlanticcouncil.org/blogs/ukrainealert/upgrading-ukraines-air-force-could-deter-russia/.
[50] Jon Chicky, "Black Hawks to Ukraine," email to Glen Howard (president, The Jamestown Foundation), April 24, 2021.

and limited capacity to act independently. The battalion structure required by the US for training is much larger than any Ukraine has. With the current severe manpower shortages, three or four battalions are required to make up one training battalion.[51] This means that many commanders, who arguably need training the most, are excluded, and their soldiers train without them. After the training, the unit is disbanded, and the soldiers return to their respective barracks. On return, they are told to forget what they learned because the official battle pamphlets (that are law) are still Soviet. No coherence exists. Additionally, Ukraine has no systemic ability to take the best soldiers from Yavoriv and make them instructors so that they could then continue to improve things.

Advisors

Ukraine benefits from advisors at multiple levels, from (previously) Gen. John Abizaid to the Ministry of Defense advisors (MoDA) group supposedly working inside the Ukrainian Defense Ministry. The challenge is that, almost without exception, those advisors come from parts of the US system that are large, sophisticated and fully functional. Then, they are then dropped into a system that is equally complex but outdated and broken, with little human or technical capacity and no authority to carry out change. Former lead MoDA Steve Silverstein comments that the US MoDA program has been poorly led in training and support, while the US Department of Defense office responsible for US policy in Ukraine does not support MoDA efforts. Selection of MoDAs who are truly subject-matter experts has historically been hit or miss. The additional key attribute is being a self-starter and sensitive to relationships and communications. MoDAs are only selected initially for one-year terms, which is ineffective.[52] And many military advisors are chosen for only six-month tours, without preparatory training, which is even less effective.

---

[51] Military staff (Come Back Alive), discussions with author, Kyiv, March 30, 2021.
[52] Steve Silverstein, discussions with author, April 2021.

Courses for Ukrainian Officers in the US

Major problems exist for graduates of the US International Military Education Training (IMET) program, running since 2015. Adm. Kabanenko comments that Ukrainian commanders do not want to send their officers to these courses. Those officers who are chosen are often those with no future perspective in the Ukrainian military, and on return, the system will not put these officers into significant positions or places where they can have influence. They never have an opportunity to implement their knowledge. The senior leadership also demands a different approach from the US with a "close-your-mouth-and-follow-orders" style. This creates cognitive dissonance and stress in the brains of those returning, and many leave early. Clearly, the culture needs to change.[53]

Defense Institution Building

After the war began in 2014, the initial Defense Institution Building (DIB) activities—developed by the Pentagon-linked Institute for Security Governance—were conducted by a small group of defense officials and contractors. These contacts were regulars with aims to learn the system, gain trust and work with Ukrainian defense ministry officials to change key documents and rewrite laws. Success was extremely slow, but doors were opening. In 2015, DIB management altered its approach and started using more short-term reform inputs from organizations such as the RAND Corporation. These were incoherent. The burgeoning close relationship was lost and has since not been regained.

---

[53] Ihor Kabanenko, Volodymyr Havrilov and Glen Grant, "Ukrainian Military Reform: Can the Armed Forces Escape their Soviet Past?" (video discussion with Glen Howard, president, The Jamestown Foundation), March 25, 2021, https://jamestown.org/event/upcoming-virtual-roundtable-ukrainian-military-reform-can-the-armed-forces-escape-their-soviet-past/.

34 | BLACK SEA BATTLEGROUND

People, Selection and Training

Many disparate groups of people from the US arrive ostensibly to support Ukraine. These include the embassy staff (together with the large defense attaché team and the Office of Defense Cooperation), regular Armed Forces, the National Guard, senior officers and defense officials, mid-level defense officials and contractors. With few exceptions, none are properly prepared for this specific task. The system primarily selects those who are suitable for Washington, not those who can deal effectively in Ukraine. In the early stages of support until 2015, it was enough just to be a US passport holder to be heard. But as the Ukrainians have gained knowledge from the war, they are increasingly less willing to accept weakness from foreign advisors and interlocutors.

Success with trying to help Ukraine reform is commensurate with political will. This means gaining high-level trust over time, the ability to develop personal contacts at all levels and possessing relevant professional knowledge specific for this complex task, not just US-centric "Gold Standard" offerings. These should be the selection criteria.

Gaining trust is probably the hardest to achieve. This takes at least six to seven years to develop, three years is just scratching the surface of relationships and understanding and the six-month postings of many US military personnel is seen as a grievous insult. Those who only have single Gold Standard solutions to offer or have not been to war are soon identified and ignored. Contractors who come for one or two weeks are seen as a joke unless they return repeatedly over many years. To Ukrainians, this shows that the US does not take the country or the war seriously. These transitory officers are sidelined.

Required skills also include the ability to speak English in a way that interpreters can translate. To be blunt, most US and Western military leaders speak a unique language (often foreign to even native-English speakers) that Ukrainian translators cannot deal with without constant exposure. When antithetical concepts are being considered, after translation, the reverse of what is being said can easily be both sides' takeaway.

Many advisors who show an ability to deal with the complexity and harshness of Ukraine are not kept in the job long enough to gain trust. Or, because there is no proper oversight, they are rarely recognized by the US system for their value.

US Bureaucracy

The US system has little or no agility to deal with fast-moving support requirements. Consequently, many critical areas where the US could provide help are long gone by the time the system responds. Support is over-bureaucratic, slow and turgid. For example, the Defense Security Cooperation Agency requires over a month to process paperwork. The US government appears to have no systemic trust in its front-line workforce. Ideas must go through multiple levels of checking, sometimes even all the way to the Office of the Secretary of Defense, before they are accepted; or they may simply disappear into the bureaucratic black hole. Congressional funding rules have been simplified, but perverse incentives still work. Bidding for innovative support means increasingly more work for an already excessively overworked chief of the Office of Defense Cooperation (ODC).

A key challenge is that the ODC chief is the prime driver of support, but he is far too overloaded to follow the strategic needs of the Ukraine defense system, other than superficially. He is expected to provide strategic thinking but without the support to do so. As such, there is a clear need for US political and military agents to ensure that support is coherent.

Conclusions of US Support and What to Do Next

The US system needs a Ukrainian advisory team of native Ukrainians with connections who can tell Washington what is actually going on within the country. They must be people with no oligarchical, political or financial interests except the well-being of Ukraine.

36 | BLACK SEA BATTLEGROUND

US support for Ukraine should be treated as a military operation. Historically no one has been responsible for the effectiveness and efficacy of the $2 billion in public money, and this needs to change. A robust, no-nonsense one- or two-star commander with war fighting credibility should be nominated to oversee US support and provide military advice to the president of Ukraine. Moreover, he should be nominated as a full-time commander who actually resides in Ukraine. The officer needs to be sufficiently close to modern combat developments to understand the future needs of the Ukrainian military. This person must work separately from the US Embassy to avoid being diplomatically sensitized into supinity. This uniformed officer should provide the military strategic overview and guidance for the support coming to Ukraine from all US agencies.

Additionally, the US political overview must include hard conditionality. Without this, there will be no change. The Ukrainian responses to US aid are all surface-level and more for PR than real. The senior leadership in Kyiv is willing to accept everything Washington offers; but when it comes to calls for real change, the Ukrainian side tries to keep the US and other allies at arms-length. Unless the Ukrainian president is convinced of the need for reform and change, nothing will happen. Political messaging needs to be clearer. Ambiguity surrounding possible US support helps no one.

The DIB program from the Institute for Security Governance, the MoDA and military advisor programs all need a total rethink from first principles based on the multiple challenges described above. If support for Ukraine becomes an operation, then the decision-making process and consequent stultifying bureaucracy should be streamlined through hard delegation of spending to the frontlines to make the support process more agile and responsive to needs.

Comprehensive training is required for most US personnel coming to Ukraine. Any who will be involved in complex areas such as policy, planning, doctrine, training or defense reform in general need a full understanding of the Ukrainian defense system, culture, societal and social mores, the antithetical nature of concepts and how this relates to change, change management skills in general and simply, how to speak to be understood.

Military Support

A number of concrete and general proposals for more effective support to the Ukrainian Armed Forces are worth considering.

The Ukrainian military needs ammunition, especially for its artillery.

All US personnel must be appropriately trained and briefed on the environment and cultural norms before deploying.

Tour lengths should be maximized. One military person living and working in Ukraine full time for five years is worth 100 short tours.

A need exists for a general officer course to help Ukrainians bridge the gap with NATO, the West and to reform.

The equipment and methodological support for front-line troops must concentrate on refining what is already there with simple improvements, not trying to create a Western analog. This could involve providing equipment to upgrade current systems, including artillery, surveillance and communications. Effective training could be supported with a huge influx of simulators from field equipment such as MILES and complex trainers for brigades and battalion headquarters to supplying barrack equipment for developing skills like low-level air-defense shooting, driving and indirect-fire observation.

The training support for front-line soldiers *en masse* should be reassessed from first principles and other models considered, such as the brigade training advisor model used in Afghanistan.

Conditionality for all tactical-level support should reflect the need that it must be embedded in the main Ukrainian training processes of units deploying on operations and career paths. Training support should not be given as "in addition to"—how

38 | BLACK SEA BATTLEGROUND

Yavoriv is now—since this does not create systemic improvement. It is also vital to modify the training of initial officers and recruits. It is a lost cause trying to reeducate ethics and values, tactics and leadership skills after they have been badly taught in the first place.

Operational battle courses that teach the Western style in the field are needed for company, battalion and brigade commanders.

Fundamental changes are needed to doctrine and the education system. This cannot be left alone, as it adversely affects all US support and thus wastes serious money. The Ukrainian education and training system needs new doctrine, pamphlets and instructors and integral support for a sustained period. Setting up a regional staff college similar to the Baltic Defense College, initially run by the US, would be extremely useful. Other considerations may be a US or UK two-star officer to run the Ukrainian NDU for five years, with a clear mandate to clean shop top to bottom.

Finally, the US should devote more political energy and finance to supporting those civil society NGOs and activists serving front-line needs. The knowledge gained from them would greatly help US advisors improve support and provide vital understanding to help change the main system.

Appendix A: Special Operations Forces Reform—Little Operational Gain So Far

The following survey was compiled from the author's experiences, comments from US officers who have served and worked in Ukraine with the Ukrainian special forces since 2014 and conversations with two current and one retired member of the Special Operations Forces (SOF) Command HQ. This overview of the Ukrainian SOF is a microcosm of the larger failure of Ukraine's defense reform as a whole.

Until 2016, standalone SOF did not exist in the Ukrainian defense forces. The units were all part of the various vertical structures within the army, air force and navy. No coherent SOF existed, nor did Ukraine even have a doctrine about what the SOF should be and do. When the war broke out in 2014, the special elite units that did exist were effectively the best-trained infantry in the Ukrainian Armed Forces. They were not used for classic SOF tasks but were sent where most pressingly needed to engage in tactical battles in eastern Ukraine. Much of the initial US support provided in 2014–2015 was wasted, as the system had no SOF structures or understanding and the senior-level Ukrainian military had little or no grasp about what US and NATO were offering or even suggesting.

In 2016, the Army SOF was formed. These units were effectively a consolidation of forces under one commander. This included the special infantry units, psychological operations (Psy Ops) forces and some reconnaissance detachments. Huge resistance existed, however, from the Ukrainian General Staff to the idea of creating a separate SOF command as a fifth branch of the armed forces, at the same command level as the army, parachute forces, navy and air force. This was despite considerable US and NATO lobbying for Kyiv to do so. A command headquarters was set up, but it had limited authority. The one officer who had real SOF experience and could have truly built up the capabilities of the force, then-Col. Serhii Krivonos (now a general), was "relegated" to deputy commander and thus effectively sidelined during much of the conflict.

40 | BLACK SEA BATTLEGROUND

The new commander, Gen. Ihor Luniov, a parachute officer, was unimaginative but reliable; and over four years, he successfully consolidated the special forces into one organization. The US is highly commended by the Ukrainian SOF for being a serious part of this reform. The SOF is now inarguably the most reformed and professional organization in the Ukrainian Armed Forces. One battalion has passed NATO certification, and, as of May 2021, this unit is on-duty for the NATO Response Force. However, a serving SOF officer ironically commented that they were certified for NATO but not used by Ukraine.

The reasons for this are many and political. In the first place, special forces of any kind have historically not been trusted by post-Maidan Ukrainian governments. For example, the former Russian-backed Ukrainian government extensively employed the elite Interior Forces during the 2014 protests, when many demonstrators died. Thus, these elite units are not seen as the sharp military tool that the US or UK views their own special forces. Like the rest of the system, the SOF still suffers internally from legacy thinking and the daily whims and orders of an unreformed General Staff. When they are deployed by the General Staff, it is not to conduct SOF tasks but usually to serve on the frontline in a tactical reconnaissance role alongside other infantry battalions. The SOF headquarters has no operational responsibility for the war, so it has no capacity to develop or properly use the SOF units as a strategic weapon.

Another problem is that there is yet no proper legal basis for the SOF in Ukraine. No one, including the Ukrainian president, can take responsibility for using the SOF in strategic or deep-strike tasks. With the current legislation in force, if SOF personnel kill a Donbas separatist not in self-defense, they would be liable for the murder of a Ukrainian citizen and could face prosecution by the Ukrainian legal system. Lacking an adequate SOF law and, consequently, SOF doctrine, special forces units have no proper operational tasks or tasking. Therefore, the SOF is not really considered by the National Security Council or Ukrainian General Staff as anything more than enhanced infantry.

The SOF is also not prescribed fully in the laws on intelligence in Ukraine. As an operational intelligence tool, these elite units need special authority to be used. This authority is often not forthcoming from risk-averse officers in the system. As a result, whatever the US teaches other than soft skills, there is, at best, a random chance of Ukrainian special forces being used in combat.

Obstacles also exist in the Ukrainian Defense Ministry's Central Military Intelligence (GUR). This organization effectively runs its own life and uses its own reconnaissance units on the frontlines outside other parts of the armed forces. The SOF is judged to be a competitor for power and resources both by the GUR and other branches of the Ukrainian Armed Forces. The GUR has an operational focus with authority to conducting operation, whereas the SOF still do not have that operational freedom or even authorization.

Without deep-attack and strategic doctrine, equipping and training also remains at the tactical level, and resources are limited to simply low-level support. Little or no coordination also exists with the naval and air assets needed to develop proper understanding of how to conduct strategic tasks beyond a single, short annual exercise.

US Support

The SOF desperately needs US support to be raised from the tactical to the political, legal, strategic and operational levels. This will require much greater study and understanding of the SOF and the surrounding environment. The current level of US advocacy to develop the Ukrainian special forces is simply too little and too weak.

SOF officers are disappointed about the poor response times for any backing they need. In conversations with SOF officers for this assessment, many commented that, when they have a serious requirement, it takes two years for the US system to produce what is needed; and often by then, the moment has passed. This is not only an SOF conclusion.

42 | BLACK SEA BATTLEGROUND

The Ukrainians wish for a much more visible US SOF presence in the country to not only better educate the leadership but also to act as a visible deterrence to Russia. Some also suggest that Ukrainian facilities could be used to train US and NATO SOF operatives, and this would help enhance cooperation and interoperability between Ukraine and Allied forces.

Conclusion

Unless there is a concerted educational push at the political level in Ukraine, the SOF will remain a tactical-level organization with no ability to develop further as a strategic tool. It will not show value from the allocated US resources or provide Ukraine with effective operational benefit.

Appendix B: Artillery Ammunition for Ukraine—The Big Challenge

The loss and failure to resupply gun and rocket artillery ammunition has been a highly contentious issue in Ukraine. Rarely a day goes by without a comment about it in the Ukrainian media. The failure is multilevel, with the government not making it a priority, the Defense Ministry only including resupply in small numbers in its annual procurement plan and the government-owned defense corporation, Ukroboronprom, failing completely to deliver a working ammunition plant.

The country, since 2015, has lost huge amounts of ammunition in warehouse explosions (see list below). It would now appear that these are linked to some of the same antecedents as those in Bulgaria and the Czech Republic (Czechia).

In late 2019, the Ukrainian parliament (Verkhovna Rada) set up a parliamentary commission of inquiry to study the circumstances of the five most significant explosions at ammunition depots between 2014 and 2018, in Ichnia, Kalynivka, Balaklia, Svatove and Kryvyi Rih.[54]

The commission deputies suggested the main version of the explosions in Balaklia was an attack by an unmanned aircraft on one stack of ammunition storage. The explosions then set off subsequent detonations in nearby storage facilities. Despite obvious evidence to the contrary, the Russian-leaning military prosecutor Anatolii Matios, in this and other cases, blamed the Ukrainian security forces of negligence. One apparently innocent

---

[54] "The Work of the TSC to Investigate Explosions at Art Warehouses Was Extended for 6 Months," *Ukrinform*, April 30, 2020, https://www.ukrinform.ua/rubric-society/3016441-robotu-tsk-z-rozsliduvanna-vibuhiv-na-artskladah-prodovzili-na-piv-roku.html?fbclid=IwAR3y1CKU8XSc78KTsqb3-YagQu9ZZLRQiuX3h4oedA2ZiXR_6iTvD-rx_Gs.

44 | BLACK SEA BATTLEGROUND

major, Olexandr Lytvynenko, was arrested and finally "confessed" his guilt.[55]

After this, the chairperson of the Rada investigative commission, David Arahamiya (who coincidentally also chairs the president's party) sided with the prosecutor, suggesting the explosions in Balaklia were the result of buried explosives with special charges. This version of events was rejected outright by the former deputy prosecutor general of Ukraine, Viktor Chumak, after he checked the security services' reports.

It is difficult not to come away with the impression that the parliamentary inquiry was set up more to confuse the public and turn the blame away from Russia than to uncover the truth. It also did nothing to raise the national priority of replenishing the huge amounts of lost ammunition. The country is now ammunition poor in most artillery types but especially 152-millimeter (mm) rockets.

Failure to Produce New Ammunition

Upon achieving independence on December 2, 1991, Ukraine inherited seemingly unlimited amounts of artillery ammunition from the Soviet Union. The government-owned factories remained in place but effectively as conduits for laundering government money. As there was little need for new ammunition, by 2000, the country suffered a major deterioration in everything to do with producing defense stocks. Additionally, Ukraine saw a vast loss of human expertise moving into other better-paying industries. After 2014, some factories were also lost to the Russians in Donbas, though these had long stopped working. Early investors, such as Oerlikon, left well before the war started. Ukrainian artillery expert Vladimir Shchetinin puts things bluntly: "Since the collapse of the Soviet Union, for 30 long years,

---

[55] Igor Burdiga, "Terrorism or Negligence: How Explosions at Military Depots Are Being Investigated in Ukraine," *Hromadske*, October 9, 2018, https://hromadske.ua/posts/iak-v-ukraini-rozsliduiutsia-vybukhy-na-viiskovykh-skladakh.

Ukraine has ceased to be a country developing modern weapons."[56]

For several decades, the legacy was squandered. Shells were disposed of, sold, stored, drowned and exploded. The deterioration intensified as the US and NATO spent considerable funds on helping reduce weapon and ammunition stocks as part of anti-proliferation efforts (something this author saw NATO perversely continue after the war was in full flow).

Regeneration of capacity is not so simple. To support the current Ukrainian defense system would mean recreating Soviet technology. But since this time, artillery has developed hugely with new gunpowder, steel, forms of ammunition and smart fuses. Also, manufacturing tools and management systems have made colossal development gains with modern technologies. In effect, recreating the old system is now impossible. For Ukraine, the redevelopment of any new capacity is a major task; and it has only started to appear in the government-owned defense production sector after more than seven years of war. Private businesses that could achieve new production are either not supported by the Ukrainian government or are unwilling to invest while the prevailing climate of corruption continues.

Former Ukrainian ministerial adviser Andrii Ryzhenko told this author that there were several early attempts after the war started in 2014 to build a factory to produce new ammunition and repair an old factory. A state defense order allocated $8 million for the project. But that money apparently disappeared. A scandal followed that was connected with former Deputy Minister of Economic Development Viktor Brovchenko. He was arrested, but charges were never laid.

In 2014, the private firm DynCorp intended to invest an unspecified amount of US funding to upgrade a Ukrainian state

---

[56] Vladimir Shchetinin, "Prospects for the Development of Ukrainian Artillery," Mil.in.ua, September 28, 2020, https://mil.in.ua/uk/blogs/perspektyvy-rozvytku-ukrayinskoyi-artyleriyi/.

factory to repair and produce ammunition, including gun ammunition. The offer came to nothing likely because the identified risks of corruption were too high. US weapons manufacturer Bushmaster was also planning to invest money to build a factory to produce 12.7–155 mm munitions. But after some studies, Bushmaster decided not to proceed with the project.

The state-owned company Artem now says it is capable of producing both 152 and 155 mm shells by the end of 2021. However, Artem is not due to start testing until June 2021, and it needs to use test facilities in Slovakia. The company's chairperson noted that the firm has experienced problems producing Ukrainian 152-mm ammunition shell casings and special chemicals such as metal powders and high explosives.[57] According to Shchetinin, they also have not solved the technical problems of design.[58] Artem could apparently produce only 14,000 rounds a year. This is a small number if the war becomes serious again. No state defense order exists for ammunition[59]; given the heavy bureaucracy, none will likely be bought from this company before mid-2022.

Five Main Warehouse Explosions

<u>Krivoy Rog, Dnipropetrovsk region</u>

In March 2014, in Kryvyi Rih, the tank warehouse caught fire. The tanks inside were fully fueled and loaded with ammunition. As a result, two (at the time extremely precious) T-64 tanks were destroyed. No one was injured. Police blamed faulty wiring.

---

[57] Vladimir Shchetinin, "By the End of the Year: Artem Will Deliver a Batch of 152-mm Shells of the Armed Forces," Mil.in.ua, March 2, 2021,https://mil.in.ua/uk/news/artem-do-kintsya-roku-postavyt-partiyu-152-mm-snaryadiv-zsu/.
[58] Vladimir Shchetinin, various discussions with author, 2021.
[59] Pagulich and Rebriy, "Ammunition Famine of the Armed Forces."

Svatov, Luhansk region

On October 29, 2015, a fire broke out at the ammunition depot near Svatov. This detonated 3,500 tons of ammunition of various calibers, including scarce rocket launcher ammunition. Fifty-nine high-rise buildings and 3,314 houses were damaged. One civilian woman and three servicemen were killed and 16 injured. Then–Chief Military Prosecutor Matios noted, "The cause of the fire at the ammunition depot in Svatovo was the negligence of officials, including the chief of this warehouse."

Balaklia, Kharkiv region

In March 2017, in Balaklia, a fire broke out at the military arsenal followed by a detonation of ammunition and further explosions outside the arsenal. About 36,000 people were evacuated from the affected area around the artillery depots. Three hundred and ninety-two buildings were destroyed, affecting over 3,900 city residents. The fire was extinguished after three days.

The subsequent investigation found witnesses who saw something dropped from an unmanned aerial vehicle, causing the detonations.

Kalinivka, Vinnystsia region

In September 2017, a fire in the ammunition warehouse at Kalynivka was followed by the detonation of ammunition. More than 30,000 people were evacuated from the military unit and settlements in a 10-kilometer zone. All modes of transport were closed. The explosions lasted two days, stopping road and rail traffic. In November 2017, the Military Prosecutor Office blamed the senior officer for failing to control access. It said employees of a private enterprise entered the area where ammunition for tank guns was stored carrying "flammable substances." A Ukrainian officer was prosecuted, although it is now believed that those who entered were GRU.

48 | BLACK SEA BATTLEGROUND

<u>Ichnia, Chernihiv Oblast</u>

In October 2018, a fire forced the evacuation of 12,500 people from the center of Ichnia and 30 surrounding villages. As a result, over 300 buildings were destroyed or damaged. Luckily, no casualties were reported.

Conclusion

No quick solution is available. The heavy artillery ammunition previously stored in Ukraine is largely gone. The stocks of Soviet ammunition in other former Communist East European countries have also been degraded by Russian actions. Poland still has such stocks, but it also needs them for its own defensive purposes. Ukraine could possibly make a change to 155-mm (NATO standard) systems to replace the 152-mm systems they have. But new 155-mm guns would be expensive. Perversely, Kyiv just ordered second-hand refurbished 152-mm weapons from Czechia, which may arguably exacerbate existing ammunition problems. The problem of heavily reduced rocket-launcher ammunition remains unsolved and apparently beyond Kyiv's ability to rectify.

A major US step could be to lease or sell cheap 155-mm M109 systems plus spares, of which the US still has many. At the gun-crew level, Ukrainian artillery units are well trained and could adjust to the M109 quite quickly. This would give the Ukrainians the options of purchasing two calibers of ammunition, with 155 mm being greatly more effective.

2.

Blind, Confuse and Demoralize: Russian Electronic Warfare Operations in Donbas

Sergey Sukhankin

August 27, 2021

Moscow's rapid and mostly bloodless annexation of Ukrainian Crimea in February–March 2014, followed a month later by the Russian-fueled instability and military confrontation in Donbas, marked the first serious test of Russia's (para)military efforts abroad since the Russo-Georgian conflict and the launch of military reforms in 2008. In addition to Russia's use of shadowy paramilitary outfits (e.g., private military contractors including the Slavonic Corps and Wagner Group), the early escalation of the Donbas conflict was marked by Russia's use of Information Operations (IO) and Electronic Warfare[1] (EW).

The following chapter specifically discusses the use of EW by the integrated Russian-"separatist" forces in Donbas since 2014 and the role of this conflict in the overall trajectory of Russia's development of EW capabilities. To this end, the chapter covers:

---

[1] In the Russian literature, EW is referred to as "radio-electronic confrontation" (*radio-elektronnoye protivoborstvo*).

1. The general course of Russian development of EW capabilities throughout history,
2. The refinement of the conceptual-theoretical foundations of Russia's EW thinking in the post-2008 period,
3. A detailed outline of EW systems used by Russia in Donbas, and
4. Speculation on future steps that Moscow might take in Donbas in case of potential military escalation there.

Development of Russia's EW Capabilities: A Historical Perspective

Since the beginning of the 20th century, electronic warfare has constituted one of the main pillars of Russia's military strength, as still reflected in the country's current capabilities. The pre-1991 period of Russian EW development can be divided into three main stages.

The first stage (1902–1917) was marked by several groundbreaking achievements. The earliest recorded (in world practice) conceptual study addressing EW's strategic importance dates back to January 1902.[2] Whereas, the rapid development of the sector reached a symbolic milestone during the Russo-Japanese War (1904–1905) when the Tsarist Russian Navy—for the first time in history (April 15, 1904)—employed EW against Japanese naval vessels. During World War I (1914–1918), EW was one of the few components (if not the only one) in which the Russian Armed Forces held primacy over their opponents.[3]

The second stage (1918 to mid-1950s) was marked by a rollback on both the theoretical and practical fronts. Despite some advances—the first unit tasked with EW operations was created in November 1918, in Serpukhov, and the integration of radio

---

[2] N. A. Kolesov and I. G. Nosenkov, *Radioelektornnaya borba. Ot eksperimentov proshlogo do reshayushego fronta budushego* (Moscow, Russia: Center for the Analysis of Strategies and Technologies, 2015).
[3] "Istoriya radioelektronnoy borby," *Nauka Tehnika*, August 24, 2019, https://naukatehnika.com/istoriya-radioelektronnoj-borby.html.

direction finders in the Red Army and naval forces started in 1919; however, necessary attention was not paid to their further implementation and development.[4] Nevertheless, EW did play a notable role in the Soviet Union's confrontation with Japan in the Far East in the late 1930s, where EW systems not only helped the Soviets acquire important data about Japanese military capabilities (intelligence gathering function) but also assisted in gathering information about the relocation of Japanese military formations. At a serious level, however, the first fundamental step was not made until the middle of World War II, in December 1942, when the first specialized units for radio-electronic suppression were introduced into the Red Army.[5]

The third stage (mid-1950s to 1990) was heavily influenced by the Cold War and mushrooming (proxy) regional conflicts. Specifically, the Korean (1950–1953) and Vietnam wars (1955–1975)—where the Soviet-backed sides encountered a technologically advanced opponent—became a watershed that triggered a boom in the development of new Soviet EW capabilities. Between 1954 and 1959, the Soviet Armed Forces received the first battalions tasked with radio-electronic interference, radio-location and radio-navigation.[6] Arguably, the zenith was reached between 1967 and 1977, when the Soviet Union made fundamental advancements on both theoretical and practical levels. In particular, the following developments should be highlighted:[7]

---

[4] Kirill Vostokov, "Rozhdeniya radiorazvetki," Nvo.ng.ru, August 18, 2000, https://nvo.ng.ru/history/2000-08-18/5_radio.html.
[5] "Izbrannyye voprosy radioelektronnogo podavlenija tsifrovykh signalov system radiosviazi," *Voronezh*, 2010, http://www.sozvezdie.su/science/izdaniya/izbrannie_voprosi_radioel ektronnogo/.
[6] Yuri Gorbachev, "REB w operatsiyakh XX i XXI veka," Vpk-News.ru, November 17, 2004, https://vpk-news.ru/articles/944.
[7] Ilya Kramnik, "111 let pomekh," Lenta.ru, April 15, 2015, https://lenta.ru/articles/2015/04/15/ew/.

- Adoption of a concept on the further development of EW, which resulted in the unification of state policies in this area;
- The launch of a series of military exercises (Efir-72, Efir-74, Elektron-75 and Impuls-76) to test ways to increase the effectiveness of EW in military operations; and
- A structural realignment within the Soviet military, which included the formation of tactical EW units.

Nevertheless, despite massive financial injections, starting from the late 1970s, the Soviet Union started losing its competitiveness in the EW space. During the 1982 Lebanon War, the growing gap between Soviet and Western EW capabilities became especially apparent. This fact also partially became evident from the war in Afghanistan (1979–1989). Russian military experts have argued that this negative trend primarily resulted from "long-dated views on EW coming from the 1940s–1950s that were widespread among members of the Soviet General Staff"—*de facto* leading to a "petrification."[8] Yet, the genuine bottom would be reached later, in the 1990s.

The Post-1991 Period: From (Near) Collapse to a New Boom

Following the dissolution of the Soviet Union in 1991, EW remained chronically underfinanced and understaffed. Many qualified professionals left for the private sector, with some joining semi-criminal structures and "private armies" organized by the nascent class of oligarchs.[9] As a result, a vacuum on both

---

[8] Mikhail Liubin, "K voprosu ob istorii razvitiya i perspektivakh radioelektronnoy borby," Cyber Leninka, 2009, https://cyberleninka.ru/article/n/k-voprosu-ob-istorii-razvitiya-i-perspektivah-radioelektronnoy-borby.
[9] Sergey Sukhankin, "A Black Cat in the Dark Room: Russian Quasi-Private Military and Security Companies (PMSCs)—'Non-Existent,' but Deadly and Useful," *Canadian Military Journal*, 19, no. 4 (Fall 2019).

theoretical and practical levels emerged.[10] But while Russia's capabilities continued to degrade, Russian military thinkers and practitioners were dazzled by the United States' advances in EW and informational-psychological operations, showcased between 1991 and 2003 in regional conflicts in the Persian Gulf region, Afghanistan and the Balkans.[11] This trend persevered until 2008–2009, when three occurrences helped usher in a new era in the development of Russian EW capabilities.[12]

The first was the initiation of dramatic military reforms (triggered in large part by the Russian Armed Forces' experience in the August 2008 Russian-Georgian War), which resulted in the emergence of a vertically integrated system of EW command and control (C2).[13] Ultimately, EW companies were created in virtually all reformed rifle and tank brigades and divisions, the Airborne Troops and special forces.[14]

Second, in his address to the Federation Council (the upper chamber of the Russian parliament) on November 5, 2008, then–President Dmitry Medvedev—speaking about potential responses to US plans to deploy elements of strategic missile

---

[10] Russian military thinkers started to allocate both offensive and defensive qualities to EW. Specifically, it was argued that "radio-electronic intelligence and *maskirovka* [military deception]—as a part of information warfare—in the military domain also have offensive and defensive components." For more information see: "Informatsionnoye protivoborstvo i maskirovka voysk," *Voyennaya mysl*, 2003, 74.

[11] Sergey Makarenko, "Informatsionnoye protivoborstvo i radioelektronnaya borba w setetsentrichsekikh voynah nachala XXI veka" (Saint Petersburg, Russia: 2017).

[12] Although, some steps toward transformation were made in the early 2000s. For instance, in July 2003, the Federal Agency of Government Communications and Information—specifically tasked with radio-electronic intelligence—was fully transferred under the jurisdiction of the Federal Security Service (FSB). This led to the formation of the 16th Center of the FSB.

[13] "Reforma Vooruzhennykh Sil (2008–2012) i ee nekotoryje itogi," Oboznik, September 17, 2018, http://www.oboznik.ru/?p=20067.

[14] Russian Ministry of Defense, "Spetsialnyye voyska," https://structure.mil.ru/structure/forces/air/structure/spec.htm.

54 | BLACK SEA BATTLEGROUND

defense in Central Europe—emphasized the role of Kaliningrad Oblast in contributing to Russia's "asymmetric response."[15] Russian military experts assumed that one such "response" would translate into deploying a "special EW center" equipped with up-to-date means of radio-technical intelligence gathering and radio-electronic suppression.[16]

Third, the creation of the Radio-Electronic Technologies Concern (KRET)[17]—within the Russian state-owned Rostec defense-industry corporation—resulted in a vertically integrated company offering a complex and diversified product in line with prospects for commercialization, an element nonexistent in the Soviet Union. KRET is specifically tasked with developing and manufacturing specialized military radio-electronic capabilities; state identification, aviation and radio-electronic equipment; multipurpose measuring devices; detachable electrical connectors; and civil products.

Furthermore, special attention was paid to EW research and the nurturing of a qualified cadre. For this purpose, a special military-scientific committee for EW troops was created in October 2015. This was followed by the creation of the Scientific Institute of EW in Voronezh in 2016.[18]

Thus, by the second half of the 2010s, Russia had arguably managed to overcome the consequences of the turbulence of the two preceding decades and—in some categories—took

---

[15] Dmitry Medvedev, "Poslaniye Federalnomu Sobraniyu Rossiyskoii Federatsii" (address, Russian Federal Assembly, November 5, 2008), http://kremlin.ru/events/president/transcripts/1968.

[16] Liubin, "K voprosu ob istorii razvitiya i perspektivakh radioelektronnoy borby."

[17] As of late 2019, the main players composing Russia's EW production were: KRET (60 percent), JSC Concern Sozvezdie (20 percent), JSC Central NII Radio technical Institute of A. I. Berg (10 percent), JSC Scientific-Technical Centre of Radio Electronic Confrontation (5 percent), and Special Technological Centre (5 percent).

[18] "Den spetsialista po radioelektronnoy borbe: Dosie," *TASS*, April 15, 2016, https://tass.ru/info/3204583.

qualitative steps forward in comparison with the pre-1991 period.

Theoretical-Methodological Foundations of Russia's EW Strategy

Russia's contemporary (post-2008) defense-industry and military-science literature divides EW into three main interconnected domains[19]:

1. Radio-electronic defeat (*radioelektronnoye porazhenie*), which is an offensive side of EW with the ultimate goal of achieving partial-to-full destruction of the enemy's critical (digital/information) infrastructure;
2. Radio-electronic defense (*radioelektronnaya zashita*), which is primarily concerned with minimizing the effect produced by the adversary's EW forces; and
3. Radio-electronic suppression (*radioelektronnoye podavleniye*), a concept somewhat close in meaning to "radio-electronic defeat" but primarily focused on decreasing the effectiveness (not complete destruction) of the opponent's assets through spoofing and imposing other types of radio-electronic interference.

In this regard, one crucial aspect must be highlighted: In Russian theory, EW constitutes an integral element of a larger phenomenon, so-called "information confrontation" (*informatsionnoye protivoborstvo*), which combines political, economic, diplomatic and military means but is comprised of two essential elements.[20]

---

[19] "Evolutsia radioelektronnoy borby," Rostec, February 27, 2018, https://rostec.ru/analytics/evolyutsiya-radioelektronnoy-borby/.
[20] Sergey Sukhankin, "Russia's Offensive and Defensive Use of Information Security," *Russia`s Military Strategy and Doctrine* (Washington, DC: Jamestown Foundation, 2019), https://jamestown.org/wp-content/uploads/2019/02/Russias-Military-Strategy-and-Doctrine-web-1.pdf?x97632.

1. *Information-technological* confrontation consisting of:
   a. EW and electronic intelligence,
   b. Electro-optical warfare (*elektronno-opticheskaya voyna*),
   c. Acoustic warfare and offensive and defensive use of information security, and
   d. Computer warfare (so-called "hackers' warfare").
2. *Information-psychological* confrontation, which envisages targeting:
   a. Human consciousness;
   b. Neurological systems (both individual and collective, including military formations);
   c. State ideology; and
   d. National consciousness.

Another essential aspect to Russia's understanding of the role of EW within the wider "information confrontation" phenomenon is articulated in a 2017 article in *Kommersant*, which underscores a so-called "innovative approach" to building up EW capabilities. In particular, the following areas are to be additionally boosted in the nearest future:[21]

- Creating "managed radio noise" (*upravliayemiye radiopomekhi*) on the enemy's territory, which is to be achieved through integrated use of unmanned aerial vehicles (UAV) and special jamming transmitters (*peredatchiki pomekh*);
- Boosting offensive EW capabilities via electromagnetic radiation; and
- Allocating special attention to the imitation of radio-electronic environments (*radioelektronnaya obstanovka*) and integration of disinformation in the enemy's command and control as well as the system of control of automated weaponry.

---

[21] "Nauchnyye printsipy radioelektronnoy borby," *Kommersant*, February 24, 2017, https://www.kommersant.ru/doc/3211081.

Importantly, nearly all the aforementioned aspects have been tested in the fullest possible way in Ukraine and Donbas, in particular.

Donbas as a Testing Ground: The 'Active Phase' of Military Confrontation

The active phase of military confrontation in the Donbas war zone occurred between 2014 and 2017. In facing off against the Ukrainian Armed Forces (UAF), the Russian-backed "separatist" forces (actively supported by Moscow economically, politically and militarily) relied on various instruments of warfare ranging from nonmilitary (disinformation) and paramilitary to conventional military elements. Arguably, three main factors secured the survival of the so-called Luhansk and Donetsk "people's republics" (LPR, DNR):

1. The near complete unpreparedness of the UAF to engage in combat, whether militarily or psychologically;
2. The rapid deployment and participation of Russian paramilitary contractors (PMCs), which spearheaded and coordinated all major military operations carried out by the "separatists"[22]; and
3. The employment of Russian-delivered means of EW, which played a key role in the defeats suffered by the UAF between 2014 and 2015.

Within the last element, five main operative tasks or functions should be indicated:

1. *Sabotage* of (Russian-manufactured) radios employed by the UAF;

---

[22] Sergey Sukhankin. "Unleashing the PMCs and Irregulars in Ukraine: Crimea and Donbas," in *War by Other Means: Russia's Use of Private Military Contractors at Home and Abroad* (Washington, DC: Jamestown Foundation, September 3, 2019), https://jamestown.org/program/unleashing-the-pmcs-and-irregulars-in-ukraine-crimea-and-donbas/.

58 | BLACK SEA BATTLEGROUND

2. *Interception of communication*;
3. *Jamming*, primarily employed against radio stations (with frequency bands of 137–180 and 400–470 megahertz) and GPS navigation;
4. *Spoofing*; and
5. Pursuing a combination of *informational-technological* (hacking smartphones and information systems, cyberattacks against critical infrastructure, etc.) and *informational-psychological* (disinformation, misinformation, provocations, dispatching malign content and texting UAF members[23]) confrontations.

The main means of EW employed by the separatist forces in their engagements with the UAF between 2014 and 2017[24] included:

- The RB-341B "Leer-3" complex is designed for jamming GSM (cellular) signals with the support of Orlan-10 UAVs and transmitting information. It had been tested in military engagements in Ukraine (spotted in Donbas during the spring and summer of 2015) even before its official introduction into the Russian Armed Forces (October 2015).[25] Later (May 2016), this advanced system was spotted several times near the city of Donetsk.
- The RB-301B "Borisoglebsk-2" complex is one of Russia's most advanced systems of electronic suppression. It is designed for radio intelligence and for jamming of HF/UHF (both terrestrial and aircraft) radio channels as well as mobile terminals and trunked radios at the tactical and operational-tactical command levels. It was

---

[23] "U Debaltsevomu rzsilayut panishni SMS pro proriv boyovykiv," Lb.ua, February 6, 2015, https://lb.ua/society/2015/02/06/294740_debaltsevo_rassilayut_pan icheskie.html.

[24] "Rossiyskie sredstva REB w boyevykh deystviyakh na Donbasse," *Inform Napalm,* May 2, 2016, https://informnapalm.org/22868-reb-v-donbasse/.

[25] "Rossiyskii complex 'Leer-3' snova zafiksirovali na Donbasse," *Inform Napalm*, April 6, 2019, https://informnapalm.org/46722-rossijskij-kompleks-leer-3-snova-zafi/.

introduced into the Russian Armed Forces in 2013 (even though it was created in 2009), when the first units were deployed to the Southern Military District.[26] This complex was first used in Donbas in November 2014 (near Stakhanov, Luhansk Oblast).[27] Also, complexes of this type frequently appear near the Anti-Terrorism Operation (ATO—the Ukrainian military's term for its armed activities against Russia-backed separatist forces) zone. Allegedly, this complex played a decisive role in the Battle of Debaltseve (January 2015), one of the heaviest defeats suffered by the Ukrainian Armed Forces to date.

- The R-934UM automated jamming station (put into service in 2008–2010) was first spotted near Luhansk in 2015, where it was working with an F-330KMA command unit. Previously, this station appeared near the eastern Ukrainian cities of Horlivka and Makiivka.[28]
- The R-330Zh "Zhitel" automated jamming station was given a particularly key role in the Donbas operation. This piece of EW technology has a long history of service in the Russian Armed Forces, having allegedly been employed during the assassination of the former president of Ichkeria (Chechnya), Dzhokhar Dudayev (1996); the Russo-Georgian War (2008); and Russia's annexation of Crimea (March 2014).[29] It was recorded being used by the

---

[26] "'Borisoglebsk-2' – novii complex REP," *Sozvezdie*, December 2009, http://www.sozvezdie.su/newspaper/ 22 dekabr 2009 g/borisoglebs k2 noviy kompleks/.

[27] "Stantsiya pomekh 'R-378bB' compleksa REB 'Borisoglebsk-2' na Donbasse," *Inform Napalm*, May 8, 2016, https://informnapalm.org/22954-kompleks-reb-borisoglebsk-2-stahanov/.

[28] "Russian electronic warfare stations in Donbas," *Inform Napalm*, June 5, 2016, https://informnapalm.org/en/russian-electronic-warfare-stations-donbas/.

[29] "REB 'Zhitel': kak 'vykluchit' amerikanskiye bespilotniki odnim nazhatiem knopki," Tvzvezda.ru, September 18, 2015, https://tvzvezda.ru/news/forces/content/201509180822-s1gq.htm.

60 | BLACK SEA BATTLEGROUND

Russian side in Donbas between 2014 and 2017.[30] On many occasions, it was spotted in Horlivka, Makiivka and Zaytsevo. This equipment may also have been used by separatist forces near Debaltseve in 2015.

- The R-381T2 UHF radio monitoring station (R-381T "Taran" complex) and "Torn" radio intelligence complexes were observed with joint Russian-separatist forces in 2015 near the Donetsk International Airport and the "Sparta" impromptu military base, located on the territory of the Donetsk National Technological University.[31]
- The PSNR-8 Kredo-M1 (1L120) portable ground reconnaissance station was adopted by the Russian army in 2002. This system is designed to detect moving targets on the ground or water and to support artillery fire at any time of day, year-round. Importantly, this system can also be used in conditions of low visibility. It has repeatedly been spotted on the territory of Luhansk Oblast (Blahodatne, Olhynka, Buhas, Volnovakha and Olenivka).[32]

These, by and large, technical descriptions require some further context, which can be deduced from analyses provided by two prominent Ukrainian military experts specializing in electronic warfare.

---

[30] "Na okkupirovannom Donbasse zafiksirovana rossijskaja stantsia pomekh 'Zhitel,'" *RBC*, November 14, 2017, https://www.rbc.ua/rus/news/okkupirovannom-donbasse-zafiksirovana-rossiyskaya-1510658089.html.

[31] "Donetsk: Kompleksy radiorazvedki WS RF 'Torn' i 'Taran' na baze 'Sparta,'" *Inform Napalm*, October 30, 2015, https://informnapalm.org/14245-radyorazvedka-ukv-dyapazona-na-baze-sparta/.

[32] "Russian Kredo-M1 Radar System in Olenivka," *Inform Napalm*, March 11, 2016, https://informnapalm.org/en/russian-kredo-m1-radar-system-olenivka/.

Col. Ivan Pavlenko, the deputy chief of Combat Support Units of the Joint Forces Headquarters,[33] admitted the overall effectiveness of Russian EW in Donbas. He also noted an important role played by Moscow jamming Kyiv's use of GLONASS (Russia's satellite global positioning navigation system) as well as spoofing Ukrainian GPS signals. According to Pavlenko, as a result of Russia's actions, between 2015 and 2017, the UAF lost—among others—about 100 small UAVs.[34]

A more detailed analysis, presented by Maj. Gen. Borys Kremenetskyi, underscored three additional important details.[35] First, he named additional EW assets employed by the Russian-backed separatists in the Donbas—the RB-531B "Infauna"; the SPR-2M "Rtut-BM" interference and jamming station; the "Shipovnik-Aero" jamming station; the "Murmansk-BN"; the 1L269 Krasukha-2, designed to jam S-band signals (2.3–2.5 and 2.7–3.7 gigahertz); the 1RL257 Krasukha-C4, and the RP-377LA Lorandit station—underscoring their role in operations.

Second, he emphasized some other key functions performed by Russian EW units, including degrading radio communications (sudden disappearance of radio communication due to unknown reasons), blocking cellular (GSM) radio signals without their further restoration, defining the points of access and targeting the areas of mass access to GSM communication, using radio-electronic warfare capabilities to spot the location of counterbattery radars, using new physical principles to destroy electronic equipment (the Murmansk-BN played a special role), sending cellular text messages to private phones of Ukrainian

---

[33] Between 2009 and 2017, Pavlenko served as chief of the Electronic Protection Section in the Electronic Warfare Department of the General Staff of the Armed Forces of Ukraine.

[34] "Ukrainian Officer Details Russian Electronic Warfare Tactics Including Radio 'Virus,' " *The Drive*, October 30, 2019, https://www.thedrive.com/the-war-zone/30741/ukrainian-officer-details-russian-electronic-warfare-tactics-including-radio-virus.

[35] Borys Kremenetsky, "EW Lessons Learned: Russian Hybrid Warfare in Ukraine," Royal United Services Institute, March 20, 2019, https://rusi.org/sites/default/files/russian_military_jamming_in_the_a ir_environment - maj_gen_borys_kremenetskyi.pdf.

62 | BLACK SEA BATTLEGROUND

soldiers and ascertaining (through data obtained from smartphones) their location.

Third, according to Kremenetskyi, on some occasions, the Russian Armed Forces experienced "electronic fratricide" because of their jamming actions. Specifically, the Ukrainian general stated,

> I believe that they did not solve the problem of interoperability. Once they try to jam our systems, their own systems are also being jammed. Sometimes they tried to jam our frequencies, but then would also jam their own frequencies. ... For example Russian UAVs use satellite signals transmitted by the country's GLONASS [global positioning] constellation using a waveband of 1.589 GHz [gigahertz] to 1.6 GHz. In such cases, Russian forces could sometimes end up jamming their own UAV GNSS [global navigation satellite system] signals.[36]

The last element is particularly important in light of growing tensions in Donbas since January 2021 that risk the situation spiraling out of control and resulting in yet another outbreak of heavy fighting between the UAF and "separatist" forces. Should the situation along the line of contact escalate, the DPR/LPR leadership,[37] as well as leading Russian military experts and officials,[38] contend that the separatists will receive direct military support from Russia.

------

[36] Thomas Withington, "Jam and Scoot," *Armada International*, December 4, 2019, https://armadainternational.com/2019/12/jam-and-scoot/#:~:text=Major%20General%20Borys%20Kremenetskyi%2C%20Ukraine%E2%80%99s%20defence%20and%20air,three%20gigahertz%29%20tactical%20radio%20communications%20and%20cellphone%20transmissions.

[37] "V DNR zayavili ob obostrenii situatsii na linii zargranitchenia," *Interfax*, April 5, 2021, https://www.interfax.ru/world/759600.

[38] "Bolshaya igra," YouTube, March 11, 2021, https://www.youtube.com/watch?v=Mbfg5ACGs1A&ab_channel=%D0%9F%D0%B5%D1%80%D0%B2%D1%8B%D0%B9%D0%BA%D0%B0%D0%BD%D0%B0%D0%BB.

However, according to Russian experts and officials, in the case of a renewed confrontation, Moscow's actions will be mainly concerned with "providing support ... in such a way as to be able to minimize the risk of a full-fledged military escalation ... incurring a defeat on the UAF in a non-contact way of combat." This could be construed as a stern warning by the Russian side that, to "help" the LPR/DPR, Moscow is ready to employ not only conventional means of war and covert PMCs—but also unmanned aerial combat vehicles (UCAV)[39] as well as advanced EW assets.

Russia's EW Operations in Donbas: The 'Post-Conflict' Stage

The period since 2017—which could be conditionally defined as the "post-conflict" stage—witnessed a lowering intensity of (para)military engagements and the gradual "freezing" of the front-line war. This lowered intensity of confrontation did not, however, mean that Russia completely ceased testing its EW capabilities against the UAF. Both Ukrainian and international observers have indicated and reported numerous instances of Russian EW pieces being present in different parts of occupied Donbas. For instance, one of the last Organization for Security and Co-operation in Europe Special Monitoring Mission (OSCE SMM) reports mentioned three EW systems spotted by its long-range surveillance drones—R-330Zh Zhitel, R-934B Sinitsa and RB-636 Svet-KU systems—near the village of Verbova Balka (28 kilometers southeast of Donetsk).[40]

Based on the information available, it is possible to identify three areas Russia has prioritized when it comes to testing its EW capabilities in the region.

---

[39] "Mashiny voyny. Spetsialnyy reportazh," YouTube, April 5, 2021, https://www.youtube.com/watch?v=EE7n0jSYxhc&ab_channel=TVCenter.

[40] "Exclusive Data: More Russian Electronic Warfare Systems Spotted in Donbas," *Inform Napalm*, March 22, 2020, https://informnapalm.org/en/exclusive-data-more-russian-electronic-warfare-systems-spotted-in-donbas/.

64 | BLACK SEA BATTLEGROUND

1. *Radio-electronic intelligence gathering and interception*: This element is best seen in the testing of the RB-636 "Svet-KU" system, which is specifically concerned with "control ... and monitoring of radio signals ... transmitted by radio channels."[41] According to Russian sources, this complex can—under certain circumstances (GSM, CDMA2000 and UMTS networks)—independently block systems of communication.[42]

2. *Radio-electronic suppression*, which is primarily tested through the employment of the following two systems:

   - The "Tirada-2" jamming complex was first spotted in Donbas in 2019.[43] This complex has also been tested—within the scope of military exercises—on the territory of the Central Military District (CMD), in Sverdlovsk Oblast. Russian sources have claimed that Tirada-2 is primarily concerned with tasks related to locating, blocking and suppressing communications satellites. In commenting on the results of those exercises in the CMD, Russian sources have argued that this complex is capable of not only blocking but also completely incapacitating enemy satellites.

   - The R-934B "Sinitsa" jamming station, whose main tasks are concerned with disrupting target-setting for the adversary's aviation and blocking data transmission from reconnaissance aircraft.[44]

---

[41] "Komplex radioelektronnoy borbi i radiotekhnicheskaya razvedka semeystv RB-636AM2 'Svet,' " Vpk.name, https://vpk.name/library/f/svet-reb.html.

[42] "Den innovatsii UVO: complex REB RB-636AM2 'Svet-KU,' " Topwar.ru, October 19, 2015, https://topwar.ru/84389-den-innovaciy-yuvo-kompleks-reb-rb-636am2-svet-ku.html.

[43] "Noveyshee rossiyskoye radioelektronnoye oruzhie vpervyye zametili na Donbasse," Lenta.ru, March 20, 2019, https://lenta.ru/news/2019/03/20/obse/.

[44] "Spetsialisty vojsk REB kaspiyskoii flotilii w hode ucheniya podavili sviaz uslovnogo protivnika sovremennymi stantsiyami 'Sinitsa,'" Russian Ministry of Defense, February 8, 2021, https://function.mil.ru/news_page/country/more.htm?id=12342943@egNews.

Russian experts have compared the Sinitsa against the Krasukha mobile, ground-based EW system (also spotted by the OSCE mission Ukraine in 2018[45]), which is capable of disrupting low Earth orbit satellites and cause permanent damage to targeted radio-electronic devices. And according to these specialists, the Krasukha is more like a "rapier" (due to its centered angle of coverage and suppression) while the Sinitsa is more like a "club" (due to a much wider and broader coverage).[46] Interestingly, the most recent (since early 2021) reports from the front note that "the UAF is experiencing difficulties with radio connections as well as reconnaissance," which is attributed by Ukrainian sources to "actions of the Russian EW forces."[47]

3. *Informational-psychological operations*—not a new phenomenon—have acquired some new traits.

First, apparently, the combined Russian-separatist forces have attempted to use the Leer-3 complex together with the Orlan-10 UAV in an integrated manner to indicate and imitate the work of a radio station, which, in turn, might enable them to send text messages with malign or disinformation content.[48] However, some experts have argued that "since 2015, the effectiveness of

---

[45] "Latest from the OSCE Special Monitoring Mission to Ukraine (SMM), Based on Information Received as of 19:30, 10 August 2018," Organization for Security and Cooperation in Europe, August 11, 2018, https://www.osce.org/special-monitoring-mission-to-ukraine/390236.

[46] "Stantsia REB R-934Y 'Sinitsa'. Kogda 'Sinitsa' w pole, zhuravliam w nebe tiazko," November 3, 2017 https://warshistory.ru/raznoe-2/r-934-stanciya-reb-r-934u-sinica-kogda-sinica-v-pole-zhuravlyam-v-nebe-tyazhko.html.

[47] "Ukrainskiye SMI: REB rossiyskikh vojsk nachali glushit sredstave sviazi VSU w Donbasse," Argumenti.ru, March 16, 2021, https://argumenti.ru/army/2021/03/713848.

[48] Pavel Shishkin, "Na Ukraine obvinili voyennykh RF w rassylke SMS-soobsheniy boytsam VSU," Vonnoedelo.com, March 23, 2021, https://voennoedelo.com/posts/id10423-921,9fpj77gbmbbwg06es.

such efforts has decreased significantly, and they have nearly lost their negative psychological impact. ... Many soldiers even collect such texts for fun."[49]

Still, the potential impact of these disinformation efforts must not be downplayed for two reasons. On the one hand, most recent reports have vividly demonstrated the extent of Russia's determination to sow propaganda and disinformation in Ukraine (especially in the southeast), using all resources available (including local loyalists and covert defectors).[50] Were the military confrontation between the Ukrainian and DPR/LPR forces (supported by Russia) to significantly intensify—and especially with growing military casualties—Russian propaganda and disinformation efforts could start playing a more visible role. On the other hand, leading Russian media outlets have strengthened another side of their informational-psychological campaign, amplifying the opinions of foreign experts who argue that Ukraine cannot hope to defend itself against a (potential) Russian attack and urge their own governments not to become involved in a conflict with Russia over Ukraine, since the latter is not part of the North Atlantic Treaty Organization (NATO).[51]

---

[49] Yuri Lapaiev, "Russian Electronic Warfare in Donbas: Training or Preparation for a Wider Attack?," *Eurasia Daily Monitor* March 17, 2020, https://jamestown.org/program/russian-electronic-warfare-in-donbas-training-or-preparation-for-a-wider-attack/.

[50] Alla Hurska. "Zaporizhia Oblast: The Next Flash Point in Russia's 'Hybrid' Aggression Against Southeastern Ukraine?," *Eurasia Daily Monitor*, July 28, 2020, https://jamestown.org/program/zaporizhia-oblast-the-next-flash-point-in-russias-hybrid-aggression-against-southeastern-ukraine/; Alla Hurska, "Pro-Russian Disinformation Operations in Kherson: A New-Old Challenge for Ukraine's National Security," *Eurasia Daily Monitor*, June 29, 2020, https://jamestown.org/program/pro-russian-disinformation-operations-in-kherson-a-new-old-challenge-for-ukraines-national-security/.

[51] Alla Hurska, "Russian 'Bot Farms'—The New-Old Challenge to Ukraine's National Security," *Eurasia Daily Monitor*, March 3, 2020, https://jamestown.org/program/russian-bot-farms-the-new-old-challenge-to-ukraines-national-security/.

The second noteworthy development that coincided with the new round of growing tensions in Donbas was the appearance of a narrative supported by Russia's main information outlets about instances of suicide among UAF soldiers.[52] In effect, earlier—especially in 2014, amid the most intensive military engagements—Russian information outlets had actively circulated allegations of low morale among Ukrainian military personnel and their pervasive unwillingness to serve their country. Incidentally, the same narrative has forcefully reappeared in early 2021.[53] In the future, Russian-backed forces might try to reactivate this and similar narratives during periods of sharp escalation along the frontlines.

Conclusion: Lessons and Future Plans

Russia's experience in Donbas is inseparable from two related factors. First is the extent of Russia's involvement and objectives pursued. In general, to date, Russia's paramilitary and conventional military involvement in eastern Ukraine has been rather limited. This is equally true with regard to the use and testing of radio-electronic confrontation capabilities. By and large, the main aspects of information confrontation extensively tested by Russia in Ukraine—both in Crimea and Donbas—have actually been informational-psychological operations as well as the radio-electronic suppression of enemy EW. Consequently, the war in Donbas provides only a narrow window on Russia's offensive capabilities in electronic warfare; its full potential in this space is yet to be discovered.

That said, one must not ignore that, since 2017, Russia has achieved visible progress in EW. Specifically, by early 2021, the Russian Armed Forces received 1,000 pieces of various EW

---

[52] "Ukrainskii soldat-srochnik pokonchil s soboy na postu," *Rossiyskaya Gazeta*, April 5, 2021, https://rg.ru/2021/04/05/ukrainskij-soldat-srochnik-pokonchil-s-soboj-na-postu.html.
[53] "Ukraintsi ne hotiat klast golovy za polskije I amerikanskije interesy," Vpk-news.ru, April 7, 2021, https://vpk-news.ru/news/61610.

systems and 19 mostly up-to-date complexes; moreover, during this period, the military performed more than 200 special-tactical trainings, simulating both defensive and offensive operations.[54] Should heavy hostilities in Donbas break out anew, Russia is likely to employ this growing potential accumulated over the past three to four years.

The second factor is Russia's short-to-medium-term EW strategy, which has been shaped by the experience its armed forces gained in various recent regional conflicts—namely, Syria, Libya, Ukraine and Karabakh. At this juncture, it is worth citing the chief of Russia's EW forces, Maj. Gen. Yuri Lastochkin. In April 2020, when referring to a nexus between experience and EW capabilities, Lastochkin stated that, over the coming years, Russia must embark, among other activities, on the development of robotic means of radio-electronic suppression as well as disorganization of enemy radio connections and data transfer; but it must specifically prioritize the advancement of anti-drone warfare capabilities.[55]

The last element merits special attention, particularly in light of Russia's experiences in the Syrian and Libyan campaigns and, perhaps, even more so, after the Second Karabakh War (September 27–November 9, 2020), which vividly demonstrated the strengths of aerial combat drones.[56] This latter conflict holds yet another special meaning for Russia, since during the hostilities, Turkish UCAVs played a decisive role in the military

---

[54] Aleksander Grigoriev. "REB: kak uchatsia woejvat bojtsi nevidimogo fronta impulsov," *Zvezda Weekly*, March 5, 2021, https://zvezdaweekly.ru/news/202132922-urO8Z.html.

[55] Viktor Khudoleev, "Strazniki efira na pravilnom puti," Redstar.ru, April 15, 2020, http://redstar.ru/strazhniki-efira-na-pravilnom-puti/.

[56] For more information, see Sergey Sukhankin. "The Second Karabakh War: Lessons and Implications for Russia (Part One)," *Eurasia Daily Monitor*, January 5, 2021, https://jamestown.org/program/the-second-karabakh-war-lessons-and-implications-for-russia-part-one/; Sergey Sukhankin, "The Second Karabakh War: Lessons and Implications for Russia, Part Two," *Eurasia Daily Monitor*, January 13, 2021 https://jamestown.org/program/the-second-karabakh-war-lessons-and-implications-for-russia-part-two/.

defeat of the Russian-equipped and Russian-trained Armenian side. Russian experts are especially concerned by the prospect that Turkish UCAVs purchased by Ukraine will be employed in Donbas if that war grows hotter.[57] Despite their generally defiant rhetoric, Russian military analysts by and large realize that, without direct support from Moscow, the LPR/DPR forces are likely to suffer major losses at the hands of UAF troops wielding advanced, Turkish-produced attack drones could change the battlefield—particularly since Ukrainian soldiers are now being specifically trained for these types of military operations.[58]

Therefore, in addition to already-tested EW systems, Russia could—based on the results of its Syrian experience (anti-drone warfare)[59]—deploy heretofore unseen assets to Donbas. Indeed, leading Russian military experts openly contend that this will be the case.[60] In particular, three elements are most likely to appear. First is the Shipovnik-AERO jamming station, specifically designed to counter UAVs, TV and radio-broadcasting stations, command communications centers, and cellular and other electro-magnetic band stations. This EW system generates powerful noise jamming that completely suppresses UAV control signals. And thanks to its ability to create a false navigation field by changing dynamic coordinates, the Shipovnik-AERO can place the adversary's drones under its control within minutes.[61] The second element is the "Samarkand" complex—deployed in

---

[57] Ukraina toze zakupaet turetskiye bespilotniki: 'Eto budet ugroza Donbassu,' " *EA Daily*, "October 7, 2020, https://eadaily.com/ru/news/2020/10/07/ukraina-tozhe-zakupaet-tureckie-bespilotniki-eto-budet-ugroza-donbassu.
[58] "V DNR rasskazali, kak budut sbivat turetskiye drony VVS Ukrainy," *Moskovsky Komsomolets*, February 16, 2021, https://www.mk.ru/politics/2021/02/16/v-dnr-rasskazali-kak-budut-sbivat-tureckie-drony-vvs-ukrainy.html.
[59] Vladimir Gundarov, "Siriyskiye uroki REB," Vpk-news.ru, February 16, 2021, https://vpk-news.ru/articles/60891.
[60] "Leonkov rasskazal, kakoy budet reaktsija Rossii na natuplenie VSU w Donbasse." Newsua.ru, February 19, 2021, https://newsua.ru/news/41830-leonkov-rasskazal-kakoj-budet-reaktsiya-rossii-na-nastuplenie-vsu-v-donbasse.
[61] Gundarov, "Siriyskiye uroki REB."

70 | BLACK SEA BATTLEGROUND

Kaliningrad Oblast and Belarus—whose full spectrum of characteristics is still unknown. The third EW asset that Russian experts believe might next be battletested in Donbas[62] is the Orion UCAV; although this prospect seems rather dubious because that system has, until at least late August 2021, been undergoing extensive pre-production trials.[63]

Given Russia's determined and advancing development of EW capabilities, the Western response should be concentrated on two aspects. The first is a more systematic accretion of its own capabilities in this domain. Second, the Euro-Atlantic alliance as a whole would benefit from facilitating its partner Ukraine's technological transition to becoming a significant EW player in its own right. This could be done by selling or donating the most up-to-date Western EW systems to Kyiv as well as by investing in Ukraine's domestic EW industry.

The European Union—which clearly lacks durable leadership and unity when it comes to Russia-related matters—is not a military alliance. Therefore, NATO should become the key driving force contributing to Ukraine's advancement in EW. Specifically, two actors, the United States and Turkey, are best positioned to assume leadership in assisting the Ukrainian Armed Forces develop their EW capabilities. Both countries have achieved truly impressive technological military advancements that have already been showcased in various regional conflicts.

As indicated earlier, cooperation in the EW domain should not be solely based on exporting NATO products. It would also make sense for Alliance members—with Canada and the United

---

[62] "Na turetskiye drony w nebe Donbassa Rossiya mozet otvetit 'Orionom,'" *Riafan*, October 26, 2020, https://riafan.ru/1325614-na-tureckie-drony-v-nebe-donbassa-rossiya-mozhet-otvetit-orionom.
[63] "Minoborony RF podpisalo kontrakty na postavku udarnykh bespilotnikov 'Inokhodets' i 'Forpost-R,'" Centre for Analysis of World Arms Trade, August 24, 2021, https://armstrade.org/includes/periodics/news/2021/0824/155064173/detail.shtml; "Russia to begin deliveries of latest strike drones to troops from 2023," *TASS*, August 26, 2021, https://tass.com/defense/1330349.

Kingdom, for instance, well suited to assume key roles—to provide Ukraine's defense industry with foreign direct investment as well as technology and knowledge transfer essential for boosting its production potential. That said, however, NATO actions must complement Ukraine's own efforts. Among the areas of strategic importance for Kyiv—aside from the defense industry—are improving energy security, reforming its information policies and undertaking anti-corruption/anti-oligarch initiatives. If those latter issues remain unaddressed, NATO's efforts to modernize the Ukrainian Armed Forces and their EW capabilities will have little practical effect.

3.

Guardian of the Danube: Romania's Mixed Progress in Implementing a Black Sea Strategy

George Visan

December 20, 2021

Romania's maritime environment consists of the Danube River and the Black Sea. The river links the country to the sea providing an important trade connection with the rest of the continent as well as a natural frontier. Moreover, the Danube is crucial for Romania as it is one of the country's most important sources of energy. Romania's main interests in the Black Sea are ensuring peace and stability, freedom of navigation and energy security along with exploitation of the natural resources found in its exclusive economic zone.

The major conflicts of the 20th century have affected Romania's perception concerning the importance of its maritime environment. In both world wars, the Danube and the Black Sea were strategic theaters of operations on the eastern front. Romania clashed with the great powers of the day in order to gain or secure access to the Black Sea and the Danube. Historically, however, Romania's interest in its maritime environment has been intermittent, with periods of great activity alternating with periods of relative neglect.

After the end of the Cold War, Romania chose the Black Sea as its main strategic focus. The reasons for this choice had to do with a mix of threats, risks, and opportunities that made the region attractive. Politically, Bucharest did not want to be associated with the Balkans and their turbulent history. The Black Sea offered both strategic opportunities as well as economic ones. The region is important economically as it links Asia and Central Asia to Europe, in addition to being rich in oil and gas resources. The strategic challenges consist of prolonged conflicts in the former Soviet space and Russian aggressive behavior, which culminated in the Russo-Georgian War of 2008 and the Kremlin's aggression against Ukraine since 2014.

Today, Romania is trying to counterbalance the Black Sea region's strategic challenges by consolidating its relationship with the United States and by investing in its own defense. Yet these efforts have only been moderately successful to date. The US military presence in Romania is rotational and does not have the same status as the one in the Baltic States and Poland, despite that region experiencing a comparable level of threat. Moreover, Romania's defense modernization and procurement is suffering from delays, which affect its deterrence credibility. Finally, despite significant energy production potential, most of Romania's oil and natural gas projects in the Black Sea are being delayed, negatively impacting the country's energy security.

Introduction: Romania and Its Strategic Maritime Environment

Romania's maritime interests include the Danube River and the Black Sea. The Danube is Europe's second-longest river and one of its main trading routes. One thousand and seventy-five kilometers of the lower course of the Danube runs through the country. Romania controls most of the Danube Delta and, more importantly, the mouths of the Danube, along with the main navigable Sulina canal.

The lower course of the Danube forms part of the border between Romania and Ukraine, and the latter country controls a small part

74 | BLACK SEA BATTLEGROUND

of the river's delta. In the south and southwest, the Danube divides Romania from its Balkan neighbors, Serbia and Bulgaria. The Danube–Black Sea canal, which links the river to the Port of Constanţa, shortens the route for ships and freight on their way to the Black Sea. Around 236 km of the river are Romanian internal waters.[1] The Danube-Rhine canal links the two rivers together, so that, in theory, freight shipped from Constanţa can reach the Netherland's Rotterdam, the busiest port in Europe.

Besides riverine shipping, trade links with Serbia and Bulgaria are maintained by bridges and viaducts. The main bridges over the river that link Romania and Bulgaria are at Giurgiu and Calafat. Plans exist to build another bridge to boost trade and tourism between the two countries. Serbia and Romania, in turn, are linked over the Danube by a viaduct across Iron Gates I Hydroelectric Power Plant (HPP) and via a bridge at Ostrovu Mare, in the vicinity of Iron Gates II HPP.

The Danube is important for Romania not only as a major trade route but also for the country's energy security. Two major hydroelectric dams are situated on the Danube: the aforementioned Iron Gates I and II. Both are the result of the cooperation between Communist Romania and Yugoslavia in the 1970s and 1980s. Iron Gates I is the most powerful HPP in the entire Romanian conventional energy-generating system, while Iron Gates II is the third-most powerful plant of this type. Additionally, the Cernavodă nuclear power plant (NPP), whose construction began in 1982, stands on the Danube–Black Sea canal. Water from the Danube is drawn and used in the secondary circuit of the two pressurized water reactors operated by the plant.

Strategically, the Danube separates Romania from the Balkans and forms a natural border with Ukraine in the southeast. In the past, the Danube partially defined Romania's political and diplomatic identity. Notably, during the first half of the 19th

---

[1] Mihai Panait, "Perspective de dezvoltare instituţională durabilă a Forţelor Navale Române în perioada 2016–2035," in *Buletinul Forţelor Navale*, Nr. 24, 2016, 86.

Figure 1. Danube River

Source: DANCERS

century, the principalities of Moldavia and Wallachia were known as the "Danubian Principalities" in diplomatic circles. The river also played a crucial role in all of the of conflicts that Romania was involved in during the 19th and 20th centuries.

Control of the Danube has been an ongoing issue for Romania since the creation of the state in the early modern period. The early Romanian state did not have the resources to properly manage the river. Moreover, up until 1878, the country was not independent but rather a dominion of the Ottoman Empire, and control of the river was coveted by both Austria and the Russian Empire.

Starting in 1856, navigation on the Danube became regulated by international and European commissions. Romania greatly resented this situation, as the existence of these bodies infringed upon its sovereignty over parts of the lower Danube. Two European commissions have regulated traffic on the Danube. The first one was created after the Crimean War in 1856 and functioned until 1948. It oversaw river navigation and administration of the maritime sector of the river, from Galați to Sulina. The commission raised taxes and had its own courts.

The Paris Treaty of 1856 additionally made provisions for an International Danube Commission to regulate traffic upstream from Galați, but this international body came into being only in 1918. The current Danube Commission was established in 1948 as the result of the Belgrade Convention of 1948, which reflected a Soviet vision regarding the river. Currently it is made up of Austria, Bulgaria, Croatia, Germany, Moldova, Romania, Serbia, Slovakia and Ukraine. Belgium, Greece, Georgia, Cyprus, North Macedonia, the Netherlands, Turkey, Montenegro and Czechia (the Czech Republic) have observer status. Although the Soviet Union has disappeared and Russia does not have access to the river, Moscow remains a full member of the commission. Article 30 of the Convention Regarding the Regime of Navigation on the Danube prohibits the deployment of naval vessels of non-riparian countries.[2] This provision may have a negative impact on Romania's ability to deter and defend against potential aggression as it hinders the deployment of allied forces from the United States or other non-riparian North Atlantic Treaty Organization (NATO) member states on the river.

The Black Sea represents Romania's main link with the global market. Goods to and from Romanian ports reach other parts of the world by transiting the Turkish Straits (Bosporus and Dardanelles) into the Mediterranean Sea and then on to the Atlantic and Indian Oceans. The Black Sea is additionally an access point to the markets of Central Asia and onward, via land routes, to the rest of Asia. Romania hopes to take advantage of its geographical position in the Black Sea and its membership in the European Union to more deeply connect with Asian markets.

The Turkish Straits and the Montreux Convention of 1936 have given the popular impression that the Black Sea is a closed sea (*mare clausum*), yet it is not landlocked like the nearby Caspian. The Turkish Straits act as much as an access point as they are a barrier. Furthermore, freedom of navigation through the Straits

---

[2] *Danube Commission*, "Convention regarding the regime of navigation on the Danube, 1948,"
https://www.danubecommission.org/dc/en/danube-commission/convention-regarding-the-regime-of-navigation-on-the-danube/.

The significance of Romania's maritime spaces is reflected in its international trade. In 2020, despite the COVID-19 pandemic, 47.2 million tons of goods transited through Romanian ports.[3] Most of this traffic passed through the Port of Constanța (83 percent) and the rest was handled by the ports of Midia and Galați.[4] Besides trade, Romanian ports double as shipyards. The main shipbuilding and repair facilities in Romania are Șantierul Naval Constanța, Midia and Mangalia (the latter two are state owned but privately managed by the Dutch company Damen). These are followed on the lower course of the Danube, close to the mouths of river, by Damen Galați, Sulina, as well as Brăila and Tulcea—the latter two owned by the Italian conglomerate Fincantieri. Further down the Danube, there are shipyards at Orșova, Turnu Severin, Giurgiu, Cernavodă and Oltenița. Romanian shipyards build, repair and modify both seagoing and riverine ships. Damen Galați is currently the only shipyard in Romania that has built and delivered military vessels for navies and coast guards around the world.

Romania's Black Sea coastline measures 245 km (132 nautical miles), and its exclusive economic zone (EEZ) has a surface of 9,700 square km.[5] Romania's EEZ is important from an energy security perspective as it is estimated to contain around 200 billion cubic meters (bcm) of natural gas, according to the most optimistic estimates.[6]

---

[3] Răzvan Diaconu, „Volumul de mărfuri încărcate/descărcate în porturile maritime românești a scăzut cu peste 11% în 2020," *Curs de Guvernare*, March 14, 2021, https://cursdeguvernare.ro/volumul-de-marfuriincarcate-descarcate-in-porturile-maritime-romanesti-a-scazut-cu-peste-11-in-2020.html.

[4] Ibid.

[5] Nicu Durnea, "Rolul Forțelor Navale Române în apărarea intereselor țării în bazinul Mării Negre la începutul mileniului III," *Buletinul Forțelor Navale*, Nr. 19, 2013, 33.

[6] Melania Agiu, "Zăcămintele din Marea Neagră, puse în pericol. Ce se întâmplă dacă investițiile în proiectul Neptun Deep nu demarează în 2022," *Adevărul*, April 8, 2021, adev.ro/qr8zxe.

78 | BLACK SEA BATTLEGROUND

After Brexit, Romania became the second-largest producer of gas in the EU.[7] Bucharest's and Ankara's gas discoveries in the Black Sea make them the most important NATO allies in the region when it comes to energy security. In the Romanian exclusive economic zone, the following potential oil and gas deposit have been identified: Neptun Deep, Neptun Shallow, Midia, Luceafărul, Histria, Pelican, Muridava, Cobălcescu, Rapsodia and Trident. Neptun Deep is considered the most valuable discovery, with an estimated capacity between 42 and 84 bcm of gas.[8] In the Turkish EEZ, exploration efforts have identified Turkali-1, Turkali-2, Turkali-3, Danube-1 and Tuna-1 oil and gas deposits. The largest find in the Turkish zone is the Tuna-1 gas field, discovered in 2021 with an estimated volume of 320 bcm.[9]

Romania and the Black Sea During the Major Conflicts of the 20th Century

In 1905, Romania received a naval wake-up call when the mutinous Russian battleship *Potemkin* entered the Constanța roadstead and demanded fuel and victuals. If these demands were not fulfilled, *Potemkin* declared it would open fire on the port. The Romanian authorities were taken by surprise by this unwanted visitor, which was being hunted by the entire Imperial Russian Black Sea Fleet. Romania's only naval assets in the Black Sea at that time were three French-built torpedo-boats, a British-built light cruiser and a school ship.[10] All of these warships were

---

[7] *Romania Insider*, "Romania remains second-biggest gas producer in EU," August 31, 2020, https://www.romania-insider.com/ro-second-biggest-gas-producer-eu-aug-2020.

[8] *Offshore Technology*, "Neptun Deep Gas Field Project, Black Sea," *Offshore Technology*, accessed November 30, 2021, https://www.offshore-technology.com/projects/neptun-deep-gas-field-project-black-sea/.

[9] Dilara Hamit, Gozde Bayar and Jeyhun Aliyev, "Turkey discovers major Black Sea natural gas reserves," August 21, 2021, https://www.aa.com.tr/en/economy/turkey-discovers-major-black-sea-natural-gas-reserves/1949231.

[10] Raymond Stănescu and Cristian Crăciunoiu, *Marina Română în Primul Război Mondial*, (Bucharest: Modelism, 2000), 28–29.

Guardian of the Danube | 79

outdated by the beginning of the 20th century and no match for a pre-dreadnought battleship like *Potemkin*. Moreover, the prospect of a naval battle between the mutinous *Potemkin* and the Russian Black Sea Fleet outside Constanţa was not something the Romanian side wished to see off its coast.

Ultimately, however, the crisis was resolved without recourse to arms. Romania gave the mutinous crew asylum or safe passage out of the country, while the latter agreed to surrender the ship to the Royal Romanian Navy.[11] When the Russian fleet arrived off Constanţa to take over or sink the fugitive battleship, the Romanian navy informed its Russian colleagues of how events unfolded with the rebels aboard *Potemkin* and then surrendered the ship to its rightful owners.[12]

This event underscored the need for a modern and capable Romanian naval force in the Black Sea. In the early 20th century, the Black Sea region was disputed between the declining Ottoman Empire and the rapidly modernizing Russian Empire. The *Potemkin* mutiny illustrated that Romania, as a young state and a small power in the Black Sea region, was vulnerable not only to the geopolitical ambitions of the established regional powers but also to internal political and social developments that took place within the latter's borders. In the aftermath of the incident, the Romanian government drew up plans for the procurement of four modern torpedo-boat destroyers but no order for maritime warships, as the policy focus shifted to the Danube.[13]

Romania simultaneously faced pressure from the Austro-Hungarian Empire regarding policing rights along the Danube. The double monarchy controlled most of the course of the river and wanted to extend this control to the lower course, which passed through Serbia, Romania, Bulgaria and the mouths of the Danube. On the eve of World War I, a naval arms race on the

---

[11] Andreea Croitoru, "Rolul ofiţerilor de marina români în soluţionarea crizei Potemkin – 110 ani de la evenimente," *Buletinul Forţelor Navale*, No. 22, 2015, 77–79.
[12] Ibid., 80–81.
[13] Stănescu and Crăciunoiu, 24.

80 | BLACK SEA BATTLEGROUND

Danube began between Romania and Austria-Hungary. Both countries invested heavily in river monitors and small riverine torpedo boats. By the time the war had broken out, Romania wielded four river monitors and eight torpedo-boats on the Danube. Furthermore, in 1915, the government finally ordered the four destroyers envisioned after the *Potemkin* incident as well as a submarine from an Italian shipyard. But when Italy entered the war that same year, the destroyers were taken over by Rome's Regia Marina.[14]

Romania entered World War I in 1916 on the Entente side. Its main priority was to establish control over the traffic on the lower Danube to protect the Turtucaia bridgehead in Southern Dobrudja. The Royal Romanian Navy tried to establish its riverine supremacy on the first day of the war by launching a surprise torpedo attack on the Austro-Hungarian monitors.[15] However, the attack failed, with only one enemy supply ship sunk. The Romanian naval doctrine at that time demanded its monitors to seek combat and sink the Austro-Hungarian monitors venturing up the lower Danube.[16] As a result of this doctrine, most of the ammunition supply of the Danube Flotilla at beginning of the war was made up of semi-armor piercing shells. However, no major clash between Romanian and Austro-Hungarian monitors occurred on the river. So instead, the monitors were used to provide naval gunfire support to Romanian troops, which quickly depleted the riverine vessels' supply of high explosive shells.[17] The Romanian monitors had to be resupplied with French-made shells via Russian ports in order to maintain readiness and defend the riverine communications.

The Russian navy, although more numerous than its Ottoman counterpart, did not seriously contest the control of the Black Sea until the first dreadnought battleships of the *Imperatritsa Marya*

---

[14] Marian Moşneagu, *Fregata-Amiral Mărăşeşti* (Bucharest: Editura Militară, 2014) 19.
[15] Stănescu and Crăciunoiu, 71–74.
[16] Stănescu and Crăciunoiu. 28.
[17] Stănescu and Crăciunoiu, 29.

class, ordered just before the start of hostilities, entered service.[18] The arrival in Istanbul in 1914 of the German navy battlecruiser SMS *Goeben* and of the light cruiser SMS *Breslau* changed the balance of forces in favor of the Central Powers. Gifted to the Ottoman Empire by Kaiser Willhelm II, *Goeben* was renamed *Yavuz Sultan Selim* and *Breslau* became *Midilli*. For most of World War I, the Central Powers dominated the Black Sea.[19]

During the disastrous 1916 campaign, Romania lost most of Dobrudja, including the Port of Constanța. It maintained only a tenuous hold over the mouths of the Danube, including its main canal, Sulina. The Danube Flotilla supported the Romanian Army during the battle of Turtucaia and during the Flămânda crossing.[20] A German submarine was damaged after a brief encounter off Sulina in October 1916, with one of Romania's torpedo boats.[21] The following year, as part of the 1917 campaign, the Romanian navy managed to sink an Austro-Hungarian river monitor, KUK *Inn*, near Brăila.[22] Romania's small liners ("packet boats") were armed and lent to the Imperial Russian Navy, which used them as auxiliary cruisers and as seaplane tenders.[23]

Following the Russian Revolution of 1917, Romania was forced to sue for a separate peace with the Central Powers in early 1918.[24] The Treaty of Bucharest imposed taxing conditions on Romania. According to this peace agreement, Romania lost part of Dobrudja to Bulgaria, and the rest, including Constanța, fell under the trusteeship of the Central Powers, although Bucharest

---

[18] Stănescu and Crăciunoiu, 52–53.
[19] Lawrence Sondhaus, *The Great War at Sea. A Naval History of the First World War* (Cambridge: Cambridge University Press) 106–107.
[20] Michael E. Barret, *Prelude to Blitzkrieg. The 1916 Austro-German Campaign in Romania* (Bloomington: Indiana University Press) 127–133.
[21] Stănescu and Crăciunoiu, 138.
[22] Stănescu and Crăciunoiu, 215.
[23] Stănescu and Crăciunoiu, 261–266.
[24] Glenn E. Torrey, *The Romanian Battlefront in World War I* (Lawrence: Kansas University Press, 2011), 281–282.

82 | BLACK SEA BATTLEGROUND

maintained formal sovereignty.[25] Romania maintained control over the mouths of the Danube and received "compensation" in the form of recognition of its union with the former Russian *gubernia* (governorate) of Bessarabia.[26] The loss of southern Dobrudja and control over Constanța, the country's main commercial port, represented a heavy blow for Romania's economic development and geopolitical ambitions. Fortunately for Romania, however, the Treaty of Bucharest never came into force, and the Entente eventually won the Great War.

After the Treaty of Versailles, Romania's coastline expanded from Cetatea Albă (today Bilhorod-Dnistrovskyi, Ukraine) up to Ecrene (Kranevo, Bulgaria).[27] The total length of the coastline was 225 nautical miles, giving Greater Romania the third-longest coastline in the Black Sea after Turkey and the newly created Union of Soviet Socialist Republics (USSR). Moreover, Greater Romania now controlled the mouths of the Danube.

The greatest security threat faced by Romania after World War I came from revisionist states that wanted to overturn the order established at Versailles. These main revisionist great powers were Germany and Soviet Russia. To complicate matters, the USSR was also Romania's largest neighbor, with which it shared the longest land border. Furthermore, Romania had to contend with two revisionist neighbors, Hungary and Bulgaria, which claimed Romania's Transylvania and Southern Dobrudja territories. In the Black Sea, the most important political development was the signing, in 1937, of the Montreux Convention, which established a special military regime concerning the straits of the Bosporus and Dardanelles.

The Romanian navy was strengthened with ships taken from its former enemy, Austria-Hungary—three river monitors and eight

---

[25] Keith Hitchens, *România 1866–1947* (Bucharest: Humanitas, 1994) 275–277.

[26] Torrey, 283-284.

[27] Nicolae Koslinski and Raymond Stănescu, *Marina Română în Al II-lea Război Mondial Vol I (1941–1942)* (Bucharest: Făt Frumos, 1996), 19.

torpedo boats[28]—as well as with ships bought from its allies. The navy procured four French-built gunboats for minesweeping operations in the Black Sea and four Italian Motoscafo Armato Silurante (MAS) anti-submarine patrol boats.[29] Of the four destroyers ordered before the war from Italy, two were commissioned into service. The other two were sold to Italy's Regia Marina in order to settle some of the war debts between the two countries.[30]

Italy would become one of Romania's major naval suppliers during the interwar years. Two more destroyers, based on the British Thornycroft-class design, were built in Italian shipyards as well as a submarine and a submarine tender.[31] However, the Great Depression greatly affected the development of the Romanian Royal Navy. Economic woes impacted the procurement of new ships, weapons system acquisitions and training. Just before the start of World War II, Romania would purchase three motor torpedo boats from the United Kingdom and a training ship from Germany (NS *Mircea*, which is still in service).[32]

The local naval shipbuilding industry also contributed to the development of the Romanian navy. Between 1938 and 1939, two submarines, *Rechinul* and *Marsuinul*, and a minelayer, *Amiral Murgescu*, were laid down in Romanian shipyards.[33] The two submarines would be commissioned later, during World War II. A number of ships were acquired or leased from Germany during the war, but some of them, like the Dutch-built Power-class motor torpedo boats, would prove ill-suited to the needs of the Romanian navy.[34]

Following the August 1939 Ribbentrop-Molotov Pact, Romania would lose Bessarabia and Northern Bukovina to the Soviet Union

---

[28] Stănescu and Crăciunoiu, 272–273.
[29] Ibidem.
[30] Marian Moşneagu, 20–21.
[31] Koslinski and Stănescu Vol. I, 22–23.
[32] Koslinski and Stănescu Vol I, 23.
[33] Koslinski and Stănescu Vol I, 20–22.
[34] Koslinski and Stănescu, Vol II, 85–91.

84 | BLACK SEA BATTLEGROUND

in June 1940. As a consequence of these territorial changes, Soviet Russia again gained access to the mouths of the Danube on the Chilia branch. Moreover, this land grab by Moscow created a vulnerable spot along Romania's defensive perimeter on the lower Danube and the Danube Delta, allowing Soviet forces to threaten navigation along the Sulina canal. Following the retreat of Romanian forces from Bessarabia, skirmishes broke out on the Danube between Soviet and Romanian naval forces, as the border arrangements were not clear.[35] The withdrawal without a fight of the Romanian Armed Forces from the provinces of Bessarabia and Northern Bukovina tempted the Soviet government to try to annex as much territory as possible.[36] The border agreement between the two countries concerning the Danube River did not follow the pre-1918 border. And this situation persisted after World War II.

When Romania entered World War II on June 22, 1941, it became the main Axis naval power in the Black Sea, playing the same role as Italy in the Mediterranean Sea. Moreover, it was the main supplier of oil and oil products to the Axis powers, as well as one of their main providers of grain and foodstuffs.[37]

The Romanian Royal Navy had to face the much larger and better equipped Soviet Black Sea Fleet. At the start of the war, the Romanian navy did not have enough modern warships and lacked intelligence concerning the strength of its enemy. With the exception of the Danube Flotilla, the navy did not train before the war in large formations.[38] In terms of equipment, it did not have enough anti-aircraft guns,[39] and its main surface combatants would fight the entire war without shipborne radar. The main missions undertaken by the Royal Romanian Navy involved protecting the Romanian coast from raids and amphibious assaults, protecting the sea lanes of the communication (SLOC),

---

[35] Jipa Rotaru and Ioan Damaschin, *Glorie și Dramă. Marina regală română 1940-1945* (București: Ion Cristoiu, 2000) 26–32.

[36] Koslinski and Stănescu Vol I, 50.

[37] Rotaru and Damaschin, 181–185.

[38] Koslinski and Stănescu Vol. I, 25–27.

[39] Koslinski and Stănescu Vol. I, 158.

mining and minesweeping operations, as well as mounting limited attacks on Soviet controlled SLOCs.

Although comparatively small, the Romanian navy lost few warships in actual combat. Despite continuous efforts by Soviet naval and air forces to sink the main Axis surface unit in the Black Sea—the Romanian four-destroyer squadron—no ship was lost to enemy action. Both Soviet and Axis forces avoided major engagements, relying instead on mines, submarines and fast attack craft. Both sides launched amphibious operations when the situation called for them and when adequate resources were in place. The Romanian Royal Navy and the German Kriesgsmarine made use of a large number of armed merchant men, armed tugboats and armed trawlers. Both Axis and Soviet forces deployed minefields in the Black Sea on and near the main sea lanes of communication, as well as on the lower course of the Danube. Minesweeping operations were intensive and carried out by both Axis and Soviet forces at regular intervals.

In several actions and operations, the small Romanian navy, aided by its Axis allies, managed to hold out against a superior enemy in terms of ships, aircraft, firepower and manpower. Relatively few surface engagements occurred in the Black Sea, as both the Axis and the Soviets wanted to conserve their major units. Moreover, the naval war in the Black Sea region was secondary to the ground war, as the latter was the decisive theater of operations. In one of the few surface engagements of the war, on June 26, 1941, the Soviet Black Sea Fleet mounted a raid against Constanța.[40] Initially, the Soviet force achieved the element of surprise, but the raid was beaten back by the quick and coordinated reaction of Romanian destroyers aided by German and Romanian shore batteries. The Soviet navy lost the destroyer leader, *Moskva*, in a minefield and another destroyer, *Tashkent*, was damaged.

An important mission of the Romanian Royal Navy during the war was the escorting of convoys between Istanbul and Constanța, Sulina and Odessa, Constanța and Odessa, and, later, between

---

[40] Rotaru and Damschin, 47-50.

Constanţa and Crimea.[41] The most dangerous operation undertaken by the Romanian navy was the evacuation from Crimea in April–May 1944 of Romanian and German troops besieged by Soviet forces. Over two thirds of Axis troops in Crimea managed to be evacuated from Crimea in what the Romanian navy dubbed "Operation 60,000."[42]

When Romania eventually switched sides during World War II, the Kriegsmarine ships present in its Black Sea ports were disarmed, while the rest were chased down the Danube, out of Romanian waters.[43] The Soviet navy confiscated and took over Romania's warships and used them against the remaining Axis forces in the Black Sea region. With few exceptions, most of the ships were returned after the war.

In 1947, the Treaty of Paris redrew the map of Romania to its 1940 borders with the Soviet Union and Bulgaria.[44] Thus, Romania became the Black Sea state with the smallest shoreline in the region, compared to the pre–World War II situation, when it claimed the third-longest coast.

In 1948, Romania's Communist government ceded Snake Island, which is actually a rock, to the Soviet Union, a move that would later complicate the maritime delimitation between Romania and Ukraine. During the Cold War, the Romanian navy, along with its Bulgarian counterpart, essentially became auxiliaries to the Soviet Black Sea Fleet, with the task of helping the latter to punch through the Turkish Straits and operate against NATO forces in the Mediterranean.

---

[41] Koslinski and Stănescu Vol. I, 186–283.
[42] Rotaru and Damaschin, 132–155.
[43] Rotaru and Damaschin, 197–223.
[44] Florin Constantiniu, *O istorie sinceră a poporului român* (Bucharest: Univers Enciclopedic, 1997), 463–466.

Romania's Black Sea Policy in the 21st Century

Romania's Black Sea policy can be divided into two main phases. The first started around 2002 and lasted until 2014. During this period, Bucharest promoted multilateral cooperation in the Black Sea, greater NATO and US presence in the region, energy security, and democratization. The highpoints of this period were the North Atlantic Alliance's Bucharest Summit in 2007, the Georgia War of 2008, and the decision in 2011 by the United States to deploy the Aegis Ashore system in Romania and Poland as part of the Phased Adaptive Approach to deal with ballistic missile threats coming from Iran.

In 2014, the illegal annexation of Crimea by Russia and the subsequent war in eastern Ukraine put an end to this phase of policy. From 2014 onwards, Bucharest's Black Sea policy emphasized deterrence against potential aggression, as well as resilience in the face of Russia's non-linear (hybrid) warfare in the region. Energy security took another dimension, emphasizing interconnectivity and offshore reserves. US presence in the region became crucial for stability and deterrence as Bucharest built up its military.

In the early 2000s, Romania was a candidate for accession to NATO and the European Union. Washington wanted Romania in NATO because of two major factors: the country's military viability as well as its potential role in stabilizing the Balkans. Of all the former Warsaw Pact members, Romania came second after Poland in terms of military potential. The second wave of NATO enlargement needed to include Bucharest in order to balance out countries such as the Baltic States or Bulgaria, whose military potential was rather limited. Furthermore, during the 1990s, the country showed that it could play a stabilizing role in Southeastern Europe. Romania supported the US-led bombing campaign against Serbia in 1999 and the intervention in Kosovo. Moreover, throughout the wars in the former Yugoslavia, Bucharest deployed peacekeepers to the region.

The military and political reforms necessary to become a NATO member moved slowly in the early 2000s. However, the attacks of 9/11 changed priorities on all sides. Washington needed allies to pursue the Global War on Terror, and Romania's relative proximity to the Middle East and Central Asia was considered an asset for US policy. Consequently, the NATO integration process was accelerated and, in 2004, Romania, Bulgaria, Estonia, Latvia and Lithuania became seen as potential intermediate staging bases for the military campaigns in Afghanistan and Iraq. Moreover, Romania was interested in receiving US troops on its territory and had its own agenda regarding the Black Sea.

Romania Chooses the Black Sea as a Strategic Focus

In geopolitical terms, Romania wanted to avoid becoming associated with the Balkan Peninsula, despite US plans and analyses to the contrary. For policy architects in Washington, Romania, along with Greece in the south, which was already in NATO and the EU, were seen as major stabilizing forces in the region. Besides its military potential, US officials believed that Romania could constitute a role model for the countries that made up the former Yugoslavia in terms of its treatment of minorities living within its borders. Previously, in the early 1990s, it was posited that Romania could soon follow the example of its neighbor Yugoslavia due to the existing tensions between the Romanian majority and Hungarian minority. However, by the middle of the decade, those tensions had been peacefully solved and the local Hungarian political organization seamlessly integrated into local political system. For prestige reasons, therefore, Bucharest consciously did not want to be lumped together with the Balkans. The region's instability as well as the history of ethnic cleansing could have negatively impacted Romania's image abroad should it decide to play a larger role in the region. Furthermore, Bucharest did not see eye to eye with Washington on the recognition of Kosovo's independence, fearing it could set a dangerous precedent that could be used by the Kremlin in the case of Transnistria. Moreover, the main threats and opportunities for Romania's foreign policy did not come from the Balkans.

Romania's concerns about Russia are not based on simple Russophobia, despite the difficult history between the two countries. Certainly, Romanians often justify their fears regarding the Kremlin's foreign policy behavior by pointing out that Russia invaded Romanian territory twelve times between the 18th and 19th centuries and that Romania was subordinated to Soviet control in the secret Ribbentrop-Molotov Pact of 1939. The imposition of Communism in Romania after 1945 with the help of the Soviet Red Army is another cultural and historical point of tension in relations between both countries. Conversely, there is a tendency in Romanian public discourse to minimize the country's alliance with the Axis powers during World War II and a limited understanding of the character of the war on the Eastern Front. That said, the main point of contention between Bucharest and Kremlin is not cultural or historical but geopolitical in nature. Russia, besides claiming preeminence in the former Soviet space, would like to have a say over the foreign policy of the countries in Central and Southeastern Europe.[45] For Romania, this is unacceptable and the main reason why, in 1997, it formed a strategic partnership with the United States and ultimately joined NATO. Moreover, in order to diminish Russian influence and apply pressure in the Black Sea, Romanian foreign policy has sought to attract a US and NATO presence in the region.

The dissolution of the Soviet Union was a geopolitical boon for Romania, but it also came with its own set of challenges. The sudden disappearance of the predominant military and ideological power in the Central and Eastern Europe in 1991, coupled with the fall of Communism in 1989, allowed Romania to choose for the first time since 1945 the course of its foreign policy. However, the disappearance of Soviet power did not mean the end of Russian attempts to maintain some sort of control over the political developments in what the Kremlin dubs its "near abroad." Part of these attempts are now commonly called "frozen conflicts"—unresolved military struggles that developed in the former Soviet republics just as the USSR was crumbling. These conflicts notably broke out mainly in the Black Sea and the South

---

[45] Janusz Bugajski, Pacea Rece. Noul Imperialism al Rusiei" (Bucharest: Casa Radio, 2005), 183.

90 | BLACK SEA BATTLEGROUND

Caucasus region: Karabakh (1988) between Armenia and Azerbaijan, Transnistria in Moldova (1990), as well Abkhazia (1989) and Ossetia (1991) in Georgia. The Kremlin drove and/or exploited these localized wars to compromise the sovereignty of the newly minted independent states and to anchor them securely into Russia's sphere of influence.

Of all the post-Soviet frozen conflicts, the 1990–1992 war in Transnistria posed the greatest and most direct security threat for Romania. The proximity of the fighting and Russian support for the breakaway Republic of Transnistria were Bucharest's main concerns. In this war, the industrial and Russian-speaking region of Transnistria wanted to gain independence from the newly created Moldovan state. Rebels in the breakaway republic were directly supported by the Russian 14th Army, which also assumed the role of *de facto* peacekeeping force after the end of hostilities in 1992. After Romania joined NATO in 2004, it sought to put the issue of the Black Sea frozen conflicts on the international agenda.

When it comes to the frozen conflict in Transnistria, Romania initially hesitated between linking the issue to the Black Sea region or to the Balkans. In the early 2000s, the latter option seemed viable due to the diplomatic focus of Western governments. At the same time, Romania hoped to pave the way for Moldova to join the EU at some point in time; while the European enlargement process in the former Yugoslav region (now dubbed the Western Balkans to erase the memories of political instability, war and ethnic cleansing) seemed to offer the best opportunity for simultaneously pushing Chisinau's prospects along. However, Western doubts and opposition to Romania linking Moldova's European integration path to the Western Balkans meant that this issue defaulted to Romania's policy in the Black Sea.

The dissolution of the USSR made newly independent Ukraine Romania's largest neighbor as well as the country with which it shared the longest border. Although Romania recognized the independence of Ukraine and its borders, the relationship nonetheless suffered from bilateral tensions over *inter alia* the rights of the ethnic-Romanian minority in Ukraine and maritime border delimitation in the Black Sea. The maritime delimitation issue was solved in Romania's favor in 2009 by the International Court of Justice, in a trial that began in 2008, after all avenues of resolving the matter through bilateral negotiations had been exhausted.[46] In spite of these differences, Bucharest championed Kyiv's Western ambitions. In 2008, at the Bucharest Summit, Romania supported giving Georgia and Ukraine membership action plans (MAP).[47] However, despite strong US support for this move, a consensus within the Alliance could not be reached.[48]

Ensuring and maintaining freedom of navigation in the Black Sea is another fundamental interest for Romania since it is a prerequisite for maintaining access to global markets for Romanian goods while permitting foreign goods and natural resources to reach Romanian ports unhindered. Moreover, freedom of navigation plays an important role in energy security—namely, allowing oil and liquefied natural gas (LNG) tankers to deliver their cargoes. Unfortunately for Romania, however, Turkey does not allow the transit of LNG tankers through the straits of Bosporus and the Dardanelles.[49]

In terms of energy security during 2002–2014, Romania's main interests in the Black Sea had been the Nabucco and Azerbaijan–Georgia–Romania Interconnector (AGRI) natural gas projects. Both pipelines aimed to diminish Europe's dependence on Russian gas supplies. Yet ultimately, neither came to fruition.

---

[46] *Ministerul Afacerilor Externe*, "Prezentarea cazului Delimitarea Maritimă în Marea Neagră (România c. Ucraina)," https://www.mae.ro/node/24347.
[47] Adrian Vierița, "The Bucharest Summit: Romania's Perceptions of NATO's Future," *Wilson Center*, March 26, 2008, https://www.wilsoncenter.org/event/the-bucharest-summit-romanias-perceptions-natos-future.
[48] *NATO*, "Bucharest Summit Declaration," April 3, 2008, https://www.nato.int/cps/en/natolive/official_texts_8443.htm.
[49] Murat Temizer, "Can Ukraine receive LNG via the Bosphorus?" *Anadolu Agency*, March 31, 2015, https://www.aa.com.tr/en/energy/natural-gas/can-ukraine-receive-lng-via-the-bosphorus/11002.

Nabucco was put forward by Romania, Austria, Bulgaria, Hungary and Turkey, but it lacked a supply source. Various options were proposed, such as gas fields in Iraq, Egypt, Turkmenistan and Azerbaijan, but all proved merely theoretical. Despite being supported by the EU and the United States, Nabucco lost in 2011 to the Trans-Anatolian Natural Gas Pipeline project (TANAP), an Azerbaijani initiative supplied with offshore Caspian gas from Azerbaijan.[50] Nabucco lingered for a while under a less ambitious form called Nabucco-West, but the project was canceled in 2013, at which point Baku threw its support behind the Trans-Adriatic Pipeline (TAP), which links up to TANAP's western end.

The AGRI pipeline project was put forward in 2010 and aims to bring Azerbaijani gas to European markets. If completed, AGRI could deliver between two billion and eight billion cubic meters of gas to European consumers.[51] However, the high cost of LNG terminals, coupled with Romania's limited project management capacity, mean that the project has yet to leave the drawing board.[52]

Romania encountered strong opposition from Russia and Turkey regarding an increased NATO and US presence in the Black Sea. The idea of extending NATO's Active Endeavour anti-terrorism and maritime policing mission in the Mediterranean Sea to the Black Sea was opposed by both Ankara and Moscow. Instead, Turkey came up with the Black Sea Harmony Initiative in 2004, which grew to encompass all of the region's riparian states.[53] Another maritime security initiative that Romania became part of during the early 2000s was the Black Sea Naval Force, better

---

[50] "Gas pipeline deal sidelines original Nabucco project," *EurActiv*, June 28, 2012, https://www.euractiv.com/section/energy/news/gas-pipeline-deal-sidelines-original-nabucco-project/.
[51] Eugenia Guşilov, "BLACK SEA LNG: Dreams vs Reality," *ROEC*, April 17, 2019, https://www.roec.biz/project/black-sea-lng-dreams-vs-reality/.
[52] Ibid.
[53] "Turkish -Russian declaration on Operation Black Sea Harmony," *OSCE*, January 25, 2007, https://www.osce.org/fsc/23842.

known by its acronym BLACKSEAFOR.[54] From a Romanian perspective, this initiative has three main disadvantages: it involves Russia, it is not permanent, and the US and other Western members of the North Atlantic Alliance did not participate.

Although Romania promoted regional cooperation between 2002 and 2014, the rest of the NATO and EU member states in the region did not necessarily share its outlook. Turkey and Bulgaria had their own agendas concerning Russia, making cooperation difficult even when the Kremlin's behavior became indisputably belligerent. Romania tried to build a working relationship with Russia to gain leverage regionally and within NATO and the EU. However, these efforts led nowhere.

A major weak point in Romania's Black Sea policy has been its inability to modernize its naval forces. In order to have a credible maritime policy, a state needs a navy. Without a modern navy, Romania's interest in maintaining freedom of navigation cannot be effectively upheld. In the early 2000s, the future looked promising as Romania acquired two mothballed Type 22 frigates from the UK. And by 2004, the Romanian Naval Forces became the first branch of the armed services to be fully professionalized.[55] In 2006, the authorities drew up plans for the procurement of three multi-role corvettes and four mine hunters in order to recapitalize the ageing fleet with new surface combatants.[56] However, these plans fell apart due to the financial and economic crisis of 2007–2010 and because, after Romania joined NATO, the political elite put further defense modernization investments on the back-burner.

---

[54] W. Alejandro Sanchez, "Did BLACKSEAFOR Ever Have a Chance?" *E-International Relations*, November 8, 2012, https://www.e-ir.info/2012/11/18/did-blackseafor-ever-have-a-chance/.
[55] "Istoric," *Forțele Navale Române*, accessed November 30, 2021, https://www.navy.ro/despre/istoric/istoric_10.php.
[56] Indira Crăsnea, "O cronologie a referirilor privind programul de achiziție și dotare cu corvete a Forțelor Navale Române," *Defence &Security Monitor*, January 13, 2019, https://monitorulapararii.ro/o-cronologie-a-referirilor-privind-programul-de-achizitie-si-dotare-cu-corvete-a-fortelor-navale-romane-1-9081.

Figure 2. Maritime Delimitation of Black Sea

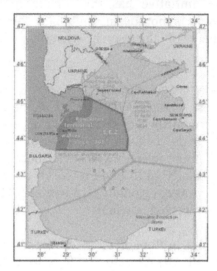

Source: Shtiu.ro

This trend continued even after the Russo-Georgian war of 2008. The Type 22 frigates, which were supposed to undergo a refit in 2009, never did. The Romanian authorities twice tried to modernize these ships but failed both times: the first time, the tender had to be called off because of the economic downturn, while the second time, the winner of the tender, an association between the Turkish company STM and a Romanian firm, discovered that they were not licensed by the producers of the weapons systems to install them on the ships.[57]

Throughout the 2002–2014 period, Romania was moderately successful in raising the Black Sea region to the attention of the United States. US troops were deployed on a rotational basis at Mihail Kogălniceanu (MK) Air Base, near Constanța, on the Black

---

[57] Mariana Iancu, "Cheltuiala fabuloasa fara finalizare. De ce n-a reusit statul roman in 11 ani sa modernizeze doua nave de lupta pentru care a platit 116 milioane de lire sterline," *Adevărul*, May 8, 2017, https://adevarul.ro/locale/constanta/cheltuiala-fabuloasa-finalizare-n-a-reusit-statul-roman-11-ani-modernizeze-doua-nave-lupta-achitat-116-milioane-lire-sterline-1_59106f485ab6550cb8e7b098/index.html.

Sea shore. MK notably supported US deployments in the Middle East and Afghanistan. The most important US military deployment to Romania was the Aegis Ashore ballistic missile defense system, with the basing agreement signed in 2011. Construction of the Deveselu facility began in 2013, and it became operational in 2015.[58] However, Bucharest's main aim—securing a permanent deterrent US presence on Romanian territory—was not achieved.

Deterring Russia

Russia's forcible annexation of Crimea and the beginning of the proxy war in eastern Ukraine in February 2014 represent the greatest security threats faced by Romania since 2014. First, the covert and then overt use of force followed by territorial conquest upended what Bucharest considered the main features of the post–Cold War order: the peaceful resolution of international conflicts and the inviolability of state borders. Second, although Romania did not share a close relationship with its largest neighbor, the compromising of Ukraine's territorial integrity was not in Bucharest's interest and posed a regional security challenge. Third, Russian control over Crimea means that Moscow has *de facto* control over a part of Ukraine's exclusive economic zone. In fact, Romania's EEZ now borders Russia's (claimed) EEZ in the Black Sea. In the future, there is a risk that the Kremlin may not recognize the result of the International Court of Justice's adjudication concerning maritime delimitation in the Black Sea.

As the building of the bridge over the Kerch Strait and the virtual closing of the Sea of Azov have shown, Russia's ambitions in the Black Sea are not limited to Crimea. In 2014, then–Romanian president Traian Băsescu expressed anxiety that Russia

---

[58] "Participarea României la Sistemul de apărare antirachetă," Ministerul Afacerilor Externe, accessed November 30, 2021, https://www.mae.ro/node/1517.

ultimately aimed to reach the mouths of the Danube.[59] These fears were justified by Russia's actions in 2014–2015 in southwestern Ukraine, in the Crimea and Odesa regions,[60] as well as Moscow's use of the concept of *"Novorossiya"* (a term dating back to tsarist imperial times) to denote these territories.[61] Had Russian-backed rebels been successful in taking over Odesa in 2014 and the Black Sea Fleet occupied Serpent's Island, the Kremlin would have been in a position to interdict all maritime traffic near the mouths of the Danube.

Following the annexation of Crimea, Russia proceeded to beef up its military presence in the newly acquired territory. Today, Crimea is being used as a power projection springboard to the Black Sea region and the Eastern Mediterranean. Indeed, Russia's interventions in Syria and Libya would arguably have been much more difficult without Crimea.

The Black Sea Fleet was modernized with diesel-electric submarines and new surface combatants. And Russia deployed long-range air-defense systems like the newly introduced S-400 system, alongside long-range land-based anti-ship missiles, creating an anti-access and area denial (A2/AD) zone.[62] The purpose of this bubble is to protect the newly acquired territories and keep NATO out of the region. The transatlantic alliance's maritime access to the Black Sea was already constricted by the Montreux Convention, which limits the number, type and time

---

[59] "Traian Băsescu: Nu s-a schimbat dorința Rusiei de a ajunge la gurile Dunării, ci putința," *Digi24*, December 12, 2014, https://www.digi24.ro/stiri/actualitate/politica/traian-basescu-nu-s-a-schimbat-dorinta-rusiei-de-a-ajunge-la-gurile-dunarii-ci-putinta-337818.

[60] Roman Goncharenko, "The Odessa file: What happened on May 2, 2014?" *Deutsche Welle*, May 5, 2015, https://www.dw.com/en/the-odessa-file-what-happened-on-may-2-2014/a-18425200.

[61] Sergei Loiko, "The Unraveling Of Moscow's 'Novorossia' Dream," *Deutsche Welle*, June 1, 2016, https://www.rferl.org/a/unraveling-moscow-novorossia-dream/27772641.html.

[62] George Vișan and Octavian Manea in "Black Sea in Access Denial Agea. Special Report," edt. E. Gușilov, January 2016, https://www.roec.biz/project/black-sea-in-access-denial-age/, 5-21.

spent by military vessels belonging to non-riparian states; but it has now been further hampered operationally by the deployment of Russian A2/AD systems. Furthermore, Russia reinforces its dominance of the northern basin of the Black Sea by regularly designating large swaths of water as no-go-zone exercise ranges for its ships and aircraft.[63]

The Kremlin has been deploying the Kalibr family of missiles on its Black Sea Fleet surface combatants and on submarines, in both land-attack cruise missile and anti-ship variants.[64] An innovative solution to compensate for Russia's inability to build surface combatants larger than guided-missile frigates has been the deployment of Kalibr missiles in vertical launchers on corvettes and fast-attack craft. In Western navies, long-range tactical land-attack missiles are deployed on guided-missiles frigates, destroyers and nuclear-attack submarines. Russia's innovative solution allows it to exercise control in the Black Sea region with limited means and minimum effort.[65] Furthermore, since 2018, the shipyards in occupied Crimea have begun building surface combatants for the Black Sea Fleet, the air-bases on the peninsula are being modernized, and Russia has deployed high-performance multi-role and strike aircraft.[66] Russia's actions in the past seven years have tipped the military balance in the region in its favor and transformed Crimea into a bastion from which the Kremlin can project power both within and outside the region.[67]

---

[63] Jeff Seldin, "US, NATO Slam Russian Plan to Block Parts of Black Sea," *Voice of America*, April 16, 2021, https://www.voanews.com/a/europe_us-nato-slam-russian-plan-block-parts-black-sea/6204673.html.

[64] "The Military Balance 2020," *IISS*, (Routledge: London, 2020), v.

[65] Benjamin Brimelow, "Russia's Navy is making a big bet on new, smaller warships loaded with missiles," *Business Insider*, April 1, 2021, https://www.businessinsider.com/russian-navy-betting-big-on-new-smaller-warships-with-missiles-2021-4.

[66] "The Military Balance 2020," *IISS*, 170.

[67] Igor Delanoe, "Tracking Black Sea Security Issues. Crimea, a Strategic Bastion on Russia's Flank", December 18, 2014, Russian International Affairs Council, https://russiancouncil.ru/en/blogs/igor_delanoe-en/1588/

98 | BLACK SEA BATTLEGROUND

The Russian takeover of Ukraine's EEZ off Crimea and the cordoning off of the Azov Sea raise serious questions concerning maritime security for Romania. Bucharest's plans regarding offshore exploitation may be thwarted by the Kremlin's use of hybrid warfare tactics and legal obstruction. In 2020 the State Duma passed a law that allows the Russian government to ignore decisions taken by international bodies if they run contrary to its interests.[68] The presence of naval special forces (Naval Spetsnaz) in Crimea, trained in assaulting offshore oil rigs and in taking control over civilian vessels, means that Russia has the means to interfere with the offshore activities of the rest of the Black Sea riparian states.[69]

Romania's response to Russian revisionism and revanchism in the Black Sea region has been twofold. On one hand, Bucharest began a process of internal balancing by investing in the modernization of its armed forces. On the other hand, it initiated a process of external balancing by promoting a Black Sea agenda within NATO and the EU.

In 2015, Romania pledged it would begin allocating 2 percent of its GDP to defense beginning in 2017.[70] The purpose of this decision was to jump-start the process of modernizing the Romanian Armed Forces, which had been neglected in the past. Defense expenditures were neglected after Romania joined NATO and became an afterthought when the 2008 economic crisis

---

[68] "Russia approves bill allowing national law to trump international treaties," *Reuters*, October 28, 2020, https://www.reuters.com/article/us-russia-politics-law-idUSKBN27D1AF.

[69] H.I. Sutton, "Naval Spetsnaz in Hybrid Warfare. Illustrated analysis of near-term Russian maritime Special Forces underwater vehicles and capabilities," *Covert Shores*, December 2, 2014, http://www.hisutton.com/Naval%20Spetsnaz%20in%20Hybrid%20Warfare.html.

[70] "Acord politic naţional privind creşterea finanţării pentru Apărare (13 ianuarie 2015)," *Presidency.ro*, January 13, 2015, https://www.presidency.ro/ro/presedinte/documente-programatice/acord-politic-national-privind-cresterea-finantarii-pentru-aparare-13-ianuarie-2015.

erupted. Consequently, most of Romania's military equipment was obsolete and the Armed Forces faced serious readiness challenges. The purpose of increased military spending was not just to increase Romanian military capabilities but to signal Bucharest's determination to its allies regarding a greater regional role.

Defense expenditure is presently concentrated in big-ticket items such as long-range air-defense systems, multi-role fighters or long-range mobile fires necessary for territorial defense. In 2017, the parliament approved an ambitious $10 billion procurement program for Romania's Armed Forces; however, most of these acquisitions suffer from delays due to acquisition and administrative issues.[71] The Romanian navy is the most affected by these procurement delays. For example, the flagship naval modernization program, the procurement of four multi-role corvettes, has been stalled for the past four years due to litigation. Conversely, the programs that are being delivered on time are those that have been awarded to US defense contractors through the Pentagon's Foreign Military Sales system: Patriot-long range air-defense missiles ($3.9 billion), HIMARS rocket systems ($1.5 billion), F-16 AM/BMs from Portugal (with US support) and Naval Strike Missiles ($286 million). Despite being oriented toward territorial defense, Romania's modernization plans have yet to address areas where the country is vulnerable or faces equipment deficits, such as modern self-propelled artillery systems and heavy armored fighting vehicles (tanks and infantry fighting vehicles).

---

[71] Victor Cozmei, "Ministrul Apararii cere Parlamentului sa aprobe un program de 9,3 miliarde de euro pentru inzestrarea Armatei. Printre tintele programului: Reluarea achizitiei corvetelor, doar 94 de transportoare blindate si sisteme de rachete pentru aparare anti-aeriana," *Hotnews*, April 11, 2021, https://www.hotnews.ro/stiri-esential-21709213-ministrul-apararii-cere-parlamentului-aprobe-program-9-3-miliarde-euro-pentru-inzestrarea-armatei-printre-tintele-programului-reluarea-achizitiei-corvetelor-doar-94-transportoare-blindate-sisteme-rach.htm.

100 | BLACK SEA BATTLEGROUND

After 2020, Romania's defense sector began investing in its defense-industrial base and barracks infrastructure. This is an important part of the country's defense policy as it seeks to attract the US and other NATO allies to base their troops on its territory. The most ambitious base modernization project involves extensions and upgrades for the MK air base, valued at €2 billion ($2.25 billion) over ten years.[72] After the base is finished, it will be able to accommodate both US and Romanian troops. The extension of the MK base represents, politically and symbolically, a Romanian response to Russia's fortification of Crimea.

On the diplomatic front, Bucharest has renewed its efforts to maintain allied focus on the Black Sea region. Romanian authorities were disappointed by NATO's decision to deploy rotational, rather than permanent, forces along the Alliance's Eastern Flank in 2014. And perhaps even more critically, Bucharest lamented the divergent statuses of Allied deterrence postures between the northern and southern portions of the Eastern Flank. On the northern (Baltic) sector of the flank, the status of the US and allied presence is that of Enhanced Forward Presence. This is in part justified by the vicinity to Russia's Western Military District—its best equipped military district and the one with the most troops.[73] The Russian exclave of Kaliningrad, the Baltic Fleet and the Suwałki corridor add to the strategic importance of the northern end of the Eastern Flank, raising the necessity of maintaining a credible deterrence posture there, particularly given that the four northeastern NATO member states share a direct border with Russia.

On the southern (Black Sea) sector of the Eastern Flank, in contrast, the US and allied presence has the status of "Forward Tailored Presence." The main deployments are in Romania and Bulgaria and consist mostly of US troops, with some Polish troops

---

[72] Mircea Olteanu, "MApN organizează o licitație în valoare de 2,1 miliarde lei pentru lucrări de infrastructură la Mihail Kogălniceanu," *Umbrela Strategică*, March 8, 2021, https://umbrela-strategica.ro/mapn-organizeaza-o-licitatie-in-valoare-de-21-miliarde-lei-pentru-lucrari-de-infrastructura-la-mihail-kogalniceanu/.

[73] "Military Balance," *IISS*, (London: Routledge, 2021), 167.

deployed as part of the Multinational Brigade South-East. In order to give more weight to Bucharest's military status on the Eastern Flank, Romania has hosted the HQ Multinational Headquarters South-East at Sibiu and in the country's capital since 2020.[74] Although the Russian Southern Military District does not have as many troops or firepower as the Western Military District,[75] the Black Sea and Crimea are the starting points of Moscow's power projection into the Eastern Mediterranean.

Romanian efforts to encourage a single approach within NATO toward the Eastern Flank have been negatively impacted by the differing approaches to Russian security policy among the Black Sea allied member states themselves. Bulgaria did not support Romania's idea of a NATO flotilla in the Black Sea, while Turkey alternates between cooperation and competition with Russia.[76] Ankara has shown it can confront Moscow in the Eastern Mediterranean, Ukraine and the Caucasus without generating a strong counter-response. Although Turkey's confrontations with Russia serve only its interests, they show that a strong posture toward the Kremlin has benefits. Building and consolidating a single strategic vision for the Black Sea riparian member states remain an ongoing challenge for Romanian diplomacy.

After 2014, Romania redoubled its efforts to promote Black Sea issues within NATO and the EU by helping establish several major multilateral groupings. In 2015, Romania and Poland created the Bucharest 9 format, which brings together all the member states on the Eastern Flank to better coordinate their actions within the Alliance. Bulgaria, Czechia, Estonia, Latvia, Lithuania, Hungary, Slovakia, Poland and Romania meet periodically as part of this forum to work out their differences and influence decision-making decisively within the Alliance. The inclusion of Bulgaria,

---

[74] *Headquarters Multinational Corps South-East,* https://mncse.ro/app/webroot/en/pages/view/73.
[75] "Military Balance," IISS, (London: Routledge, 2021), 167.
[76] "Bulgaria respinge, din nou, ideea unei flotile în Marea Neagră," *Digi24*, August 14, 2016, https://www.digi24.ro/stiri/externe/ue/bulgaria-respinge-din-nou-ideea-unei-flotile-in-marea-neagra-549714:

Figure 3. Russia's Anti-Access/Area Denial Capabilities in the Black Sea Region

Source: CSBA

Hungary and, to a lesser extent (particularly recently), Czechia, which want cooperative relations with Russia despite its aggressive moves, ensures that differences are smoothed over or at least that these states have an avenue where they communicate their points of view without necessarily compromising wider Alliance consensus.

The other format promoted by Romania since 2014 is the Three Seas Initiatives (3SI), which is also the result of *inter alia* cooperation between Bucharest and Warsaw. 3SI reunites states that border the Baltic, the Black Sea and the Adriatic Sea: the Baltic States, Poland, Austria, Bulgaria, Slovenia, Croatia, Czechia, Slovakia, Hungary and Romania. The aim of this format is the economic development of both Central and Southeastern Europe via regional cooperation and interconnectivity. In this way, member states hope that the region will gain more substance and clout in the EU.

Relations between Romania and Ukraine have improved after 2014, but there are still tensions regarding Ukrainian language law[77] and administrative reforms.[78] In a sign of the changing security environment, both countries have begun conducting naval exercises regularly on the Danube.[79] Moreover, in August 2020, the two governments signed a technical agreement concerning defense cooperation.[80] The agreement entered into force in 2021.

Romania's interest in finding a solution to the frozen conflicts around the Black Sea has not abated. The persistence of these conflicts 30 years after the dissolution of the Soviet Union represents a major security challenge and threat to European security. The possibility of Russia trying to "freeze" the current fighting in Ukraine would create the largest frozen conflict in the region and increase regional instability and insecurity. Romanian diplomacy is attempting to put the frozen conflicts on the EU foreign policy agenda.[81] Heretofore, the frozen conflicts in the Black Sea region have been mostly ignored by the EU and generally considered part of the "cost" of doing business with Russia. But as Bucharest contends, the extension of such conflicts in the former Soviet space near the borders of the EU should not

---

[77] Dan Alexe, "Ucraina limitează învățământul în limbile minoritare, inclusiv româna," *Radio Europa Liberă Moldova*, January 3, 2021, https://moldova.europalibera.org/a/ucraina-limiteaz%C4%83-%C3%AEnv%C4%83%C8%9B%C4%83m%C3%A2ntul-%C3%AEn-limbile-minoritare-inclusiv-rom%C3%A2na/31031467.html.
[78] "Convorbirea Președintelui României, Klaus Iohannis, cu Președintele Ucrainei, Volodîmîr Zelenski," *Presidency.ro*, May 12, 2020, https://www.presidency.ro/ro/media/comunicate-de-presa/convorbirea-presedintelui-romaniei-klaus-iohannis-cu-presedintele-ucrainei-volodamar-zelenski.
[79] "Riverine 2018, exercițiu româno-ucrainean pe Dunăre," *Statul Major al Forțelor Navale*, September 6, 2018, https://www.navy.ro/eveniment.php?id=318.
[80] "Ucraina și România, au semnat un acord de cooperare tehnico-militar," Embassy of Ukraine in Bucharest, September 5, 2020, https://romania.mfa.gov.ua/ro/news/ukrayina-ta-rumuniya-pidpisali-mizhuryadovu-ugodu-pro-vijskovo-tehnichne-spivrobitnictvo.
[81] Bogdan Aurescu, "Tackling frozen conflicts in the EU's own neighbourhood," *EUObserver*, January 19, 2021, https://euobserver.com/opinion/150638.

104 | BLACK SEA BATTLEGROUND

be neglected in Brussels as it has direct impact on the security of all member states.

On the energy front, Romanian authorities have been dragging their feet regarding offshore oil and gas extraction. In 2018, the parliament finally passed a law regulating offshore oil and gas extraction, but the foreign companies involved in offshore projects in Romania have roundly criticized it for being too cumbersome and imposing rather high royalties.[82] Despite promises that the law will be amended, the Romanian parliament has yet to take any action. Exxon, the company that had obtained rights to exploit the most important offshore gas and oil field in the Black Sea, Neptune Deep, withdrew from the project, citing excessive regulation.[83] The window of opportunity regarding offshore gas extraction is rapidly closing as the EU is trying to move away from fossil fuels and wants to transform the European economy to reflect this objective.

A positive development in terms of energy security has been cooperation with the United States in nuclear energy. Bucharest and Washington will work together to build Units 3 and 4 of the Cernavodă nuclear plant and modernize Unit 1.[84] The project, worth $8 billion, should be implemented in 2021–2031.[85] The US convinced the Romanian government to give up on a similar

---

[82] Kevin Crowley and Bryan Gruley, "The humbling of Exxon," *Bloomberg*, April 30, 2020, https://www.bloomberg.com/features/2020-exxonmobil-coronavirus-oil-demand/.

[83] "Popescu: Romgaz poate prelua participația Exxon la Neptun Deep, are o capacitate financiară mai mare decât Petrom," *Energynomics*, November 20, 2020, http://www.energynomics.ro/ro/popescu-romgaz-poate-prelua-participatia-exxon-la-neptun-deep-are-o-capacitate-financiara-mai-mare-decat-petrom/.

[84] Roxana Petrescu, "Acordul de 8 mld. $ dintre România și SUA pentru energia nucleară a trecut de Parlament: Proiectele nucleare vin cu dublu avantaj: costuri competitive și zero emisii de CO2. Vor fi create 9.000 de locuri de muncă," *Ziarul Financiar*, June 24, 2021, https://www.zf.ro/companii/energie/acordul-8-mld-s-dintre-romania-sua-energia-nucleara-trecut-parlament-20155114.

[85] Ibid.

agreement reached with China.[86] Furthermore, both countries have decided to conduct research in civil nuclear energy and develop small modular reactors. The implementation and success of these projects, however, depend on improving the Romanian government's administrative capacity.

Conclusion

Romania has been moderately successful in its bid to put Black Sea issues on NATO's and the EU's agendas. It has also managed to more tightly involve the United States in the region. Romania plays host to the US Aegis Ashore missile-defense system and to American troops; however, these troops are deployed on a rotational basis. Bucharest thinks that the foreign soldiers currently stationed on its territory are not enough to deter potential aggression. Moreover, it looks to change the status of this deployment to match the US and Allied deployments in Poland and the Baltic States. Yet Bucharest faces an uphill battle on both counts: Washington's strategic priority is the Indo-Pacific region, and US rotational deployments to the Black Sea may well be the best that can be achieved in the current security environment. A more attainable option for Romania might be to call on its allies in Europe to send their troops to the southern sector of the Eastern Flank.

The level of ambition of Romania's Black Sea policy is decoupled from the means available to the state. The most striking feature of this situation is reflected in the lack of meaningful investment in Romania's Naval Forces to enforce and defend the country's offshore claims and interests. Romania's inability to modernize its navy has diminished its capability to pursue its interests in the Black Sea as well as undermined its credibility as a net security provider in the region. A shortage of modern ships and other naval means reduces the opportunities for cooperation with the

---

[86] "Chinezii, înlocuiți cu americanii pentru energia nucleară din România," *Digi24*, October 9, 2020, https://www.digi24.ro/stiri/economie/energie/chinezii-inlocuiti-cu-americanii-pentru-energia-nucleara-din-romania-138206.

106 | BLACK SEA BATTLEGROUND

US and other NATO countries on whose naval presence Bucharest counts for deterrence in the Black Sea. Romanian decision-makers have yet to truly internalize that a maritime policy requires a navy.

The strategic and economic linkage between the Danube and the Black Sea has also not been realized. The river and the sea represent a single geopolitical space and should be viewed as a whole. Any serious maritime policy needs to recognize this simple fact and factor it into a final analysis. Looking at this issue through a historical lens, it seems that Romania, mostly for want of resources, failed to fully exploit the strategic and developmental potential of the Black Sea. This is one of the main lessons of the 20th century for Romania's policymakers.

Finally, energy security remains a sore point for Romania. Despite ambitious plans and efforts, it has few demonstrable achievements. The most important Romanian project concerning energy security, the development of offshore gas and oil reserves, has yet to begin, and the window of opportunity is rapidly closing as the EU and the global economy prepare to move away from fossil fuels. In nearly every major facet of security in the Black Sea region, therefore, time for Bucharest to address these mounting challenges is running out.

4.

Bulgaria's Black Sea Dilemma: NATO Ally or Russian Giveaway?

Valeri R. Ratchev and Todor Tagarev

January 13, 2022

For the European Union, North Atlantic Treaty Organization (NATO) and United States, the growing strategic importance of the wider Black Sea region—an area at the crossroads of the Balkans, the Caucasus and Central Asia—stems in part from witnessing the aggressive actions of the Russian Federation there.[1] For three decades, by utilizing direct military operations and a wide range of tools, including economic coercion and corruption, the Kremlin has created an atmosphere of tension in the region, seeking to exploit vulnerabilities and frictions within and between neighboring countries. Moreover, in several parts of the wider Black Sea area, the smell of gunpowder is strong.

---

[1] For a comprehensive explanation of the evolving Wider Black Sea concept, see Ian. O. Lesser, *Global Trends, Regional Consequences: Wider Strategic Influences on the Black Sea* (Athens, International Centre for Black Sea Studies, 2007), https://icbss.org/books/xenophon-paper-no-4/; Dimitrios Triantaphyllou, ed., *The Security Context in the Black Sea Region (London and New York:* Routledge, 2016); Marat Terterov, John van Pool, and Sergiy Nagornyy, "Russian Geopolitical Power in the Black and Caspian Seas Region: Implications for Turkey and the World," *Insight Turkey* 12, no. 3 (2010): 191–203.

108 | BLACK SEA BATTLEGROUND

In its policy toward the region, NATO pursues three main objectives: (1) to prevent Russia from using the Black Sea as a platform to expand its influence in neighboring areas; (2) to provide direct political, economic and military support to the regional member states and democratic partners; and (3) to help Black Sea nations resist Russian "hybrid" threats and strategic corruption.[2] Achieving these objectives requires decisive contributions from regional allies and partners.

Yet, NATO ally Bulgaria's focus seems to be away from the escalating tensions. The previous Bulgarian government's[3] interests and policies were limited to providing uninterrupted import flows of natural gas, oil and tourists from across the Black Sea and exports in the opposite direction. Any regional problems were considered essential to deal with only if they impacted these flows. Even the Russian invasion and annexation of Crimea in 2014 was not a strong enough signal to compel the Bulgarian leadership to reevaluate the country's poisonous ties with Russia.

The following chapter outlines the critical security considerations of the Bulgarian leadership over the past 10 years, Sofia's policies in practice, as well as the consequent impact of those policies on strengthening Russia's grip on crucial sectors of the Bulgarian economy. Then, it assesses Bulgaria's latest strategic documents and policy acts, demonstrating how the Russian threat is underplayed in Sofia and illuminating the essential channels of Russian influence over the Bulgarian national security sector. The final section explains the importance of Bulgaria for regional, European and transatlantic security and outlines the challenges

---

[2] The term "Strategic corruption" is used according to Philip Zelikow, Eric Edelman, Kristofer Harrison, and Celeste Ward Gventer, "The Rise of Strategic Corruption. How States Weaponize Graft." *Foreign Affairs* July/August 2020, accessed August 25, 2021, https://www.foreignaffairs.com/articles/united-states/2020-06-09/rise-strategic-corruption.

[3] The government of then–prime minister Boyko Borissov. At the time of writing this article (November 2021), Bulgaria has a caretaker government and just held its third parliamentary election in one calendar year.

The Black Sea in the Bulgarian Perspective

The Russian Federation poses a growing strategic threat to the countries in the Black Sea region. Its ambitions of reestablishing geopolitical control over the post-Soviet space are well-publicized and have been reiterated recently as President Vladimir Putin's famous "red lines."[4] However, diplomatic attempts consistently fail to resolve any of the protracted conflicts in Moldova, Ukraine and the South Caucasus that were sparked or exploited by Moscow. Meanwhile, energy resources originating from Russia and transiting those conflict areas are of significant importance for many European economies, several of which are trapped in strategic dependence on Russian supplies. The Kremlin qualified the pro-European social upheavals in Georgia, Ukraine and other regional countries as a Western conspiracy to weaken Russia and destabilize its neighborhood. And it remains openly opposed to any democratic and pro-European movements in what Russia considers its "near abroad," striving to prevent these outcomes by weaponizing almost every tool at Moscow's disposal—from gas and electricity to migration and vaccination. Gradually but decisively, using every opportunity, Russia has turned the land and maritime domains between the Western Balkans and Central Asia into a "hybrid warfare" battlefield.

Further complicating the situation for the Western alliance are the ambiguous future of Afghanistan and the expected new wave of mass migration bound for Europe; the unpredictable behavior of a critical ally, Turkey; as well as the uncertain perspectives on relations with Iran. All these factors raise the relative importance of the region, both as a knot of challenges and as a bridge to other

---

[4] "Putin Explained the 'Red Lines' in Relation to NATO," *Vedomosti*, November 30, 2021, https://www.vedomosti.ru/politics/news/2021/11/30/898300-putin-rasskazal-o-krasnih-liniyah (in Russian).

110 | BLACK SEA BATTLEGROUND

strategic regions. Nevertheless, the outstretched wings of the Russian imperial double-headed eagle routinely tend to overshadow every serious discussion on wider Black Sea security.

Members of Bulgaria's foreign and security policy establishment share many of their allies' attitudes vis-à-vis the wider Black Sea region, though with some intra-regional and country-specific considerations. Critically, Bulgaria never faced up to the problem of recognizing the Black Sea as a region with a unique identity and grave security dimensions. As such, it never developed a specific policy toward this region, nor did it see the need to play an active role as an EU and NATO member in drafting a Euro-Atlantic strategy for the Black Sea. Sofia's regional interests and policy are primarily limited to energy, tourism and trade, and these are the lenses through which it tends to view any regional security problem. Its essential national security concerns have been limited to preventing mass migration from the territory of Turkey and averting domestic religious radicalization. Even Russia's invasion and annexation of Crimea and the consequent military buildup of the peninsula were not a strong enough signal to compel the Bulgarian leadership to take more seriously the military dimension of Black Sea security and Russia's toxic role there.

Instead of a rational threat assessment, the central perspective of Bulgaria's regional policy is the belief that the country sits at the intersection of three integration projects—European, Russian and Turkish. European (including NATO) integration provides everything essential for the country in political, economic and security terms. Whereas Russia advances Bulgaria's geopolitical control over the "near abroad" and beyond, applying systematic economic and political pressure and using direct or subtle military threats. The Turkish project, in turn, is based on "Neo-Ottomanism" and seeks to gain influence across the wider region's Muslim and ethnic-Turkic communities and their political formations, using various soft power means.

Three consequences derive from this perspective. First, Bulgarian economic interests overshadow political and security considerations to an unacceptably high level. Second, governments in Sofia may sacrifice important political values and principles to access energy resources and markets. And third, in an economic context, Russia and Turkey have opposite meanings for Bulgaria—Russia is a source of energy dependence and a high trade deficit, while Turkey is a comprehensive market and a gateway to other regions.

Bulgaria is one of the few portals through which Russian interests can easily access Europe. The problems for national security and Bulgaria's role in the Black Sea come from economic relations with Russia that are not market-based. On the contrary, those interactions are highly politicized and implemented through strategic corruption. According to estimates presented in the 2016 "Kremlin Playbook" study, "Russia's economic presence [in Bulgaria] averaged over 22 percent of GDP between 2005 and 2014, [and] there are clear signs of both political and economic capture, suggesting that the country is at high risk of Russian influenced state capture."[5]

One of Bulgaria's most strategically important captured sectors is the supply of natural gas. Imprudent Bulgarian authorities have provided Gazprom with a series of lucrative, decades-long contracts while blocking projects for alternative deliveries. Thus, for 30 years, Russia successfully gained control over the entire Bulgarian energy sector apart from one strategic asset—the ownership of gas pipelines. However, former Prime Minister Borissov ultimately also resolved this issue in favor of Gazprom: In 2020, Bulgaria paid $1.59 billion to build a length of pipe across its territory, extending Russia's TurkStream all the way to the border with Serbia. The Bulgarian government built this pipeline, which will be used exclusively by Gazprom, to implement the widely advertised "Roadmap," signed in 2017 by Bulgaria's energy minister and Gazprom's CEO. However, during parliamentary hearings in August 2021, the caretaker energy

---

[5] Heather A. Conley, James Mina, Ruslan Stefanov, and Martin Vladimirov, *The Kremlin Playbook: Understanding Russian Influence in Central and Eastern Europe* (Washington, D.C.: Center for Strategic and International Studies and Rowman & Littlefield, 2016), https://www.csis.org/analysis/kremlin-playbook.

minister stated that "the roadmap cannot be found."[6] At the time of writing this text, Bulgargaz was utilizing less than a quarter of its quota for the cheapest gas delivered to Europe, that coming from Azerbaijan, while increasing the import of Russian gas, at double the price.[7]

The Lukoil-owned refinery in Burgas has a similar monopoly position on the Bulgarian energy market. Knowingly overlooked by the Bulgarian authorities, the company has been importing oil through its unsupervised terminal for years. With billions of dollars in annual turnover, Lukoil nonetheless regularly reports a deficit to avoid taxes, while its international marketing and trading unit, LITASCO SA, realizes profits in Switzerland.

Furthermore, the company does not hesitate to exploit its monopolistic position to the detriment of Bulgaria's national security. In 2011, the state attempted to install monitoring devices in "Lukoil Bulgaria," which immediately led to difficulties in supplying civilian airports with aviation fuel. The government had to release aviation kerosene from the state reserve to prevent serious air traffic problems.[8] Overall, Russia's sponsorship of unprofitable energy contracts generates significant and chronic trade deficits for Bulgaria—between $1.5 billion and $4 billion a year, depending on energy prices.

---

[6] "The roadmap for 'Turkish Stream' still undiscoverable in Bulgaria," *mediapool.bg*, August 6, 2021, https://www.mediapool.bg/neotkrivaema-ostava-patnata-karta-za-turski-potok-u-nas-news324988.html – in Bulgarian.

[7] Ilian Vassilev, "How much ignoring the Azeri gas costs the Bulgarian users?" *Analyses & Alternatives*, August 1, 2021 – in Bulgarian. See also Ilian Vassilev, "Tsunami warning," *Analyses & Alternatives*, August 9, 2021, https://altanalyses.org/en/2021/08/09/tsunami-warning/. Both sources were accessed on August 26, 2021.

[8] "The Government agrees on the delivery of aviation kerosine from the reserve for another 10 days," *BTV News*, August 3, 2011, accessed August 26, 2021, https://btvnovinite.bg/508599512-Pravitelstvoto_otpuska_kerosin_ot_rezerva_za_oshte_deset_dni.html – in Bulgarian.

Over the past two decades, Turkey has been among Bulgaria's most important economic partners outside the EU, with a trade turnover of about $4 billion–$5 billion and a positive trade balance. Direct relations between then–prime minister Borissov and President Recep Tayyip Erdoğan were instrumental for Bulgaria to avoid being affected by the mass migration crisis that hit Europe in 2015–2016. That said, Turkey is the only country that officially intervenes in Bulgaria's domestic politics. In December 2020, Erdoğan delivered a video address to the Movement for Rights and Freedoms political party conference; and in June 2021, he hosted that faction's leader in a meeting closed for the media. Boyko Borissov, the former prime minister, also visited President Erdoğan one week before the Bulgarian parliamentary elections in July 2021.[9]

The second consequence of Bulgaria's aforementioned "intersections" understanding of its geopolitical position is that Sofia cannot separate the Black Sea from the Balkans. For about 10 years, the former governing elite saw the country as a regional hub that combines the interests of various actors—Russia and Turkey from the East with the Western Balkans and further onward to the large Central European consumers of Russian gas. The self-generated illusion that Bulgaria will be entrusted with the privilege to manage gas flows via the "Southern Corridor" feeds the Sofia elite's engagement in relationships of strategic corruption. Knowing the importance of "being a hub," the Kremlin played to this desire in Bulgaria by infiltrating the country with political proxies, oligarchs and corrupt media. That strategic corruption encompasses crucial sectors such as Bulgaria's second nuclear power plant project,[10] long-term gas contracts and transit taxes, crude oil delivery and processing, and the defense industry, creating a robust web from which it is difficult to extract any

---

[9] Krassen Nikolov "Former Bulgarian PM Borissov meets Turkey's Erdogan ahead of elections," EURACTIV.bg, July 5, 2021, https://www.euractiv.com/section/politics/short_news/former-bulgarian-pm-borissov-meets-turkeys-erdogan-ahead-of-elections/.
[10] The current one, "Kozloduy," was built during the Soviet era, and four of its six reactors have been closed down in the beginning of the century.

114 | BLACK SEA BATTLEGROUND

element. Corruption is worth the money for Moscow since having a foothold in the Balkans means having a say over European strategic matters of Russian interest.[11]

These two consequences have a combined impact on the Bulgarian elite's inability to appropriately manage relations with Russia and Turkey, on one hand, and with the EU, NATO and the US, on the other. As a result, almost everything that Sofia does is viewed differently in Brussels and Washington. The former governing majority undermined and neglected policy cohesion with the Euro-Atlantic community and replaced it with former Prime Minister Borissov's authoritative leadership and "black box" manual management. In their 2020 *Foreign Affairs* article on state-weaponized graft around the world, Philip Zelikow *et al.* specifically define this "black box" and authoritarian leadership as examples of "strategic corruption."[12]

Similar contradictions influence Bulgarian official policy toward the Russian military buildup in Crimea and across the Black Sea region. From one side, Bulgaria contributes essentially to regional military cooperation in Southeastern Europe and the Black Sea. The US-inspired Southeastern Europe Defense Ministerial Process (SEDM),[13] launched in 1996, resulted in establishing an international mechanized brigade (SEEBRIG)[14] and a Black Sea

---

[11] Dimitar Bechev, *Russia's Strategic Interests and Tools of Influence in the Western Balkans* (Riga: NATO Strategic Communications Centre of Excellence, 2019), accessed August 26, 2021, https://stratcomcoe.org/publications/russias-strategic-interests-and-tools-of-influence-in-the-western-balkans/46.

[12] Zelikow, *et al.*, "The Rise of Strategic Corruption. How States Weaponize Graft."

[13] The South-East Europe Defense Ministerial (SEDM) Process began with a meeting of Ministers of Defense in Tirana in March 1996, followed by a series of meetings that brought together the Ministers of Defense, Deputy Ministers of Defense and senior militaries of the member states. For details, see https://www.sedmprocess.org/.

[14] The Multinational Peace Force South-Eastern Europe, called SEEBRIG, was established by the defense ministers of Albania, Bulgaria, Greece, Italy, North Macedonia, Romania and Turkey in 1998 and

Naval Force (BLACKSEAFOR).[15] Also, in 2020, Bulgaria inaugurated the Maritime Coordination Center in Varna to facilitate greater NATO and regional cooperation in the Black Sea region.[16] The Naval Forces of the Republic of Bulgaria regularly contribute to annual Sea Breeze exercises as well as NATO and EU operations in the Mediterranean Sea.

The Bulgaria-US 2006 Defense Cooperation Agreement was a major step for Sofia's national strategic culture. The established joint military infrastructure at Bezmer Air Base, Novo Selo Range, Graf Ignatievo Air Base and Aytos Logistics Center is unique since the country had heretofore never hosted a long-term deployment of foreign forces. The strategic decision not only had a military value for the "ally in need," but pro-Western experts and political and societal forces saw it as a point of no return for the country's strategic orientation. Initially, the facilities were part of the redeployment of US forces from Central Europe to forward positions in the context of the Global War on Terror. Currently, they are used intensively for national, bilateral, and international combat exercises in the region and are seen as a strategic asset in any potential Black Sea military confrontation.

On the other hand, prior to NATO's 2016 Warsaw Summit, Romania, backed by Turkey, raised the idea of establishing a permanent Black Sea "flotilla" to counter Russian in-theater naval activities after the annexation of Crimea, but Bulgaria did not support that proposal. Then–Prime Minister Borissov

---

activated in Plovdiv, Bulgaria, in 1999. SEEBRIG conducted its first mission, as Kabul Multinational Brigade, under International Security Assistance Force Command. For details, see http://www.seebrig.org/.
[15] The Black Sea Naval Cooperation Task Group, or BLACKSEAFOR, was initiated by Turkey at the second Chiefs of the Black Sea Navies meeting in Varna, Bulgaria, in 1998, and operationalized in 2001, with the participation of the Russian Federation, Turkey, Romania, Bulgaria, Ukraine and Georgia. For additional information, visit https://www.mfa.gov.tr/blackseafor.en.mfa.
[16] "Official Inauguration of the Maritime Coordination Center in Varna," US Embassy in Bulgaria, July 21, 2020, accessed August 26, 2021, https://bg.usembassy.gov/official-inauguration-of-the-maritime-coordination-center-in-varna/.

116 | BLACK SEA BATTLEGROUND

demonstrated a risk-averse culture, stating that he would like to see "yachts, tourists and pipelines" in the Black Sea and not an arena of military confrontation. He added, "I do not need a war in the Black Sea."[17] The Bulgarian prime minister's words effectively illustrated how the Russian strategy works—through fear and corruption, equivalent to the carrot and stick approach. And clearly, it can work quite well.

In sum, due to strategic corruption combined with limited knowledge and leadership capacity, the outgoing political elite were unable and unwilling to orient the country's security and defense policies toward the Black Sea region. In 2021, the NATO, EU, and US approaches differ significantly from Bulgaria's. The country is losing influence in the Balkans and does not recognize the new realities across the Black Sea. The threat of Bulgaria becoming a weak link for NATO in the Black Sea is real.

The Russian Threat in Bulgaria's Risk Assessment Versus Practice

Two contradictory practices complicate Bulgaria's foreign and security policies. First, strategic documents and policy positions approved by the government and parliament are not treated as binding by the governing majority. Hence, in practice, they do not directly guide security and defense planning. Second, while Sofia openly supports NATO and EU decisions made in Brussels, it often pursues unannounced policies at home. Such confusion is particularly evident in *de facto* and *de jure* coalition

---

[17] "Borissov for the Black Sea: My dream was for boats, yachts and gas pipelines," Interview for Darik Radio, February 20, 2017, https://dariknews.bg/novini/bylgariia/borisov-za-cherno-more-mechtata-mi-beshe-da-ima-platnohodki-lodki-tryba-za-gaz-2004899 – in Bulgarian. The statement was made one day after the Kremlin warned against the development of an enhanced NATO presence in the Black Sea.

governments—i.e., most of the Bulgarian governments of the past three decades.[18]

Demagogy of the Official Risk Assessment

Bulgaria's two capstone security and defense documents, the National Security Strategy (revised in 2018) and the National Defense Strategy (2016), were adopted after the Russian occupation of Crimea, the outbreak of the Donbas crisis, the downing of Malaysia Airlines' MH17 passenger plane over Donbas, the Russian intervention in Syria on the side of dictator Bashar al-Assad, the poisoning of Sergei Skripal on British soil and other covert operations of the Russian special services in Bulgaria and the Balkans, the intensive Russian military buildup in Crimea, countless politically aimed cyberattacks originating from Russia and other major developments. Nevertheless, the two documents do not reflect any of these threats.

The National Security Strategy builds on the assessment that "a full-scale military conflict against the Republic of Bulgaria is still unlikely, but the threat of hybrid actions and cyberattacks is growing."[19] Meanwhile, the Black Sea region is interpreted in contradictory ways. On the one hand, the region is seen "in a broad European and Euro-Atlantic context," permitting regional actors to "deepen the cooperation between countries in the fields of economy, trade and security."[20] On the other hand, the Strategy acknowledges that "the crisis in Ukraine and the illegal

---

[18] In April 2018, the leader of the parliamentary party "Attack" (on whose support the governing coalition depended in 2013–2014) and then–deputy speaker of the Bulgarian parliament, Volen Siderov, visited occupied Crimea. In an interview in Yalta, broadcast by major Russian media outlets with an audience of over 500 million, Siderov stated that Crimea has not been occupied and that Bulgaria should leave NATO. The parliament and the government did not react to his visit or his statements contradicting Bulgaria's official position.

[19] Revised and amended National Security Strategy (March 23, 2018), art. 9. Available in the Bulgarian language at https://mod.bg/bg/doc/strategicheski/20180330 Aktualizirana SNSRB 2018.pdf.

[20] Ibid., art. 39.

annexation of the Crimean Peninsula are leading to a permanent disruption of the geostrategic and military balance in the Black Sea region."[21] This neutral observation misses the point that Bulgaria contributes to the military balance and, if it is disrupted, the government should take adequate measures. Instead, the Strategy claims that "NATO's increased presence in the Black Sea region demonstrates allied solidarity and determination to defend the Alliance's territory in the event of aggression,"[22] without making it clear how Bulgaria shares the burden of that effort.

Rather than analyzing the essential changes in Bulgaria's strategic environment, the National Defense Strategy notes that "the military aspects of the security environment are taking on new dimensions due to the conflicts in the Middle East and Africa and the crisis in Ukraine and proliferating asymmetric and hybrid actions."[23] In particular, the document assesses that "the importance of the Black Sea region for international security, including for the Republic of Bulgaria, is growing due to its role as a link between Europe, the Middle East and Asia."[24] Such a role can, indeed, be discussed, but more from the US, NATO and EU perspectives. For Bulgaria, the regional military context should be seen as more critical because it lowers the real threshold of conflict. Furthermore, "the long-term effects of the Ukrainian crisis and the deterioration of Russia's relations with NATO *have the potential to develop a trend* toward a return to 'power politics' in Europe."[25] Russia's power politics are a continuation of the Soviet Union's policies by the same means; but that fact is simply not recognized or noted by Sofia.

---

[21] Ibid., art. 40.
[22] Ibid., art. 145.
[23] National Defense Strategy, adopted with Decision # 283 of the Council of Ministers, April 18, 2016, art. 14, accessed August 26, 2021, https://mod.bg/bg/doc/strategicheski/20160419_Natsioanalna_otbra nitelna_strategia_RMS_283_18.04.2016.pdf, - in Bulgarian.
[24] Ibid., art. 23.
[25] Ibid., art. 30, italics added by authors.

According to the 2020 Annual Report on the State of Defense and the Armed Forces, "the main destabilizing factors are the continuing conflict in Eastern Ukraine, the militarization of illegally annexed Crimea, the regional strategic balance and the 'frozen' conflicts in Transnistria, Abkhazia and South Ossetia. The potential for significant military confrontation has been preserved, which creates preconditions for growing regional instability."[26]

Sofia does not dare anger Moscow, even on paper. And yet such eclectic documents have a detrimental impact in several directions:

- They tell the people in Bulgaria that nothing of real importance is happening in Georgia, Moldova, Ukraine, Crimea and the Black Sea and that Russian tourists are more important to them than missiles and submarines.
- They tell Russia that Bulgaria accepts its military actions and preparations with "no comments" and has no intentions to react adequately.
- They tell the NATO and EU allies that Bulgaria sees no serious reasons to support decisive joint countermeasures across the Black Sea area.
- They do not provide necessary guidance for strategic security and defense planning.

Against this background, the Russian political, economic, information and intelligence forces seek to manipulate the Bulgarian security and defense decision-making process in a myriad ways.

---

[26] Ministry of Defense, Annual Report on Defense and Armed Forces 2020, April 2021, p.4,
https://www.mod.bg/bg/doc/drugi/20210405_Doklad_otbrana_2020.pdf – in Bulgarian.

120 | BLACK SEA BATTLEGROUND

Russian Penetration of the National Security System

Leadership

The Kremlin systematically influences the Bulgarian defense and security sector via political, economic and media engagements. Senior actors, including the president, government ministers, military commanders, law enforcement officers, attorneys general and others, are all high-value targets for Moscow. As some observers noted, President Rumen Radev has repeatedly taken positions aligned with the Kremlin's interests.[27]

Bulgaria's judicial branch is also not immune to Russian pressure. In 2015, then–Defense Minister Nikolay Nenchev turned to Poland to overhaul MiG-29 fighter planes to avoid dependence on Russia and to control costs. But two years later, he was accused by the prosecution[28] of "endangering Bulgaria's air sovereignty." He was acquitted of the charges by a decision of the Supreme Court of Cassation in 2019;[29] yet the earlier actions of the Bulgarian judicial branch sent a clear signal to anyone in the country who supported (and was willing to act on) eliminating Bulgaria's military dependencies on Russia.

Russian sway among the Bulgarian elite further translates into policy statements, or the lack thereof, as well as negative resource allocation decisions that cascade down the security and defense organizations' hierarchies, impacting their daily choices. These channels of Russian influence on Bulgaria's leadership, main combat capabilities, defense industries and personnel come in various forms.

---

[27] Daniel Smilov, "Rumen Radev: Composition on a Painting by Reshetnikov," *Deutsche Welle*, February 7, 2019 – in Bulgarian.
[28] In Bulgaria, the prosecution is considered part of the judicial branch.
[29] "The Supreme Court of Cassation finally acquits Nikolay Nenchev for the MiG-29 overhaul," mediapool.bg, May 10, 2021, accessed August 26, 2021, https://www.mediapool.bg/vks-okonchatelno-opravda-nikolai-nenchev-za-remonta-na-mig-29-news321654.html – in Bulgarian.

For example, in 2014, the Bulgarian Ministry of Defense published its draft "Vision: Bulgaria in NATO and European Defense 2020." The document specifically pointed to the Russian "hybrid warfare model" as a direct threat to Bulgaria's security. Velizar Shalamanov, who then served as minister of defense, explained that all relevant agencies agreed on the text. However, upon pressure from the highest political levels, the document was further edited. The version adopted by the Council of Ministers[30] notably avoids the reference to Russia posing a direct threat to Bulgaria and sets the security challenges in a broader European and regional context.

Officially, Bulgaria supports the positions and declaration of NATO and the EU on the illegal annexation of the Crimean Peninsula, the introduction of sanctions against the Russia, as well as the conducting of military exercises on NATO's eastern flank and in the Black Sea. Yet in practice, Borissov's "yachts, tourists and pipelines" policy prevails.

This effect is visible in the post-2014 defense allocations. Notwithstanding Russia's increasingly aggressive posture and investments in naval, anti-access and area-denial (A2/AD) and medium-range strike capabilities in the Black Sea and on the Crimean Peninsula, Bulgaria's defense budget continued to decline until 2018. The government only then approved a plan to meet the NATO pledge to spend at least 2 percent of GDP on defense by 2024. However, the ministers conspicuously left the steepest budget increases for the years beyond Borissov's governmental term.

Likewise, in the Skripal case, though Sofia supported the declaration of the European Council, it decided, in a "balanced and moderate" position, not to expel Russian diplomats until it could be provided with "compelling evidence" of Russia's involvement.[31]

---

[30] *Bulgaria in NATO and in European Defence 2020*, Sofia, September 2, 2014.
[31] "The Great Expulsion," *Information Centre of the Ministry of Defense*, April 1, 2018 – in Bulgarian.

122 | BLACK SEA BATTLEGROUND

Officers and associates of the former, Communist-era Bulgarian security services—which were practically subordinated to the Soviet KGB and the Russian Defense Ministry's Main Intelligence Directorate (GRU) during the Cold War—provide another venue for influencing Bulgaria's security sector today. At the end of 2006, the Bulgarian parliament adopted a law on making public the names and positions of Bulgarian citizens associated with the Communist-era state security and intelligence services. With the implementation of the law, it became clear that a considerable number of Bulgaria's contemporary senior military officers, civilian staff and political appointees in the security sector were formerly officers or agents of the coercive apparatus of the Communist regime.

The scale of the phenomenon is massive, and it succeeds in perpetuating itself through the promotion and appointment of like-minded military officials and civilians. For example, two active-duty and three retired military officers were arrested in March 2021 for spying for Russia. A former military intelligence officer trained by the GRU coordinated the group. Some of the detained served in the Bulgarian Ministry of Defense, others had been clerks in the parliamentary office for classified information. According to the prosecution, the group succeeded in delivering classified documents to the Embassy of the Russian Federation in Sofia.[32]

On occasion, it does not become clear where the actual loyalties of such individuals lie until after they leave military service. In several cases, upon retirement, flag officers have joined parties running on anti-US/anti-NATO and pro-Russia agendas, or they otherwise actively spread anti-Western and pro-Russian sentiments. For example, a former military intelligence officer, who had served as a director for defense planning and a defense

---

[32] "For pennies: Former and active military personnel arrested for spying for Russia," *Svobodna Evropa*, March 19, 2021, accessed August 26, 2021, https://www.svobodnaevropa.bg/a/31159352.html – in Bulgarian. The court procedures started in November 2021. Public information on measures taken by the defense ministry or other agencies in response to this case is not available.

advisor in the Bulgarian Mission to NATO, gave a series of interviews regarding the NATO exercises in the Black Sea. He claimed, among other things, that the Crimean Peninsula is Russian, and the British warship HMS *Defender* (while passing through internationally recognized Ukrainian territorial waters in June 2021) had "provoked" Russia. Hence, Russia had the right to fire warning shots, and that such skirmishes could lead to war.[33] While the cited interview was likely intended for the domestic audience, dozens of Russian media outlets picked it up, stating that NATO is preparing for war against Russia.[34]

Critical Defense Resources

Bulgaria's defense is also vulnerable to Russian influence when it comes to maintaining major combat systems. Even while Bulgaria was part of the Warsaw Pact, the defense industry was not granted certificates and know-how for extending the life cycle of airframes and missiles. The problem became painfully clear at the turn of the 21st century, when the defense ministry announced an international tender for upgrading a squadron of MiG-29 fighters. Large Western companies prepared their bids. However, instead of developing the indigenous capacity or seeking reliable cooperation for certifying airworthiness, the Bulgarian Ministry of Defense added a requirement late in the procedure stipulating that any aircraft modifications need to be certified by the original designer or manufacturer. With this decision, the Bulgarian minister of defense eliminated all competitors to the Russian company RSK MiG. Thus, it solidified the dependence on Russia for any overhaul and life extension works, including the delivery of spare parts and components. For obvious reasons, RSK MiG never modernized the fighters to NATO standards, while Bulgaria

---

[33] "In the Black Sea, Russia and NATO train for war," Interview with Brigadier General Valentin Tsankov, Dir.bg, July 6, 2021, accessed August 26, 2021, https://dnes.dir.bg/obshtestvo/brigaden-general-valentin-tsankov-pred-dir-bg-v-cherno-more-rusiya-i-nato-trenirat-za-voyna – in Bulgarian.

[34] See, for example, Victoria Starostina, "Bulgarian General declared that NATO is preparing for war with Russia," Gazta.ru, July 8, 2021, accessed August 26, 2021, https://www.gazeta.ru/army/news/2021/07/08/16218704.shtml – in Russian.

124 | BLACK SEA BATTLEGROUND

remained dependent on Russia for a critical capability. The situation is similar when it comes to Bulgaria's Soviet-made helicopters, guided missiles and air-defense units.

In 2018, the Bulgarian defense minister extended plans to use all Soviet-made airframes in service until the end of their anticipated life cycle.[35] To implement this decision, the Ministry of Defense will have to allocate a significant amount of money. On the one hand, this will make rearmament even more challenging. On the other hand, money will feed into the Russian military-industrial complex, despite it being under sanctions from Bulgaria's major NATO and EU allies.

The situation with the country's main naval platforms is not much different. In 2008, Bulgaria and France signed a "strategic partnership" agreement that included the delivery of two Gowind-class corvettes built by Armaris. However, during a visit to Paris in October 2009, then–Prime Minister Borissov canceled this part of the agreement.[36] The main reason given was the reduction in the defense budget due to the 2008 financial crisis. Instead, attention shifted to modernizing the two second-hand Wielingen-class frigates, acquired in 2005 from Belgium, potentially using French suppliers. Although it would have come at a much-reduced cost, that modernization also never materialized, and the Bulgarian navy continues to contribute to NATO missions and exercises "with limitations."

The saga of upgrading the fleet endures. In June 2016, the Bulgarian parliament approved the navy's top-priority project for acquiring two multi-purpose modular patrol ships at a cost of 820 million levs (just under $500 million). However, the Value Added

---

[35] "The Council of Ministers Approved the Projects for Overhaul of the MiG-29 and Su-25 Airplanes," *News.bg*, November 28, 2018, https://news.bg/politics/ms-odobri-proektite-za-remont-na-samoletite-mig-29-i-su-25.html – in Bulgarian.

[36] "Bulgaria Puzzled Anew by Arms Deal for French Corvettes," novinite.com, November 29, 2010, accessed August 26, 2021, https://www.novinite.com/articles/122656/Bulgaria+Puzzled+Anew +by+Arms+Deal+for+French+Corvettes.

Tax (VAT) law was amended during the competitive procedure. According to the interpretation of this amendment, the $500 million had to include 20 percent VAT. On this basis, the best bidder withdrew from the contract negotiations in December 2017. In July 2018, the parliament approved an amended investments project. At the end of 2020, the defense ministry signed a contract with a German shipbuilding company. However, after Borissov's government stepped down, it became clear that the contract had not included delivery of the main combat systems and other critical capability components.[37] Curiously, over all these years, Bulgaria never officially discussed the opportunity for cooperative "smart defense" procurement with Romania, which is also acquiring frigates.

Defense Infrastructure

The defense industry is another priority area for Russian influence. Traditionally, Bulgaria has a mostly export-oriented defense industry. It could nevertheless provide critical support to the Bulgarian Armed Forces and other security services under duress. Albeit slowly, Bulgarian defense companies started to cooperate with European and North American partners, diversified their products, introduced new technologies and occasionally competed with Russian companies in third countries.

However, the Russian Federation regularly raises the issue of license-based defense production by Bulgarian companies. In addition, it requests remuneration and the authority to sanction deliveries to international markets. Bulgaria never recognized these demands; yet, the pressure in recent years has been growing. According to former defense minister Boyko Noev, Borissov's government was close to acknowledging at least some

---

[37] Momchil Milev, "Are the armed forces buying 'trip boats' for 1+1 billion levs," *Capital*, June 10, 2021, accessed August 27, 2021, https://www.capital.bg/politika_i_ikonomika/otbrana/2021/06/10/4219396_kupuva_li_si_armiiata_lodki_za_razhodki_za_11_mlrd_lv/ – in Bulgarian.

126 | BLACK SEA BATTLEGROUND

of the Russian claims,[38] which would have had a detrimental impact on Bulgaria's defense industry.

In April 2015, an attempt was made to poison a defense company's owner, Emil Gebrev, and two of his associates. The Bulgarian authorities ignored the case, and the investigation into the assassination attempt was quickly closed. New information in early 2019 linked the poison used to the weapons-grade Novichok-class chemical weapons deployed against Sergei and Yulia Skripal in Salisbury. Furthermore, "Fedotov"—likely a GRU officer, who visited England at the time the Skripals were poisoned—was also in Bulgaria when the attempt on Gebrev's life was made.[39] Nevertheless, the prosecution and security services hesitated to reopen the case or link it to the Salisbury attack and GRU officers' involvement.

Russia also tries to coerce Bulgarian defense companies through international propaganda. Russian media often disseminates "discoveries" that are later proven fake. Among the examples are the alleged use of a Bulgarian portable ground-to-air missile to shoot down a Russian Su-25 Frogfoot as well as the story of Bulgarian-made munitions found in Aleppo, Syria, and supposedly used to attack the civilian population. Additionally, indications reveal the involvement of Russian competitors in a series of recent accidents at Bulgarian defense production facilities or test ranges, some involving casualties.[40]

---

[38] "Boyko Noev: Russia's Interests to Control Bulgaria's Defence Industry are openly Stated," *FrogNews*, February 13, 2019, accessed August 27, 2021, https://frognews.bg/novini/boiko-noev-interesite-rusiia-kontrolira-balgarskata-otbranitelna-industriia-otkprito-zaiaveni.html – in Bulgarian.

[39] Rossen Bossev, "A GRU Agent visited Bulgaria when Gebrev was poisoned," *Capital*, February 8, 2019, https://www.capital.bg/politika_i_ikonomika/bulgaria/2019/02/08/3 387392_agent_na_gru_e_bil_v_bulgariia_po_vreme_na_otravianeto/ – in Bulgarian.

[40] "Boyko Noev: Russia's Interests to Control Bulgaria's Defence Industry Are Openly Stated."

Personnel

The people working in the defense and security fields in Bulgaria are particularly sought-out and, it turns out, vulnerable targets. Both Bulgaria's "foot soldiers" and civilian experts are subject to pro-Russian influence established by institutional factors, propaganda and disinformation campaigns within traditional and electronic media, including social networks and, last but not least, manipulative elements in the specialized educational system. From one side, the Bulgarian leadership's mixed messages regarding the national security environment, threats and responses create an environment that certainly impacts security and defense personnel. Bureaucrats and lower-level officials follow the leadership's messages more than the statements found within state strategic documents. Moreover, such messages are seen as guidance for promotions, especially for the senior military and civilian employees. It is clear that the president, who has the final say on general promotions across the security sector, is unlikely to back officers who disagree with his political views; this is not a legal consideration, but it is common practice.

On the other hand, Russian military-oriented propaganda, especially after the annexation of Crimea, has penetrated virtually all media in Bulgaria. The focus is on "historical justice" and the "right" to intervene militarily as well as on "ultra-advanced" new weapons, to which the West purportedly has no answer. The information disseminated is mostly historical or technical (rarely political) and is promptly reproduced by the Bulgarian media.

Another vehicle for perpetuating legacy dependencies and attitudes is Bulgaria's unreformed military education system. Having long escaped political attention while exploiting academic freedom and protection, Bulgarian military academy faculty members from different generations routinely demonstrate in publications a commitment to theses from the Kremlin playbook.[41] They widely use Russian sources to argue that NATO and its member states are fighting a hybrid war against Russia.

---

[41] *Bulgarian Science* 117, Special National Security Issue (February 2019).

The annexation of Crimea is a "restoration of historical justice," but sanctions against the Kremlin are illegal. The "color revolutions," "Maidan," peoples' struggle for better democracy and honest governance, not to mention any partnership with NATO and EU, are seen through Moscow's conspiracy prism.

Even *Military Journal*, the official publication of the Bulgarian Ministry of Defense (first published in 1888 in 2,000 copies), has lost its capacity to connect the political and command leadership with the officer corps. Bulgaria's first civilian defense minister reestablished the magazine in 1991 as a symbol of new civil-military relations. It was to be the *primary* source of information, analysis, and ideas on the changing post–Cold War security environment, defense reform, and NATO membership for the military, security-sector organizations, and broader society as well. But in 2016, the G. S. Rakovski Defense and Staff College took over publishing authority from the Ministry of Defense, which led to a decline in the publication's importance and popularity. Currently, the journal is printed in fewer than 300 copies per issue and delivered solely within the defense system or for commercial release. The magazine is not available to read online. Several specialized periodicals on naval, air and general military matters, together with the associated websites, discussion forums, and social network profiles, also actively promote anti-Western and pro-Russian sentiments.

Ultra-Nationalists

Russian influence also occurs via ultra-nationalistic Bulgarian organizations, some with suspected links to and sponsored by Moscow. These organizations seek to cooperate with active military personnel to take on the trappings of an ostensibly influential paramilitary outfit. And such groups call for all kinds of anti-systemic actions: military coups, exiting NATO, discharging political parties and the parliament, as well as killing Bulgarian politicians, diplomats, journalists and academics.[42]

---

[42] "There is no Place in Bulgaria for Para-military Formations, Assassination Threats, and Russian Media Aggression," Declaration of the Atlantic Council of Bulgaria, November 14, 2017 – in Bulgarian.

Currently, the "ultras" are mobilized for propaganda against COVID-19 vaccinations, which they claim are an instrument for establishing mental control over people.[43]

The noisiest of these formations include the National Salvation Committee "Vasil Levski" and Soldiers Union–Bulgarian National Army of Volunteers (Opalchennie) BNO "Shipka." These are not true paramilitary formations, but their members wear camouflage uniforms to be perceived as such. The groups use aggressive rhetoric on online social networks and have undertaken a couple of public marches in the streets and against government institutions. They claim that the "democrats" sold Bulgaria to NATO and devastated the Army, thus destroying the nation's ability to resist aggression. Moreover, they assert that the main disadvantages of modern Bulgaria are its multi-party system and the country's distance from Russia. Their adherents' brutal anti-Semitism, xenophobia, and cruelty to migrants mean that these formations much more closely resemble the Western European ultra-nationalist network known as Patriotic Europeans Against the Islamicization of the Occident (PEGIDA)[44] than to any typical paramilitary group.

To sum up, Bulgaria recognizes various threats to its security shared within NATO—cyber and terrorist attacks, mass refugee flows, nuclear arms proliferation and others. However, even though these threats are duly considered within various strategy documents, they do not represent priority risks to Bulgaria. Official risk assessments by the government are sluggish and superficial, neither managing to appreciate the Black Sea security

---

[43] A Facebook group of the Military School for Artillery and Air Defense/Faculty of Artillery, Air Defense, and Communications and Information Systems, https://www.facebook.com/groups/170205543031802/ – in Bulgarian.

[44] Representatives of PEGIDA from Germany and the Netherlands participated in the persecution of illegal migrants on the Bulgarian-Turkish border, supporting another illegal volunteer "border patrol" organization. See https://sofiaglobe.com/2016/07/07/concern-grows-over-bulgarian-paramilitaries-and-border-patrols/, accessed November 20, 2021.

dynamics nor identify the domestic predisposing conditions that increase the likelihood of those threats reaching their goals and leading to significant losses. The major consequence of such poor risk awareness is unrealistic defense planning, exemplified by the wishful "Program for the Development of the Defense Capabilities of the Bulgarian Armed Forces" (adopted by Borissov's government in February 2021). At the same time, it facilitates the demoralizing impact of Russian propaganda. Gradually, Bulgaria's defense decision-making has turned into an impenetrable "black box," in which shady political considerations or corrupting influence routinely substitute for important national security factors as well as afford space for authoritarian, manipulative securitization. The "black box" and authoritarian leadership are precisely what Zelikow *et al.* refer to as "strategic corruption."

Bulgaria Matters But Is Undermined by Political Corruption

Several strategic issues reveal the value of Bulgaria to NATO, the US and the EU in the context of Russia's military Black Sea buildup. Being at the center of the wider Black Sea region, Bulgaria links the economic, political and security interests of Russia, Ukraine, the South Caucasus countries, Turkey, and Iran with those of the Balkans and Southern and Central Europe as well as, more generally, with NATO and the EU. Moreover, two strategic diagonals intersect in the country's airspace. The first— a direct connection between Russia and the Western Balkans— was first highlighted during the NATO-led operation in Kosovo.[45]

---

[45] After Russian troops unexpectedly and uncoordinatedly occupied airport "Slatina" near Kosovo's capital Pristina and created a critical situation among the coalition, Bulgaria (as well as Romania and Hungary) refused overflight rights for six Russian airplanes to deliver supplies to the contingent. As later Zbignev Brzezinski testified before the Senate, "The attempt faltered because three small European countries had the gumption to defy Moscow." See "The Lessons of Kosovo," Testimony of Zbigniew Brzezinski to the Senate Foreign Relations Committee, October 6, 1999, accessed August 27, 2021, https://csis-website-prod.s3.amazonaws.com/s3fs-public/legacy_files/files/attachments/ts991006_brzezinski.pdf.

The other diagonal connects Central Europe (Germany) to Iran. It was operationalized by the US and NATO during the War on Terror, in 2001, at the Sarafovo airbase near Burgas: 200 US military personnel operated six tanker planes there daily, in support of Operation Enduring Freedom in Afghanistan.

Bulgaria is probably the only country that successfully maintains good relationships with *all* countries in the wider Black Sea region. To a large extend, this is determined by economic interests and is supported by the sizable Bulgarian diaspora in Turkey, Moldova and Ukraine (more than 200,000 in each country).

Bulgaria may be the poorest EU member state; yet, it is in the top three in terms of the lowest budget deficit, public debt to gross domestic product and bank capitalization ratios. Despite the remaining COVID-19-related effects on the economy, real GDP growth is expected to reach 4.6 percent (EU average is 4.8 percent) at the 2021 annual base. Inflation is set to accelerate to 1.9 percent in 2021 (EU average 2.2 percent), on the back of higher foreseen energy prices. The unemployment rate for 2021 is 4.8 percent (EU average 7.6 percent), with the perspective to decline to 3.9 percent in 2022. The budget balance is planned at minus 3.2 percent in 2021 (EU averages minus 7.5 percent), with the perspective to drop to 1.9 percent in 2022.[46] In terms of economic infrastructure, two mid-size international airports operate on the Bulgarian Black Sea shore in Varna and Burgas. The most important ferry lines in the Black Sea connect Bulgaria with Russia (Chernomorsk) and Georgia (Poti). Both ferry lines are part of the maritime multi-modal transportation corridor Europe–Caucasus–Central Asia (TRACECA).[47]

---

[46] All data are according to the European Commission's economic forecast for Bulgaria, available at https://ec.europa.eu/economy_finance/forecasts/2021/summer/ecfin _forecast_summer_2021_bg_en.pdf.

[47] More information about TRACECA is available at https://www.euneighbours.eu/en/search/25?keys=traceca.

132 | BLACK SEA BATTLEGROUND

However, critical flaws in the political, moral and bureaucratic spheres compromise these trends. The heaviest deficits are in the quality of the democratic political system. Before reaching the quality of a consolidated democracy, the boundaries among the three divided powers were gradually blurred in favor of an authoritative government. Because of controlled grand political corruption and as a consequence of being captured by Russian-backed corruption schemes, Bulgaria's political elite empowered selected oligarchy. The government and oligarchy jointly serve as proxies of the Kremlin's most significant corporate instruments in this space—Gazprom, Lukoil, Rosatom, Rosoboronexport, VT Bank and others.

In the spring of 2021, US Senators Jim Risch and Robert Menendez issued a joint statement[48] in light of the US Department of the Treasury's Office of Foreign Assets Control sanctioning of three Bulgarian oligarchs "for their extensive roles in corruption in Bulgaria, as well as their networks encompassing 64 entities."[49] The senators sent a strong message: Bulgarian society and Bulgaria's strategic allies will no longer tolerate grand corruption or suppression of the rule of law.

These deficits have the most devastating effects on society, bringing monopolization of the economy's main sectors, obstacles to the development of medium- and small-sized businesses, the elimination of economic competition through controlled public procurement, as well as other forms of grand corruption. The tendency to favor an authoritarian style of government and Russian influence in the country logically go hand-in-hand and reinforce one another.

---

[48] Joint Statement from Ranking Member Risch and Chairman Menendez on U.S.-Bulgaria Bilateral Relationship, https://www.foreign.senate.gov/press/ranking/release/joint-statement-from-ranking-member-risch-and-chairman-menendez-on-us-bulgaria-bilateral-relationship.

[49] "Treasury Sanctions Influential Bulgarian Individuals and Their Expansive Networks for Engaging in Corruption," US Department of Treasury, June 2, 2021, https://home.treasury.gov/news/press-releases/jy0208.

However, the political landscape in Bulgaria underwent significant changes in the 2020–2021 period. Mass protests in 2020 against grand corruption and compromised democratic governance gave rise to the "protest" parties "Democratic Bulgaria" and "Stand up, BG!" and to the newly created populist, anti-systemic party "There Is Such a People." After the July 2021 parliamentary elections, these political actors managed to position themselves as a viable alternative to the "status quo" parties (the governing GERB,[50] the Bulgarian Socialist Party and the Movement for Rights and Liberties).

Moreover, before the simultaneous presidential and parliamentary elections in November 2021, two ministers from President Roumen Radev's caretaker government (both Harvard University alumni) formed the "We Continue the Change" party. Attracting the protest vote, they won most of the seats in the parliament (28 percent) and successfully negotiated with three other parties to establish a coalition government, approved on December 13. As a mentor of the new leading party, the president obtained massive direct support for his reelection.

An essential outcome of the parliamentary elections is the complete replacement of parties directly or indirectly sponsored by the Kremlin. The former nationalists (anti-EU/NATO/US and pro-Russian) remained below the electoral threshold. Moscow-backed parties failed to trigger a referendum on leaving NATO, and Russia itself was unable to offer "equal cooperation." A new parliamentary party, *Vazrazhdane* ("Renaissance"), originating from Varna, will be the Kremlin's latest "developing project" in Bulgarian politics (direct Russian support for this faction is an open secret). The party kicked off its campaign with negative energy, spreading doubts and dissatisfaction, using the ethnic issue, nationalism, xenophobia and coronavirus-denialism rhetoric. "Renaissance" received nearly 5 percent of the vote (13 seats) but has a significant capacity to absorb other elements of the protest electorate and to bolster destabilization, intrigue and

---

[50] GERB is the Bulgarian-language abbreviation of Citizens for European Development of Bulgaria.

134 | BLACK SEA BATTLEGROUND

division of society in the deepening political, post-pandemic and regional security crises.

Meanwhile, in a live televised debate with his opponent in the second presidential round (Sofia University rector and professor Anastas Gerdzhikov), President Radev revealed his positions vis-à-vis Russia and the Black Sea. According to the Bulgarian head of state, "Russia cannot be our enemy; the Bulgarians see it as a liberator. Only political losers emphasize the Russia theme. The most important thing is to seek dialogue. The EU-Russia dialogue is in critical condition. [US] President [Joe] Biden has launched a dialogue with Putin over the head of the EU." Asked by his opponent for a clear answer on Crimea, Radev said, "Crimea is Russian; whose is it supposed to be?" According to him, "the Black Sea is becoming a crossroads of geopolitical interests. We should not allow the over-militarization of the Black Sea."[51] This shocking statement provoked an immediate critical reaction from the European Commission,[52] Ukraine[53] and the US embassy in Sofia.[54]

The interim lesson from Bulgaria's failure to cope with the Russian challenges at home is that engaging with authoritarian kleptocracies, such as Russia, inevitably brings home authoritarianism and grand political corruption. It is arguably unrealistic to try to craft a workable security defense strategy that does not explicitly prohibit cooperation with undemocratic kleptocratic powers.

---

[51] "Presidential Depate Radev – Gerdjikov (Video)," Bulgarian National Television, https://bnt.bg/news/prezidentskiyat-debat-radev-gerjikov-video-300435news.html, accessed November 20, 2021.
[52] "EU on Radev's Words: Krimea is Ukraine," ClubZ, November 19, 2021, https://www.clubz.bg/120983-es_za_dumite_na_radev_krim_e_ukrayna, accessed November 20, 2021.
[53] "Comment of the Ministry of Foreign Affairs of Ukraine on the statements by President of Bulgaria Rumen Radev," MFA of Ukraine, November 19, 2021, https://mfa.gov.ua/en/news/komentar-mzs-ukrayini-u-zvyazku-z-vislovlyuvannyami-prezidenta-bolgariyi-rumena-radeva, accessed November 20, 2021.
[54] "Statement by the U.S. Embassy in Bulgaria," November 22, 2021, https://bg.usembassy.gov/statement-by-the-us-embassy-in-bulgaria-22-11-2021/.

Conclusions

The Kremlin's adherence to an archaic imperial model and its modern arsenal of conventional, nuclear and "hybrid" tools of coercion have been game-changers for security in the wider Black Sea region. Notably, all of Russia's open military or militarized conflicts are located on the southern arc from Moldova and Ukraine toward the Caucasus and the Caspian Sea. The militarization of Crimea and the Black Sea since 2014 further strengthens the Kremlin's political and economic leverage, thus forcing some countries in the region to consider accepting limited sovereignty and outside control. Consequently, Russia is more likely to continue to use military force in the wider Black Sea area than in other portions of its neighborhood.

Yet, approximately half of the Black Sea is under NATO's area of responsibility. The Alliance, EU and US are full-fledged regional actors. For the past decade, these transatlantic allies have been searching for effective approaches to the Black Sea's security problems, and they have already implemented many practical solutions. However, Bulgaria's role in this process is marginal. The government and the military leadership have habitually been unable or unwilling to raise the issue of security in the Black Sea at NATO HQ and SHAPE.

Bulgaria was eager to host US military installations and NATO structures, but these expressed goals seem to be more for domestic consumption rather than a comprehensive policy approach for tackling the challenges caused by Russia's destabilizing activities in the region. The political debate on Russian aggressive actions has frequently been hushed up so as not to undermine the government's noisy announcements of energy "triumphs." The silence is not due to a lack of information or poor awareness. It consciously takes a back seat so as not to interfere with the multi-billion-dollar deals with the Kremlin's agents, which grossly distort Bulgarian politics.

At the beginning of 2022, Bulgaria once again stood along the shores of the proverbial Rubicon—a Rubicon that separates the nation from the corrupted elite, good governance from pervasive populism, the oligarchy from business standards, the rule of law from organized crime, and security policy from speculative securitization. Having held three general and one presidential election in one year, Bulgarians made a genuine march toward democratic renewal. Four parties formed a coalition government. In a telephone conversation with the new Prime Minister Kiril Petkov on December 16, 2021, Secretary of State Anthony Blinken expressed the gratitude of the United States to Bulgaria as a reliable ally and partner. Blinken reaffirmed the US's desire to expand its partnership with Bulgaria in new areas, such as the promotion of carbon-free energy sources, modernization of defense, security of 5G networks, and other regional issues.[55] After the prime minister met with NATO Secretary General Jens Stoltenberg, he stressed that Bulgaria would continue to modernize its armed forces to meet Alliance standards and stressed his government's ambition to meet the goal of defense spending reaching 2 percent of GDP by 2024.[56]

Despite the apparent situational ambiguity and volatility, Bulgarians seem dedicated to making change happen. But to reflect this desire, the country will need to realistically address its fundamental national and allied security challenges. Only such a policy course can ultimately break Bulgaria free from the grip of Russian strategic corruption as well as overcome its growing democratic, governance and moral deficits.

---

[55] "Prime Minister Kiril Petkov talks with US Secretary of State Anthony Blinken," Government Press Office, December 16, 2021, https://www.gov.bg/bg/prestsentar/novini/ministar-predsedatelyat-kiril-petkov-razgovarya-s-darzhavniya-sekretar-na-sasht-antani-blinken.
[56] "Bulgaria is highly praised for its contribution to NATO," Government Press Office, December 17, 2021, https://www.gov.bg/en/Press-center/News/Bulgaria-is-highly-praised-for-its-contribution-to-NATO.

5.

Water Crises and the Looming Ecological Catastrophe in Occupied Crimea and Devastated Donbas

Alla Hurska

January 21, 2022

After Russia illegally annexed Ukraine's Crimean Peninsula and then sparked a military conflict in Donbas, the environmental conditions and access to clean drinking water for local populations in both territories rapidly deteriorated. These concurrent (though varying in their intensity) crises stem from a combination of factors, including long-term infrastructure problems, administrative mismanagement, corruption, ecological negligence, militarization, as well as ongoing fighting between the Russia-backed "separatists" and the Ukrainian army. Despite the fact that these mounting challenges have grown worse as a direct result of Russian-sponsored actions, the Russian side blames Ukraine for these developments. In fact, Russia says it plans to conduct a comprehensive environmental impact assessment to determine the amount of damage ostensibly done by Ukraine.[1]

---

[1] "V Krymu otsenyat ekologicheskiy ushcherb ot vodnoy blokady," [Environmental Damage from Water Blockade Will Be Assessed in Crimea], *Vesti Krym*, May 29, 2021, https://vesti-

138 | BLACK SEA BATTLEGROUND

Indeed, the occupying Russian authorities in Crimea have already put forward some preliminary estimates claiming the "damage" to be $19.4 billion[2]—more such spurious claims are surely coming.

Furthermore, the Russian Federal Security Service (FSB) seeks to initiate criminal proceedings against 12 Ukrainian citizens, including former presidents Leonid Kravchuk and Petro Poroshenko, for (among other charges) so-called "ecocide,"[3] thus shifting the blame for the water (and environmental) crisis in Ukraine's southeast to Kyiv's political elite. Nevertheless, major international organizations wholly reject those accusations: for instance, the United Nations' monitoring mission in Ukraine insists that, according to international law, Russia as the *de facto* occupier bears full responsibility for providing the Crimean population with water.[4]

Drawing on a broad array of Russian- and Ukrainian-language sources, the following chapter examines the current catastrophic water situations in Donbas and illegally annexed Crimea, paying special attention to the roots (including historical) of the present-day conditions.

---

k.ru/news/2021/05/29/v-krymu-ocenyat-ekologicheskij-usherb-ot-vodnoj-blokady/.

[2] "V okkupirovannom Krymu otsenili ushcherb ot 'vodnoy blokady,' [In the Occupied Crimea, the Damage from the "Water Blockade" Was Assessed]," Gordonua.com, March 24, 2021. https://gordonua.com/news/crimea/v-okkupirovannom-krymu-ocenili-ushcherb-ot-vodnoy-blokady-1545609.html

[3] "Vlasti Kryma prosyat vozbudit delo protiv 12 grazhdan Ukrainy za blokadu poluostrova" [Crimean Authorities Ask to Initiate Proceedings Against 12 citizens of Ukraine for Blockade of the Peninsula], TASS, April 29, 2021. https://tass.ru/politika/11272139.

[4] "Missiya OON v Ukraine o pisme Poklonskoy: 'Rossiya neset otvetstvennost za dustup k vode v Krymu," [UN Mission in Ukraine on Poklonskaya's Letter: "Russia Is Responsible for Access to Water in Crimea], *Krym.Realii*, September 3, 2020. https://ru.krymr.com/a/news-oon-poklonskaya-rossia-neset-otvetstvennost-za-dostup-krymchan-k-vode/30818404.html.

Historical Background: The Water Issue in Crimea

Due to its arid climate, the Crimean Peninsula is predisposed to water-related difficulties. That is why a scarcity of water resources has been an essential factor influencing Crimea's geo-economic and military-political situations for much of its history. In 1687, for example, lack of water proved a major hindrance to the advance of the Russian army (led by Vasily Golitsyn), which was then attempting to impose its control over Crimea and gain a foothold along the Black Sea coast. Local leaders, including Crimean Khan Selim Giray, understood that an open battle with large numbers of Russian troops would be unwise, and so, they resorted instead to "scorched earth" tactics. This turned out to be a winning strategy: Despite sufficient food supplies, Tsarist Russia's advance was halted primarily due to the lack of water, forcing its army to turn back, temporarily postponing the strategic peninsula's occupation.[5]

Water Issues Before 1917

Russia's apprehension over access to water in Crimea and its first attempts to solve the issue date back to the 18th century (the first annexation), when cartographers drew up initial maps of the Crimean Black Sea steppes, paying specific attention to the particularities of the local hydrographic network. Up until 1917, the Russian Empire engaged its best experts to try to solve the water issue, yet little practical success was achieved. One particularly notable visionary from this period was Russian botanist of Swedish descent Christian von Steven, who, for the first time in recorded history, in 1846, proposed building a canal connecting the Dnipro River and the Crimean Peninsula. Yet, the estimated costs for such a project discouraged the Russian authorities. Moreover, the issue of irrigation of the Crimean steppe was repeatedly raised in the State Duma. But again,

---

[5] V. Velikanov, "Detali pohoda armii V.V. Golitsyna v 1687 g," in "Yug Rossii i sopredelnye strany v voynakh i vooruzhennykh konfliktakh: materialy Vserossiyskoy nauchnoy konferentsii s mezhdunarodnym uchastiyem (Rostov-na-Donu, 22–25 iyunya 2016 g.), ed. Matishov G. (Rostov-na-Donu: Izdatelstvo YuNTs RAN, 2016), 32–39.

140 | BLACK SEA BATTLEGROUND

because of excessive costs, the decision was postponed until 1916. By then, however, World War I, coupled with the ensuing February Revolution (1917), thwarted these plans, and the project was never implemented.

Despite understanding the problem, the imperial Russian authorities were constrained by a lack of technology and thus could not resolve the water shortage issues. As a result devastating droughts repeatedly harmed local agriculture and inhabitants.[6]

Water Issues During the Soviet Era

After the introduction of Communism, first Soviet leader Vladimir Lenin initiated a special program aimed at irrigating the dry lands in the Russian Soviet Federative Socialist Republic (RSFSR).[7] In 1924, construction began on the Alminsky Reservoir, with a capacity of more than 6 million cubic meters of water. It was completed in 1936.[8] Following the Great Patriotic War (1941–1945), the issue of supplying more water to Crimea resurfaced, with the Soviet authorities proposing three different options:

- Constructing a water pipeline from the Kuban region;
- Desalinating the Sea of Azov; or

---

[6] Ye. Bogutskaya et al., "Sredniy mnogoletniy stok rek Yuga-Zapadnoy chasti Krymskogo poluostrova," [The Average Long-Term Runoff of Rivers in the South-Western Part of the Crimean Peninsula], *Vodnoye hozyaystvo Rossii: problem, tekhnologii, upravleniye*, no. 2 (2020), https://cyberleninka.ru/article/n/sredniy-mnogoletniy-stok-rek-yugo-zapadnoy-chasti-krymskogo-poluostrova.
[7] L. Korolyova and M. Galkina, "Predistoriya stroitelstva Severo-Krymskogo kanala," *Krymskoye Istoricheskoye Obozreniye*, no. 3 (2015): 47–58.
[8] "Mogily, kholera, stroyki: kak Krym perezhyval defitsyt vody," [Graves, Cholera, Construction Sites: How Crimea Experienced a Water Shortage], *RIA Novosti*, February 6, 2020, https://crimea.ria.ru/society/20200206/1117926431/Mogily-kholera-stroyki-kak-Krym-perezhival-defitsit-vody.html.

Water Crises and Looming Ecological Catastrophe | 141

- Building a canal from the Dnipro River (assumed to be the most rational choice).[9]

As a result, on September 21, 1950, the Soviet Council of Ministers adopted the resolution "On the Construction of the Kakhovka Hydroelectric Station, South Ukrainian and North Crimean Canals to Irrigate Areas of Southern Ukraine and Northern Crimea."[10] Yet the issue did not move forward until 1961, when the Central Committee of the Communist Party of Ukraine and the Council of Ministers of the Ukrainian SSR declared the start of "the Great Construction Projects of Communism." Thanks to these efforts, water began flowing through the newly built North Crimean Canal (NCC) and reached Krasnoperekopsk (northern Crimea) on October 17, 1963. Two years later, channeled water reached Dzhankoy; and in 1971, it flowed all the way to the Kerch Peninsula—Crimea's easternmost point.[11]

Despite these infrastructure mega-projects, the chronic water deficits were never entirely eliminated, with severe droughts recurring throughout the 1970s and 1980s—especially between 1982 and 1984—devastating local agriculture. In 1990, the authorities commissioned the second stage of the NCC and built the Mezhgornoye Reservoir, to this day the largest artificial water reservoir in Crimea. Even this failed to solve local water shortages, however, while creating additional challenges. Specifically, due to mistakes in engineering, the loss of water during transportation via the canal reached a staggering 40 percent, which was accompanied by a rise in groundwater levels, causing the salinization of soils. In general, the Soviet authorities frequently disregarded scientific principles and conducted

---

[9] Korolyova and Galkina, "Predistoriya stroitelstva Severo-Krymskogo kanala."

[10] Postanovleniye Soveta ministrov SSSR, *Gosudarstvennyy arkhiv RF*, http://krym.rusarchives.ru/dokumenty/postanovlenie-soveta-ministrov-sssr-o-stroitelstve-kahovskoy-gidroelektrostancii-na-reke.

[11] "Missiya OON v Ukraine o pisme Poklonskoy."

142 | BLACK SEA BATTLEGROUND

extremely low-quality construction works, which took a serious toll on local water security.[12]

Water Issues After Ukraine's Independence

After 1991, practically no major undertakings were carried out until the late 1990s, with the third stage of the NCC's construction accomplished in 1997. By then, the total length of the canals and irrigation pipelines in Crimea had reached 11,000 kilometers. Further works (stage four) were frozen due to a lack of funding, while follow-on stages five and six, which would have been crucial for resolving chronic water supply problems, were never built.

In spite of these shortcomings, the NCC's construction—though incomplete—made it possible to address the water supply shortages in at least parts of Crimea. Up to 80 percent of the water sent to the peninsula from mainland Ukraine was utilized for agriculture and fish farming.[13] Importantly, the NCC was seasonal, not year-round. The flow of water usually occurred between the end of March and November. Thus, until 2014, the North Crimean Canal provided the peninsula with 80 to 87 percent of its overall water intake.[14]

---

[12] "Strategiya vodosnabzheniya Kryma i kak ona osushchestvlyayetsya?," [Crimea's Water Supply Strategy and How Is It Being Implemented?], *Ostrov Krym*, May 2, 2015, http://www.mircrimea.ru/water-strategy-of-crimea/.

[13] G. Kravchenko, "Vodnyy baryer dlya krymskoy vlasti: kak reshayetsya problema vodosnabzheniya poluostrova," [Water Barrier for the Crimean Authorities: How the Problem of Water Supply to the Peninsula Is Being Solved], *Krym Realii*, April 5, 2018, https://ru.krymr.com/a/29148493.html.

[14] D. Kozlov et al., "Severo-Krymskiy kanal," [North Crimean Canal], *Voda Rossii*, https://water-rf.ru/%D0%92%D0%BE%D0%B4%D0%BD%D1%8B%D0%B5_%D0%BE%D0%B1%D1%8A%D0%B5%D0%BA%D1%82%D1%8B/883/%D0%A1%D0%B5%D0%B2%D0%B5%D1%80%D0%BE-%D0%9A%D1%80%D1%8B%D0%BC%D1%81%D0%BA%D0%B8%D0%B9_%D0%BA%D0%B0%D0%BD%D0%B0%D0%BB.

Crimea's Annexation, Continuing Water Issues and Russia's Myth-Building

Following the unlawful annexation of Crimea, Ukraine blocked the water supply through the NCC. In May 2014, at the canal's 91st kilometer, on the territory of Kherson region, near the Kherson–Armyansk section of European route E97, local farmers hastily built a temporary dam to disrupt the flow of water from the Dnipro to the peninsula.[15] Between 2015 and 2017, the authorities constructed a permanent dam at the NCC's 107th kilometer, which now restricts the flow of water into occupied Crimea.[16]

Since 2014, Crimea's entire water supply has solely depended on internal reserves, but these are proving to be insufficient, causing Crimea to face one of the most acute water shortages in 50 years. Importantly, since most of the water from the NCC was used for agriculture-related needs, this sector suffered the most.[17] To somehow alleviate these shortages, farmers started switching to drought-resistant crops (the cultivation of rice discontinued), while also relying on so-called "drip irrigation" systems. Simultaneously, water scarcity caused a dramatic decrease in

---

[15] "Pivnichno-Krymskyy kanal prypynyv podachu vody do Krymu," [The North Crimean Canal Cut Off Water Supply to Crimea], *Ekonomichna Pravda*, May 13, 2014, https://www.epravda.com.ua/news/2014/05/13/451805/.

[16] "V predstavitelstve prezidenta Ukrainy obyasnili, zachem ukreplyat dambu na Severo-Krymskom kanale," [The Office of the President of Ukraine Explained Why to Strengthen the Dam on the North Crimean Canal], *Krym.Realii*, March 23, 2021, https://ru.krymr.com/a/news-krym-korynevych-ukreplenie-severo-krymskogo-kanala/31165206.html.

[17] V. Tabunshchik, "Izmeneniye ploshchadi zerkal vodokhranilishch yestestvennogo stoka na territorii Krymskogo poluostrova (sravneniye dannykh na nachalo aprelya 2019 i 2020 goda)," [Change in the Area of the Mirrors of the Natural Flow Reservoirs on the Territory of the Crimean Peninsula], *Geopolitika i ekogeodinamika regionov*, no. 4 (2020), https://cyberleninka.ru/article/n/izmenenie-ploschadi-zerkal-vodohranilisch-estestvennogo-stoka-na-territorii-krymskogo-poluostrova-sravnenie-dannyh-na-nachalo.

144 | BLACK SEA BATTLEGROUND

water diverted for irrigation: from 700 million cubic meters in 2013 to 17.7 million cubic meters two years later. Another side effect was the rapid dwindling of irrigated land, which reduced from 140,000 hectares to a mere 13,400.[18]

The water situation became so dire that, in 2016, Andrey Nikitchenko (the head of the directorate managing the federal development program for the peninsula) announced that the issue had been taken up at the federal level. These measures included the construction of a complex system of water supply networks—a project expected to cost more than 20 billion rubles (approximately $276 million). At the same time, the authorities announced that work was already in full swing,[19] but no improvements ensued. The problem rapidly extended beyond the original irrigation needs, affecting the supply of clean drinking water as well. In the summer of 2017, the Crimea-based session of the Russian Security Council raised the issue. According to Nikolai Patrushev, in 2016 (compared to 2014), water intake on the peninsula had decreased by five times, and the area of irrigated land dwindled by 92 percent.[20]

Nevertheless, local officials continued to deny the true gravity of the dilemma. But after 2020, when the situation became critical— owing to a combination of factors such as an abnormally dry autumn and lack of precipitation during several consecutive winters—hiding the reality became next to impossible, and Crimean authorities had to publicly acknowledge that the scarcity of water in Crimea is the key problem the peninsula faces. Even Sergey Aksyonov (the region's installed pro-Russian head) did

---

[18] Kravchenko, "Vodnyy baryer dlya krymskoy vlasti: kak reshayetsya problema vodosnabzheniya poluostrova."

[19] "Proyekt po vodosnabzheniyu vostochnogo Kryma oboydetsya v 20 milliardov rubley," [The Project for the Water Supply of the Eastern Crimea Will Cost 20 Billion Rubles], *RIA Novosti*, December 12, 2016, https://crimea.ria.ru/society/20161208/1108313536.html.

[20] "Patrushev konstatiroval slozhnuyu situatsiyu s vodoy na vostoke Kryma," [Patrushev Stated a Difficult Situation with Water in the East of Crimea], Lenta.ru, June 27, 2017, https://lenta.ru/news/2017/06/27/voda/.

Water Crises and Looming Ecological Catastrophe | 145

not rule out that Moscow might classify this as an emergency.[21] Since the end of August 2020, in the Crimean regional capital of Simferopol, Bakhchisarai District, Belogorsk Region and the southern coastal city of Alushta, the authorities introduced water rationing. Other areas—including the cities of Yevpatoria and Yalta—switched to water-saving regimes.[22] A strategically critical source of water for Simferopol—"the Simferopol Sea," once one of the largest artificial water reservoirs in Crimea—has now turned into a dried-up pond.[23] The rest of Simferopol's main reservoirs were filled to a mere 14 percent of their designed volumes.[24] Experts believe that in the next 30 years, not a single freshwater lake will remain in Crimea.[25]

---

[21] Alla Hurska, "Unprecedented Drought in Crimea: Can the Russian-Occupied Peninsula Solve Its Water Problems Without Ukraine?" *Eurasia Daily Monitor* 17, no. 119 (August 12, 2020), https://jamestown.org/program/unprecedented-drought-in-crimea-can-the-russian-occupied-peninsula-solve-its-water-problems-without-ukraine/.

[22] "29 naselyonnykh punktov Kryma pereshli na podachu vody po grafiku," [29 Settlements of Crimea Switched to Water Supply According to the Schedule], Blackseanews, November 10, 2020, https://www.blackseanews.net/read/170392.

[23] Ignat Bakin, "Problema ne reshayetsya iz-za gluposti, vorovstva I zhazhdy dotatsiy," [The Problem Is Not Being Solved Because of Stupidity, Theft and a Thirst for Subsidies], *Znak*, December 18, 2020, https://www.znak.com/2020-12-18/krym_vysyhaet_lyudi_poluchayut_vodu_4_chasa_v_sutki_poka_vlast_i_strelyayut_po_tucham_i_royut_skvazhi.

[24] "Zasukha prevzoshla ozhydaniya: v vodokhranilishchakh Kryma ostalos 14% vody," [Drought Exceeded Expectations: 14% of Water Remained in Crimean Reservoirs], *Vesti Krym*, November 18, 2020, https://vesti-k.ru/news/2020/11/18/zasuha-prevzoshla-ozhidaniya-v-vodohranilishah-kryma-ostalos-14-vody/.

[25] Yevheniy Leshchenko, "Krym zalyshytsya bez prisnoyi vody i ozer: vcheni sprognozuvaly terminy," [Crimea Will Be Left Without Fresh Water and Lakes: Scientists Have Predicted the Timing], Zn,ua, October 26, 2020, https://zn.ua/ukr/UKRAINE/krim-zalishitsja-bez-prisnoji-vodi-i-ozer-vcheni-sprohnozuvali-termini.html.

146 | BLACK SEA BATTLEGROUND

Typically, Crimean reservoirs fill up with water toward the end of the winter; but 2020 was atypical.[26] The Crimean Ministry of Housing and Communal Services reported that, in February 2021, the reserves of the Simferopol and Zagorsk water reservoirs were completely exhausted and the Balanovskoye reservoir was approaching a so-called "dead volume."[27] The natural rejuvenation of local water reserves—via the melting snow and rainfall—did not occur either. Despite this, the Crimean authorities stated the peninsula was ready to welcome about eight million tourists during the summer of 2021, predicting moreover that, by 2025–2026, this number could swell to ten million.[28]

Frustratingly for locals, the much-needed precipitation that fell on Crimea last summer brought little alleviation. The abnormal rain showers in June 2021 helped mitigate some immediate, localized problems, filling reservoirs along the southern coast enough to last through the end of 2021; while Yalta and Sevastopol received a typical year's worth of water.[29] But the flooding also damaged infrastructure and profoundly aggravated

---

[26] Zarema Seitablayeva, "Problemy s vodoy v Krymu: te samye 'kamni s neba'," [Problems with Water in Crimea: The Very "Stones from the Sky"], *Krym.Realii*, February 15, 2021, https://ru.krymr.com/a/krym-nehvatka-vody-problemy-vodosnabzheniya/31095348.html.

[27] "Zapas vody v vodokhranilishchakh Kryma – vdvoye menshyy, chem byl v 2020-m," [The Water Supply in the Reservoirs of the Crimea Is Half as Much as It Was in 2020], *Khartiya97*, April 2, 2021, https://charter97.org/ru/news/2021/4/2/417113/.

[28] "Sergey Ksyonov: Krym v sostoyanii prinyat bolshe 10 millionov turistov," [Sergey Ksyonov: Crimea Is Able to Receive More Than 10 Million Tourists], *Lenta novostey Kryma*, April 15, 2021, https://crimea-news.com/society/2021/04/15/782261.html.

[29] "Yalta nakopila boleye chem godovoy zapas vody v vodokhranilishchakh," [Yalta Has Accumulated More Than a Year's Supply of Water in Reservoirs], *RIA Novosti*, June 28, 2021, https://ria.ru/20210628/voda-1738964712.html.

the quality of the water reaching consumers (the true extent of which has yet to be identified).[30]

Explaining the Reasons for the Water Crisis Post-2014

Crimea's difficulties with supplying sufficient and clean water stem from a combination of several factors. These can be broken into four main areas.

First, poor infrastructure is a long-term issue that could not have been solved (realistically speaking) in the post-2014 period. While some improvements have been completed, those did not collectively bring any noticeable qualitative change. By and large, the vast bulk of local infrastructure and equipment dates back to the 1970s and needs urgent renovation, which, in turn, would require massive investments.

The second issue is corruption and mismanagement. Following the annexation of Crimea and shutdown of the NCC, the local occupying authorities disregarded the possibility of critical water shortages. Moreover, no strategic reserves were accumulated. Additionally, in some cities, water losses—due to mismanagement and dated transportation networks—exceeded 50 percent.[31] According to the head of the Department of Geoecology at the Crimean Federal University, Tatiana Bobra, even a partial, mid-term solution would require an overhaul of the peninsula's entire water-supply system.[32] On top of that, it

---

[30] "V Krymu posle navodneniya zakryli bolee 80 plyazhey iz-za zagryazneniya morskoy vody," [In Crimea, After the Flood, More Than 80 Beaches Were Closed Due to Sea Water Pollution], *Znak*, June 29, 2021, https://www.znak.com/2021-06-29/v_krymu_posle_navodneniya_zakryli_bolee_80_plyazhey_iz_za_zagr_yazneniya_morskoy_vody.

[31] "Strategiya vodosnabzheniya Kryma i kak ona osushchestvlyayetsya?"

[32] "Ekonomit vodu v Krymu nado bylo uzhe 3 goda nazad – mneniye uchenogo," [It Was Necessary to Save Water in Crimea 3 Years Ago – the Opinion of the Scientist], *RIA Novosti*, September 22, 2020, https://crimea.ria.ru/society/20200922/1118753433/Ekonomit-vodu-v-Krymu-nado-bylo-uzhe-3-goda-nazad--mnenie-uchenogo.html.

appears that practically all funds allocated from the Russian budget to address the issue have been distributed among local influence groups. In 2020, Vladimir Garnachuk, a former advisor to Aksyonov, stated that 87.5 billion rubles (approximately $1.2 billion) were allocated between 2014 and 2020 to solve the water supply problems in Crimea. But due to corrupt practices, only a third of the money was used, and just 2 out of 37 planned projects were fully completed.[33]

Third is the demographic transformation on the peninsula. Since the annexation, Crimea has hosted large numbers of newcomers from Russia, both civilian and military.[34] Russian military service members, law enforcement officers, regulatory agency officials and inspectors, along with their families, make up a large portion of this new migration wave. Incidentally, resettlement practices in Crimea are hardly a novelty: they were used in the 1940s after the mass deportation of the local Crimean Tatars. During Soviet times, this measure was unquestionably coercive; but today, resettlement to the peninsula is seen as more of a privilege. For instance, as a reward, some military retirees are eligible for a special relocation program. Retirees from Moscow, the High North, Siberia and other wealthy Russian regions, who have bought real estate in Crimean recreation zones, are attracted by special mortgage programs.[35] Also, representatives of the Russian bureaucratic apparatus, their family members, as well as migrants from the Russia-backed Luhansk and Donetsk "people's

---

[33] A. Dorogan and A. Rudenko, "Krymu grozit zasoleniye zemel. Yest li u Rossii vodnaya strategiya?," [Salinization of Lands Threatens Crimea. Does Russia Have a Water Strategy?], *Krym.Realii*, July 30, 2020, https://ru.krymr.com/a/krymu-grozit-zasolenie-zemel-yest-li-u-rossii-vodnaya-strategiya/30733323.html.

[34] Alla Hurska, "Demographic Transformation of Crimea: Forced Migration as Part of Russia's 'Hybrid' Strategy," *Eurasia Daily Monitor* 18, no. 50, March 29, 2021, https://jamestown.org/program/demographic-transformation-of-crimea-forced-migration-as-part-of-russias-hybrid-strategy/.

[35] Yevgeniya Horyunova, "'Demohrafichna zbroya' Rossii v Krymu," *Chornomorska bezpeka* 4, no. 36 (2019): 38–43, https://geostrategy.org.ua/chornomorska-bezpeka/chornomorska-bezpeka-no-4-36-2019/844.

republics" (LPR/DPR), have contributed to migration flows into Crimea.[36]

The fourth factor—inseparable from the third issue—is the continued militarization of the peninsula and expansion of Russian military facilities there.[37] Prior to 2014, the approximate number of Russian service members in Crimea (limited to the area surrounding the Black Sea Fleet base in Sevastopol) was between 10,000 and 12,000. Today, the current number, while classified, could be close to 42,000 (excluding family members).[38] Moreover, this quantity increases during various trainings and exercises.[39] Undoubtedly, these transformations have resulted in a massive increase in water consumption, causing the further depletion of local reserves.[40]

While the exact figure of those who moved to Crimea following the annexation is difficult to determine, Russian official statistics say that from January 2020 to January 2021, the peninsula's

---

[36] Hurska, "Demographic Transformation of Crimea."

[37] "MID Ukrainy: v Krymu dostatochnovody dlya naseleniya, vinovata militarizatsiya," [Ukrainian Foreign Ministry: There Is Enough Water in Crimea for the Population, Militarization Is to Blame], *Ukrainskaya Pravda*, May 22, 2021,
https://www.pravda.com.ua/rus/news/2021/05/22/7294467/.

[38] "Rossiya uvelichila kolichestvo voyennykh v Krymu do 42 tysyach – Taran v Evroparlamente," [Russia Has Increased the Number of Military in Crimea to 42,000 – Battering Ram in the European Parliament], *Ukrinform*, April 14, 2021,
https://www.ukrinform.ru/rubric-polytics/3227859-rossia-uvelicila-kolicestvo-voennyh-v-krymu-do-42-tysac-taran-v-evroparlamente.html.

[39] "Shoygu nakazav zbilshyty kilkist viysk v okupovannomu Krymu," [Shoygu Ordered to Increase the Number of Troops in the Occupied Crimea], Espreso.tv, June 21, 2021, https://espreso.tv/shoygu-nakazav-zbilshiti-kilkist-viysk-v-okupovanomu-krimu?preview_token=GXiYHkWQybtp8jYlB5u8pAFrxeDxM1IgNO4iYP YkOgANpmYRijNvHiM2leqX3W1G.

[40] Crimean Tatars, "The Bakhchisaray Reservoir Has Almost Completely Shallowed," Facebook, November 18, 2020,
https://www.facebook.com/CrimeanTatarsEn/videos/2013301522143126.

150 | BLACK SEA BATTLEGROUND

population increased by 498,948. According to the latest Russian population census (2021), in total, at least 568,105 people have moved to Crimea since its forced takeover by Russia.[41] It is worth pointing out that some Russians are settling in Crimea without changing their registration (*propiska*) in Russian passports (because of a fear of being sanctioned or denied a visa to a foreign country), and thus, they are not included in official statistics. Ukrainian experts argue the real number of migrants to Crimea after 2014 could be between 800,000 and 1 million.[42]

Russia's Attempts to Address the Water Issue: Main Approaches

When Ukraine discontinued the flow of water southward from the NCC in early 2014, the Crimean population was confident in Russia's ability to expeditiously find a workable solution. Initially, both the federal center and the pro-Russian Crimean authorities hoped to reach some kind of agreement with the Ukrainian government. But when no deal could be struck, Moscow began—albeit reluctantly—to search for other options (though occasionally still extending overtures to Kyiv).[43]

Broadly speaking, since the annexation, Russia's main strategies and proposed projects have involved the following:

Kuban Viaduct

This project envisages the transportation of water to Crimea directly from Russia by diverting some of the flow of the Kuban River. The proposal calls for either creating a water intake system at the mouth of the Kuban or building a 300-kilometer pipeline

---

[41] "Naceleniye Kryma I Sevastopolya: chislennost, natsionalnyy sostav," [Population of Crimea and Sevastopol: Size, Ethnic Composition], Statdata.ru, March 30, 2021, http://www.statdata.ru/naselenie-krima-i-sevastopolya.

[42] Hurska, "Demographic Transformation of Crimea."

[43] A. Druzhynovich and M. Yevstifeev, "Kak defitsit vody obnazhyl nereshennye problem Kryma," [How Water Scarcity Exposed Crimea's Unresolved Problems], *RIA Novosti*, February 6, 2020, https://crimea.ria.ru/society/20200206/1117927849/Kak-defitsit-vody-obnazhil-nereshennye-problemy-Kryma.html.

Water Crises and Looming Ecological Catastrophe | 151

along the bottom of the Sea of Azov.[44] However, due to the high cost (tentatively, hundreds of millions of dollars), long distance (550 kilometers) and lack of domestic technical capabilities, the project was deemed unrealistic,[45] and the idea was dropped.

Desalination

The first desalination plant was commissioned in Sudak, on the Black Sea coast, in December 2014. Interestingly, despite sanctions, Russia received numerous proposals from foreign companies (Dutch, Swiss and German) to supply the necessary equipment.[46] The Crimean regional head, Sergey Askyonov, also drew up plans for this technology to be used in Yalta, Kerch and Feodosia.[47] The construction of desalination plants was included in the Russian government plan for the water supply of Crimea, with 8 billion rubles ($111 million) allocated for these needs in the 2021–2022 budget. At the end of November 2020, Aksyonov said the companies that would be engaged in construction had been selected, but because of the sanctions, their names could not be announced. Ultimately, the extremely high costs (both for the equipment and the large amounts of energy needed to run these facilities) precluded any of the planned desalination plants from

---

[44] Ye. Ruseykina et al., "Ustye reki Kuban – Severo-Krymskiy kanal," [Mouth of the Kuban River – North Crimean Canal], *COK* no. 11 (2018): 36–39, https://www.c-o-k.ru/articles/uste-reki-kuban-severokrymskiy-kanal-variant-perebroski-presnoy-vody-v-krym.
[45] A. Kondakov et al., "Vodnye problem I effektivnost ispolzovaniya vodnogo potentsiala Rossii s uchetom mezhdunarodnykh aspektov," *Sovremennye proizvoditelnye sily* no. 3 (2014): 134–51.
[46] V. Vasilenko, "Krym: vodnyy krizis I ekologicheskiye problem," [Crimea: Water Crisis and Environmental Problems], *EKO* 507, no. 9 (2016), https://cyberleninka.ru/article/n/krym-vodnyy-krizis-i-ekologicheskie-problemy.
[47] M. Loktionova, "'Opresneniyem zadachu ne reshyt': kak vernut vodu Krymu I Kubani," ["Desalination Cannot Solve the Problem": How to Return Water to Crimea and Kuban], *Gazeta.ru*, December 18, 2020, https://www.gazeta.ru/social/2020/12/18/13405514.shtml.

152 | BLACK SEA BATTLEGROUND

being constructed—something President Vladimir Putin admitted himself.[48]

Use of Military Engineers

This has comprised battalions of a military logistical support brigade, which has been involved in laying temporary aboveground water pipelines in various parts of the peninsula since May 2014.[49] Also, special hydraulic structures were built, making it possible to fill the portion of the NCC on Crimean territory with water from the Belogorsk and Taigan reservoirs, along the bed of the Biyuk-Karasu River. Even though, by the summer of 2014, the drinking water emergency was temporarily resolved, it still proved impossible to ensure the required amount of water for irrigation needs. As a result, Crimea lost almost its entire harvest of rice and soybeans that year.[50]

In 2020, due to an unprecedented drought in Simferopol, the Crimean authorities once again asked for help from the Russian military. In July 2020, over 300 soldiers and 140 units of equipment from the Southern and Western military districts started to lay more than 50 kilometers of temporary pipeline to supply water from the Taihinske Reservoir to the Simferopol Reservoir.[51] But already in December 2020, the connection between those reservoirs was halted because the useful volume of water in the Taihinske Reservoir had become fully depleted; and in June 2021, the Russian Armed Forces started to

---

[48] Aleksina Dorogan, "Bez vody I vodnoy strategii: kak Krym perezhyl samyy zasushlivyy za posledniye poltora stoletiya god," [Without Water and Water Strategy: How Crimea Survived the Driest Year in the Last Century and a Half], *Krym.Realii*, December 30, 2020, https://ru.krymr.com/a/deficit-vody-zasuha-krym-2020-god/31020464.html.

[49] Vasilenko, "Krym."

[50] Petr Bologov, "Zhazhda poluostrova," [Thirst for the Peninsula], *Gazeta.ru*, October 17, 2016, https://www.gazeta.ru/comments/2016/10/14 a 10250747.shtml.

[51] Hurska, "Unprecedented Drought in Crimea."

disassemble this water pipeline.[52] Additionally, specialists of Main Construction Department No. 4 of the Russian Ministry of Defense built a water intake on the Belbek River and an aboveground pipeline from the Kadykovsky quarry to a water intake on the Chorna River.[53] Those quickly and haphazardly laid pipes rupture all the time, however; and useful volumes of pumped water continue to be wasted.[54]

One reason for these failures is that the pipelines used by the Russian Armed Forces are not actually suitable for carrying water. Rather, the pipes implemented are utilized for military purposes such as supplying fuels and lubricants.[55] Also, the quality of the work performed by the military engineers, along with the quality of the water that comes out of the tap, caused many complaints from local residents. And due to the pipe breaks, some nearby settlements began to experience sinkholes; while many local roads were ruined by heavy military equipment.[56] Despite the fact that, in May 2021, Defense Minister Shoigu stated the temporary water pipelines built by the Russian military

---

[52] "U Krymu viyskovi RF rozbyrayut 60 km vodovodu, shcho podavav vodu z Bilogirska do Simferopolya," [In the Crimea, Military of the Russian Federation Dismantle 60 km of the Water Supply System Giving Water from Belogorsk to Simferopol], Blackseanews, June 15, 2021, https://www.blackseanews.net/read/177256.

[53] Yekaterina Shokhina, "Kak Krym obespechat vodoy," [How Crimea Will Be Provided with Water], *Vedomosti*, October 20, 2020, https://www.vedomosti.ru/economics/articles/2020/10/20/843978-krim-obespechat.

[54] David Axelrod, "Rzhavchina iz krana i strelba po oblakam," [Rust from the Crane and Shooting at the Clouds. Where Did the Water in Crimea Go?], BBC, September 22, 2020, https://www.bbc.com/russian/features-54250343.

[55] Dorogan, "Bez vody i vodnoy strategii."

[56] Marina Kozyreva, "'Iz pustogo v porozhnee' – iz krymskikh setey," [From Empty to Empty – From the Crimean Nets], *Krym.Realii*, August 13, 2020, https://ru.krymr.com/a/iz-pustogo-v-porozhneye-iz-krymskih-setey/30778513.html.

154 | BLACK SEA BATTLEGROUND

helped to "lift the water blockade,"[57] this approach actually turned out to be extremely ineffective and resource-consuming.

Drilling for Fresh Water Under the Sea of Azov

This idea goes back to Soviet times, when scientists assumed that reserves beneath the Azov's seabed could hold as much as 100 billion cubic meters of fresh water, which would be enough to satisfy local needs for several hundred years.[58] On May 21, 2021, Russian scientists started geological exploration and drilling of wells under the Sea of Azov. According to the Russian State Geological Holding JSC "Rosgeologia," a huge amount of fresh water is hidden under the sea, and it will be possible to produce 0.5–1.2 billion cubic meters of water annually.[59] But some experts believe the water under the Sea of Azov would require additional purification even for technical consumption.[60] This view is shared by Aksyonov. He stated that the water found under the Sea of Azov turned out to be unsuitable for transporting through Crimea's water supply networks due to its high mineralization. Moreover, Crimean cleaning stations cannot cope with the

---

[57] "Shoygu schitayet, xhto rossiyskiye voyennye spasli Krym ot 'vodnoy blokady,'" [Shoygu Believes that the Russian Military Saved Crimea from a "water blockade"], *Krym.Realii*, May 31, 2021, https://ru.krymr.com/a/news-krym-shoigu-zayavil-o-spasenii-kryma-ot-vodnoy-blokady/31282586.html.

[58] Anatoliy Komrakov, "Sovbez i geologi pytayutsya prorvat vodnuyu blokadu Kryma," [Security Council and Geologists Are Trying to Break the Water Blockade of Crimea], *Nezavisimaya*, April 14, 2021, https://www.ng.ru/economics/2021-04-14/1_8128_water.html.

[59] Pelageya Popova, "Stalo izvestvo, skolko presnoy vody mozhet poluchat Krym iz-pod Azovskogo moray," [It Became Known How Much Fresh Water Crimea Can Receive from Under the Sea of Azov], *ForPost*, May 1, 2021, https://sevastopol.su/news/stalo-izvestno-skolko-presnoy-vody-mozhet-poluchat-krym-iz-pod-azovskogo-morya.

[60] "Voda iz-pod Azovskogo moray trebuyet dopolnitelnogo ochishcheniya dazhe dlya tekhnicheskogo potrebleniya - ekspert," [Water from Under the Sea of Azov Requires Additional Purification Even for Technical Consumption – Expert], *Krym.Realii*, May 31, 2021, https://ru.krymr.com/a/news-krym-voda-skvazhyny-azovskoe-more-ozhishchenie/31282443.html.

capacity required for the peninsula's needs; therefore, this project, in Aksyonov's words, "Will have to be forgotten."[61]

Artificial Rain Production

In the fall of 2020, a Yak-42D aircraft belonging to the Russian Federal Service for Hydrometeorology and Environmental Monitoring (*Roshydromet*) was transferred to Simferopol for the purpose of trying to seed clouds to generate artificial rain. But the test failed due to unfavorable weather conditions. Moreover, according to some experts, this plan cannot be a long-term solution: Sowing the silver iodide used in such operations does not work well in coastal regions such as Crimea, where the agricultural land is separated from the sea by mountains. Environmentalists expressed concerns as well. However, after China's announcement that it would regularly employ this method by 2025—producing artificial rain over 56 percent of China's territory—hopes to use it in Crimea were revitalized.[62]

Water Rationing for the Civilian Population

In 2020, the pro-Russian Crimean authorities decided to resort to an old Soviet practice: reducing water consumption by limiting or restricting the population's access to water. The first stage of water rationing was introduced on August 24, 2020, in many parts of the peninsula, including Simferopol, Alushta, Yevpatoria and Yalta. Moreover, an hourly water supply schedule was posted, and the hot water supply was suspended completely.[63] In some

---

[61] "Aksenov soobshchil, chto voda pod Azovskim morem neprigodna dlya setey Kryma," [Aksenov Said that the Water Under the Sea of Azov Is Unsuitable for the Networks of Crimea], Blackseanews, June 11, 2021, https://www.blackseanews.net/read/177179.

[62] Andrey Samokhin, "Водную проблему Крыма решит спецавиация," *Vzglyad*, January 16, 2021, https://vz.ru/society/2021/1/16/1077433.html.

[63] Vadim Rebrina, "V Krymu vvodyat zhestkiy etap ogranicheniy podachi vody. OON vozlagayet otvetstvennost na RF," [A Tough Stage of Water Supply Restrictions Is Being Introduced in Crimea. UN Puts Responsibility on the Russian Federation], Liga.net, September 7, 2020, https://news.liga.net/society/news/v-krymu-vvodyat-tretiy-samyy-jestkiy-etap-ekonomii-vody-strogo-po-chasam.

settlements in the Bakhchisaray region, water only flowed for 15 minutes at a time, twice a day.[64] For technical reasons associated with the constant turning on and off of water, these measures led to numerous main water pipeline breakdowns, causing additional water leakage and financial costs. The Crimean republican government allocated 27 million rubles (approximately $374,000) to purchase special water containers, which were installed near residential buildings, children's educational institutions and hospitals.[65] In 2021, water rationing for civilians remained unchanged, but military bases are now fully supplied.[66]

Sewage Treatment

Crimea produces almost 150 million cubic meters of wastewater per year; and according to some specialists, improved sewage treatment could help address the water problems in at least certain industries, including agriculture. However, this, again, would require massive investments amidst an unfavorable financial environment caused by international sanctions.[67] Still, the sewer infrastructure in Crimea requires a major overhaul: clogged storm sewers caused massive flooding and an emergency

---

[64] "Ekonomiya vody v Yalte: iz-za zasukhi vodu budut podavat po chasam," [Saving Water in Yalta: Due to Drought, Water Will Be Supplied by the Hour], *Focus*, December 7, 2020, https://focus.ua/ukraine/468849-ekonomiya-vody-v-yalte-iz-za-zasuhi-vodu-budut-podavat-po-chasam.

[65] Nadezhda Datsyuk, "Grafik otklyucheniya vody v Krymu 2020: Kogda I gde vvedut novye ogranicheniya," [Water Cutoff Schedule in Crimea 2020: When and Where New Restrictions Will Be Introduced], *Komsomolskaya Pravda*, August 21, 2020, https://www.crimea.kp.ru/daily/217172.5/4274106/.

[66] Igor Sevryugin, "'Dlya voyennykh baz vody khvatayet': kak Rossiya zanimayetsya vodosnabzheniyem Kryma," ["There's Enough Water for Military Bases": How Russia Deals with Water Supply to Crimea], *Krym.Realii*, December 21, 2020, https://ru.krymr.com/a/voda-krym-zasuha-voyenniye-bazy-rossiya-naseleniye/31011448.html.

[67] "Tri sposoba naydeny: Krym smozhet zabyt o defitsite vody," [Three Ways Have Been Found: Crimea Can Forget About Water Scarcity], *RIA Novosti*, February 14, 2019, https://crimea.ria.ru/society/20190214/1116072815.html.

situation in Yalta, Kerch and other settlements following the particularly heavy rainstorms that occurred in June 2021. The republican statistical agency Krymstat notes that 56.5 percent of water supply networks need to be replaced in Crimea. In 2019, less than 1 percent were refurbished.[68]

The aforementioned list of projects and approaches notwithstanding, it appears that Russia will primarily rely on two strategies to address Crimea's water shortages. The first is drilling new artesian wells (currently, there are 3,200 on the peninsula, including illegal ones[69]). The second is water rationing and reliance on precipitation and rainwater collection. Despite economic sanctions, Western companies have facilitated Russia's policies in this space: For instance, German Siemens and Danish Grundfos have assisted local authorities in pumping water from artesian wells. And in March 2021, the Beshterek-Zuya water supply system—equipped with pumps manufactured by Western companies—was launched. This dramatically improved the water supply in Simferopol, whose residents started to receive running water for 18 hours a day. Since April 2021, Simferopol and its suburbs have been almost fully transferred to water supply from artesian wells, which have even been drilled in city parks.[70]

Assessing Ecological Repercussions

Crimea's ecological situation more generally has also worsened significantly since 2014. Extensive drilling of new wells has led to ground subsidence, affecting not only the quantity but also the quality of the water produced. Moreover, seawater started to seep in and replace the fresh groundwater pumped out via artesian

---

[68] "Minoborony RF provedet perebrosku vody iz Tayganskogo vodokhranilishcha v Simferopol," [The Ministry of Defense of the Russian Federation Will Transfer Water from the Taigan Reservoir to Simferopol], *Flot2017*, July 9, 2020, https://flot2017.com/minoborony-rf-provedet-perebrosku-vody-iz-tajganskogo-vodohranilishha-v-simferopolskoe/.
[69] Dorogan, "Bez vody i vodnoy strategii."
[70] "Okupanty perevodyat Simferopol na vodosnabzheniye tolko iz skvazhyn," [Invaders Transfer Simferopol to Water Supply Only from Wells], ARC, April 21, 2021, https://arc.construction/13497?lang=ru.

wells, resulting in changes to the water's chemical composition. High levels of mineralization of well water have gradually made it undrinkable and unusable even for irrigation,[71] also contributing to soil salinization. Additionally, outdated water purification methods and equipment do not ensure the required quality of drinking water.

Grievances about the poor water quality have gradually increased, reaching unprecedentedly high levels. Residents of Crimea have complained about rusty and salty water coming out of their taps; in some cities, drinking water even contains seaweed. According to a report from the Department of Federal Service for Surveillance on Consumer Rights Protection and Human Wellbeing (Rospotrebnadzor) in Crimea, 19 percent of drinking water on the peninsula does not meet Russian standards. In some regions, the share of good-quality drinking water is only 55 percent. Also, in some districts, the water's salinity exceeds acceptable levels by five to six times.[72]

Apart from this, in 2015–2020, the pollution of coastal seawaters from local sources increased, with the main perpetrators being urban wastewater facilities. The most dangerous situation occurred in Sevastopol. This city, the site of the main—and expanding—Russian military base in the Black Sea region, has received a constant influx of new inhabitants since the annexation. In 2015–2016, the main Sevastopol sewage treatment facility—Yuzhnye—ceased to function, and city waste is now being dumped directly into the Black Sea. The Sevastopol Naval Base and other military facilities associated with the Russian Black Sea Fleet are major sources of pollution in their

---

[71] Maksim Koshelev, "'Obezvozhennyy' Krym: chto delat s deficitom presnoy vody," ["Dehydrated" Crimea: What to Do with the Shortage of Fresh Water], *Krym.Realii*, March 10, 2017, https://ru.krymr.com/a/28361893.html.

[72] Gosudarstvennyy doklad "O sostoyanii sanitarno-epidemiologicheskogo blagopoluchiya naseleniya v respublike Krym I gorode Federalnogo znacheniya Sevastopole v 2018 godu," *Rospotrebnadzor*, 2018, http://82.rospotrebnadzor.ru/s/82/files/documents/Gosdoklad/1477 85.pdf.

own right. Oil dumps along with uncontrolled discharges of rocket fuel components, ballast and bilge water have caused a rapid deterioration in coastal seawater quality. Finally, the offshore platforms of Chernomorneftegaz, which produces natural gas and gas condensate in the northern part of the Black Sea, have become a steady source of water pollution. Currents spread these polluted waters throughout the whole Black Sea basin.[73]

Since large chemical plants (Crimean Titan, Crimean Soda Plant and Brom) need huge amounts of water for their production cycles, the water shortages they contribute to have also created severe environmental problems in the northern areas of the annexed peninsula. For example, in Krasnoperekopsk, the city's chemical plants turned once-living salt lakes into waste storage facilities. As a result, the concentration of harmful chemical substances in the air regularly exceeds the maximum allowable levels. Moreover, chemical plants have started to drill dozens of wells, inadvertently launching the process of soil salinization in the region. Seventy-five percent of the soil in these areas has become unsuitable for agriculture; and drinking water for the population acquired a salty taste.[74] Also, in August and September 2018, in the northern Crimean city of Armyansk, sulfurous anhydride from the Crimean Titanium plant, the largest chemical substances producer in Europe's East, leaked into the atmosphere. The plant's production technology requires that waste containing sulfur compounds be stored in water. But due to a lack of proper waste management, this waste was deposited in a local lake. When water shortages occurred and the lake started to dry up, harmful chemicals began to evaporate into the

---

[73] Boris Babin, "OON issleduyet morskiye ekologicheskiye problemy, svyazannye s Krymom," [UN Explores Maritime Environmental Issues Related to Crimea], ARC, March 31, 2021, https://arc.construction/12981?lang=ru.
[74] "Krasnoperekops: ekologichna katastrofa vzhe zaplanovana," [Krasnoperekopsk: An Ecological Catastrophe Is Already Planned], *Krym.Realii*, May 7, 2021, https://www.radiosvoboda.org/a/krasnoperekopsk-ekolohichna-katastrofa-vzhe-zaplanovana/31243400.html.

atmosphere. As a result, over 5,000 people, half of them children, were evacuated from Armyansk.[75]

War for Water: Will Russia Invade Ukraine to Solve Crimea's Water Problems?

Since the unlawful annexation of Crimea in 2014, many Russian and Ukrainian experts have started to discuss the possibility of a Russian military invasion from the peninsula into continental Ukraine. In recent years, chronic water shortages, the failure of Crimean and Russian authorities to resolve the growing water scarcity, increasing militarization of the peninsula and growing numbers of military exercises there have convinced both Western and Ukrainian experts and military specialists that the threat of war over water in Crimea is real.[76]

On June 5, 2020, Serhiy Nayev, the commander of Operational Command East of the Ukrainian Ground Forces, informed that the Ukrainian military and law enforcement agencies had reinforced the security and defense capabilities of water supply infrastructure objects (such as the NCC, once Crimea's lifeline) and other objects of critical infrastructure in the Kherson and Mykolaiv oblasts.[77] Also, in July 2020, the commander of the Ukrainian Navy, Rear Admiral Oleksiy Neizhpapa, confirmed that the Ukrainian Armed Forces did not exclude that Russian troops

---

[75] Sergey Gromenko, "Kto otvetit za ekologicheskuyu katastrofu v Armyanske?," [Who Will Be Responsible for the Ecological Disaster in Armyansk?], *Krym.Realii*, September 18, 2018, https://ru.krymr.com/a/kompensatsii-za-ekologicheskuyu-katastrofu-v-armianske/29495750.html.

[76] "Rossiya mozhet ppoyti na zakhvat Severo-Krymskogo kanala iz-za zasukhi," [Russia May Go to Seize the North Crimean Canal Due to Drought], *Krym Realii*, June 9, 2020, https://ru.krymr.com/a/news-krym-voina-za-severokrymsky-kanal-umland/30660465.html.

[77] Alla Hurska, "Pro-Russian Disinformation Operations in Kherson: A New-Old Challenge for Ukraine's National Security," *Eurasia Daily Monitor* 17, no. 93, June 29, 2020, https://jamestown.org/program/pro-russian-disinformation-operations-in-kherson-a-new-old-challenge-for-ukraines-national-security/.

Water Crises and Looming Ecological Catastrophe | 161

might try to break through from Crimea to southern Kherson to access the NCC. He also mentioned that when Russia starts to restore the part of the NCC that runs through Crimea, it will be a signal of a possible Russian invasion to seize the rest of the canal.[78]

Russia itself has fueled such assumptions. For example, in September 2020, during the Slavic Brotherhood 2020 military exercises, tactical groups of Russian (Pskov-based) and Belarusian paratroopers with air support carried out a simulated operation that aimed to free hydraulic systems captured by the enemy. This stage of the exercises did not go unnoticed by Ukrainian military experts.[79] Russia also intensified its "hybrid" threats—pro-Russian disinformation and cyber operations as well as the use of Cossacks, other paramilitary formations and the Russian Orthodox Church—in the strategically vital Kherson, Odesa and Zaporizhia oblasts. Agitation and pro-Russian moods would presumably make military intervention there much easier by helping Russia gain total control over these territories, secure access to the NCC and the Kakhovka Reservoir, thus enabling Moscow to redirect those water supplies to annexed Crimea. Moreover, such a military operation would physically connect Crimea (via the M14 highway, which is part of the Black Sea

---

[78] Alena Balaba, "Komanduyushchiy VMSU: amerikanskiye fregaty ne nuzhny, korvet budet dostroyen, a pervyy division 'Neptun' zhdem v 2021 godu," [Commander of the Naval Forces of Ukraine: American Frigates Are Not Needed, the Corvette Will Be Completed, and the First Battalion of "Neptune" Is Expected in 2021], *Dumskaya*, July 5, 2020, https://dumskaya.net/news/komanduyushchiy-aleksey-neizhpapa-o-razvitii-vms-119359/.

[79] "Na Ukraine: Ucheniya VDV RF I RB na gidrotekhnicheskom uzle 'mogut byt napravlenny protiv Severo-Krymskogo kanala,'" [In Ukraine: Exercises of the Airborne Forces of the Russian Federation and the Republic of Belarus at the Hydraulic Unit "Can Be Directed Against the North Crimean Canal"], *Voyennoye obozreniye*, September 22, 2020 https://topwar.ru/175330-na-ukraine-uchenija-vdv-rf-i-rb-na-gidrotehnicheskom-uzle-mogut-byt-napravleny-protiv-severo-krymskogo-kanala.html.

162 | BLACK SEA BATTLEGROUND

Economic Association transportation corridor) with the LPR/DPR, mainland Russia and Transnistria.[80]

In the fall of 2020, both Russian officials and the occupying Crimean authorities belligerently started to accuse Ukraine of creating a humanitarian catastrophe and attempting a "genocide" of the Crimean civilian population. So when Russia deployed tens of thousands of troops and advanced weapons to Crimea and near the border with the separatist (LPR/DPR) regions during the spring of 2021, many experts (including Andriy Taran, who was then the minister of defense of Ukraine) suggested that the Russian Federation was considering an attack on Ukraine to secure water supplies for the occupied peninsula.[81] In addition, news reports claimed that the Russian troops deployed near the Ukrainian borders had all the strategic means that would be required for an invasion: artillery, electronic warfare (EW) equipment, logistical support and field hospitals. Allegedly, Russia also deployed various elements of the air force necessary to create an aerial advantage over the battlefield and to support the ground forces.[82]

Torrential rainfalls in Crimea in late spring–summer refilled some of the dry rivers, lakes and reservoirs on the peninsula, temporarily relieving the drought-related disasters across the territory. The question, however, is whether this has fully

---

[80] Hurska, "Pro-Russian Disinformation Operations in Kherson."; and Alla Hurska, "Zaporizhia Oblast: The Next Flash Point in Russia's 'Hybrid' Aggression Against Southeastern Ukraine?" *Eurasia Daily Monitor* 17, no. 110, July 28, 2020, https://jamestown.org/program/zaporizhia-oblast-the-next-flash-point-in-russias-hybrid-aggression-against-southeastern-ukraine/.
[81] "Rossiya mozhet napast na Ukrainu iz okkupirovannogo Kryma – Minoborony," *Glavcom*, April 14, 2021, https://glavcom.ua/ru/news/rossiya-mozhet-napast-na-ukrainu-iz-okkupirovannogo-kryma-minoborony-749934.html.
[82] Yuriy Sheyko, "Gotovila la li Rossiya nastupleniye na Ukrainu: vyvody zapadnykh analitikov," [Was Russia Preparing an Offensive Against Ukraine: Conclusions of Western Analysts], *DW*, April 22, 2021, https://www.dw.com/ru/gotovit-li-rossija-nastuplenie-na-ukrainu-na-chto-ukazyvajut-novye-dannye/a-57284735.

eliminated the threat of a potential Russian invasion from Crimea to take the NCC and the Kakhovka Reservoir. For now, such an option seems off the table for two reasons: First, the aforementioned precipitation will relieve the situation for at least one year; second, the hypothetical costs of invading Ukraine are likely to exceed the cost of a possible solution to the Crimean water crisis.[83] Moscow has no real intention of fully invading Ukraine—at least not with the purpose of providing water to civilians in Crimea. (The Russian military is first in line when it comes to access to water, so its units are not hampered in this way.) Moreover, Western sanctions have hit the Russian economy quite painfully, and so, the Kremlin is unlikely to willingly provoke the West into imposing even more stringent measures. Finally, with the renewed large project with Western Europe—the Nord Stream Two gas pipeline—Russia will likely try to present itself as a nonaggressive international player to ensure the pipeline is accepted by the German government.

Even though, as of mid-January 2022, Russia continues to concentrate numerous military forces near Ukrainian borders (in Crimea as well), they are there mainly to blackmail North Atlantic Treaty Organization (NATO) countries and Ukraine as well as to mobilize domestic opinion behind the regime. Uncertainty certainly persists. But most likely, if Russia has real intentions to seize southeastern Ukraine, it will try to use a combination of "hybrid" and conventional forces—similar to how it acted in Donbas. Such threats require close monitoring so that the experience of Donbas does not spread to other Ukrainian territories.

Water Issues in Donbas: The War and Its Ecological Impact

Crimea's ecology is not the only victim of Russia's activities. In effect, acute water shortages and a potential ecological catastrophe are also looming in war-torn Donbas and even more

---

[83] Krym Realii, "Mozhet li Rossiya zakhvatit Severo-Krymskiy kanal, otvechaet ekspert," YouTube, April 17, 2021, https://www.youtube.com/watch?v=Xs-kElvl5jk.

164 | BLACK SEA BATTLEGROUND

widely throughout central and eastern Ukraine.[84] Specifically, according to the United Nations Children's Fund (UNICEF), more than 3.6 million people in eastern Ukraine—including 500,000 children—have unstable access to clean water and suffer poor sanitation. In part, this is due to periodic shelling of key infrastructure facilities in the area. For instance, in 2018 alone, 89 attacks on water infrastructure facilities were recorded, which resulted in several million people being left without access to clean water for a protracted period.[85]

During Soviet times, the lack of local water resources in Donbas was solved via a trans-basin diversion of surface waters through the Siverskyi Donets–Donbas Canal (133.4 kilometers in length).[86] The war has profoundly complicated the normal functioning of this canal, however: its related infrastructure—located on both sides of the contact line—has been damaged more than 300 times since 2014.[87] Moreover, continuous fighting limits the possibility for essential repairs. More than 30 workers have been killed or injured on the spot.[88]

Apart from this, the armed conflict has threatened the normal functioning of toxic and radioactive waste storage facilities, causing the ingress of toxic substances into the local

---

[84] Alla Hurska, "Donbas Without Water: The Ecology of the East Ukrainian Frontline," *Eurasia Daily Monitor* 17, no. 149, October 22, 2020, https://jamestown.org/program/donbas-without-water-the-ecology-of-the-east-ukrainian-frontline/.

[85] Anastasiya Magazova, "Dostup k pityevoy vode – odna iz seryezneyshykh problem zhyteley Donbassa," [Access to Drinking Water Is One of the Most Serious Problems of Donbass Residents], *Radio Svoboda*, March 27, 2019, https://www.radiosvoboda.org/a/accesses-to-drinking-water-in-donbass/29839304.html.

[86] Anna Tsvetkova, "Donbass. Voyna. Voda," [Donbass. War. Water], *Ecosoft*, accessed July 1, 2021, https://ecosoft.ua/blog/donbas-viyna-voda/.

[87] Hurska, "Donbas Without Water."

[88] Magazova, "Dostup k pityevoy vode – odna iz seryezneyshykh problem zhyteley Donbassa."

groundwater.[89] Now, environmentalists are warning that the contamination of the 1,000 km Don River—which further flows into the Sea of Azov—is highly hazardous, posing potential serious risks to riparian communities living up and down this major waterway.[90] Also, Donbas and areas located in dangerous proximity to the fighting are home to several environmentally unfriendly plants and industrial facilities (established before 1991), which include coal mines, landfills, chemical and metallurgical facilities, and tailing dumps (designed for the storage and disposal of radioactive and toxic waste).[91] If any of these objects are damaged—even unintentionally—the ecological impact would be catastrophic, and the harmful effects would extend far beyond Ukraine's state borders.

It is worth recalling the case of the Avdiivka Coke and Chemical Plant (Donetsk Oblast). Constant shelling since 2014 eventually led to an incident involving a hazardous ammonia leak and contamination of the surrounding area.[92] In effect, in January 2021, inhabitants of Donetsk, Horlivka and other cities in the DPR shared information (through social networks) about the poor quality of their drinking water since the incident. This was corroborated by the company Water of Donbas, which admitted that the water in the Siverskyi Donets–Donbas Canal had a much higher than normal concentration of ammonium. Regular consumption of water with an excessive concentration of ammonium leads to a number of serious ailments, including

---

[89]Hurska, "Donbas Without Water."

[90] "UNEP: Donbass – na grani ekologicheskoy katastrofy," [UNEP: Donbass – On the Brink of Ecological Disaster], *OON*, July 25, 2018, https://news.un.org/ru/story/2018/07/1334882.

[91] I. Nikolayeva, et al., "Doslidzhennya potochnogo stanu khvostoskhovyshch u Donetskiy ta Luhanskiy oblastyakh," *OBSE*, 2020, https://media.voog.com/0000/0036/1658/files/Summary_OSCE_Don bas%20TSFs%202020_ukr_upd-1.pdf.

[92] Wim Zwijnenburg, "Donbass-khimicheskaya bomba zamedlennogo deystviya," [Donbass – A Chemical Time Bomb], *Bellingcat*, April 16, 2017, https://ru.bellingcat.com/novosti/ukraine/2017/04/16/donbas-timebomb/.

166 | BLACK SEA BATTLEGROUND

disorders of the reproductive and nervous systems and diseases of the liver, kidneys and lungs.[93]

Another point of concern and a grave challenge to the local environment are flooded abandoned coal mines. According to the National Institute for Strategic Research, more than 80 percent of mines in the LPR/DPR have been flooded, presenting a huge ecological challenge to the downstream Sea of Azov.[94] For example, anthropogenic radionuclides from the Yunkom mine—which was used for a nuclear test in 1979—have already begun to penetrate local groundwater. In 2020, water samples collected 5 kilometers from the site demonstrated that radioactive water filled with heavy metals and other toxic substances had reached Debaltseve, Vuhlehirsk, Zhdanovka and Shakhtarsk.[95] Also, the hostilities in the region have significantly worsened the situation in the Pervomaiskugol (Zolote) mines, where groundwater is rapidly accumulating. Normally, this water would have been pumped out, processed and discharged into the river. However, under current circumstances, such operations are not done,

---

[93] "Kompaniya 'Voda Donbassa' poyasnila izmeneniye tsveta I zapakha pityevoy vody v regione," ["The company Water of Donbassa" Explained the Change in the Color and Smell of Drinking Water in the Region], *DAN*, January 12, 2021, https://dan-news.info/obschestvo/kompaniya-voda-donbassa-poyasnila-izmenenie-cveta-i-zapaxa-pitevoj-vody-v-donbasse.html.

[94] Tina Avdeyeva, "Donbass okazalsya nag rani ekologicheskoy katastrofy, pityevaya voda stanovitsya opasnoy: podrobnosti," [Donbass Is on the Brink of Environmental Disaster, Drinking Water Becomes Dangerous: Details], Avdeevka.city, May 25, 2021, http://avdeevka.city/news/view/donbass-okazalsya-na-grani-e-kologicheskoj-katastrofy-pitevaya-voda-stanovitsya-opasnoj-podrobnosti.

[95] Margarita Dneprovskaya, "Pityevaya voda Donbassa pod ugrozoy radioaktivnogo zagryazneniya, mezhdunarodnye nablyudateli," [Drinking Water of Donbass Under the Threat of Radioactive Contamination: International Observers], Vilne Radio, July 10, 2020, https://freeradio.com.ua/ru/pytevaia-voda-donbassa-pod-uhrozoi-radyoaktyvnoho-zahriaznenyia-mezhdunarodnye-nabliudately/.

Water Crises and Looming Ecological Catastrophe | 167

resulting in contaminated water mixing with surface waters to be subsequently carried to Mariupol.[96]

Lastly, the overall low quality of drinking water in Donbas bears mentioning. According to the Ukrainian Ministry for Reintegration of the Temporary Occupied Territories, the LPR/DPR authorities habitually dump untreated mine wastewater into reservoirs, so that "the norms for the maximum permissible concentration of oil products in the water in the Volyntsevsky drinking reservoir [became] exceeded by six times, nitrates by 5.7 times, sulfates 3.5 times, and zinc by almost four times."[97] If these reckless actions and their consequences remain unaddressed, a viable risk looms of a large-scale ecological catastrophe affecting an area extending well beyond Donbas, with the potential of dealing damage to the entire Black–Baltic Sea region (Ponto-Baltic Isthmus).

Conclusion

Russia's direct and unintended actions in southeastern Ukraine—both in Crimea and Donbas—have not only broken key principles of international law but have also had a deeply negative impact on the regional enviromental and water situations. Based on the information coming from open sources (Russian, Ukrainian and local outlets), the current poor state of the environment and

---

[96] Aleksandra Yarlykova, "Shakhtnyye vody, radiatsiya, khimikaty. Chto proiskhodit s ekologiyey na Donbasse," [Mine Water, Radiation, Chemicals. What Is Happening to the Environment in Donbass], *Rubrika*, October 28, 2019, https://rubryka.com/ru/article/donbas-ekologiya/.

[97] "Minintegratsii planuye zaprovaduty mekhanizm monitoringu ekologichnoyi sytuatsii na TOT za dopomogoyu suputnykov," [The Ministry of Reintegration Plans to Introduce a Mechanism for Monitoring the Environmental Situation at TOT with the Help of Satellites], Ministry of Reintegration of the Temporarily Occupied Territories of Ukraine, March 10, 2021, https://minre.gov.ua/news/minreintegraciyi-planuye-zaprovadyty-mehanizm-monitoryngu-ekologichnoyi-sytuaciyi-na-tot-za.

168 | BLACK SEA BATTLEGROUND

water-related problems there are bound to further to worsen due to several interdependent factors.

First, continued mismanagement, endemic corruption and the militarization of Crimea (which has now become Russia's "bastion" and anti-access/area denial bubble on the Black Sea) is likely to result in further problems with water management, which will negatively affect the local populations and agriculture. While Russia will not cut water supplies to locally deployed military formations (and their families), it still has no long-term or economically sustainable solution to local water-related issues. This means that the local (civilian) population will bear the brunt of the difficulties stemming from Russia's reckless behavior. This crisis is, however, (partly) manageable: On average, Crimean households require 200 million–250 million cubic meters of water per year, which the peninsula could generate on its own assuming weather-related drought conditions end; so the needs of the local population can be satisfied.

However, taking into account other needs—the key one being agriculture—the peninsula will require imports of water or else Crimean farming will suffer.[98] Given the most recent forecasts by local climate experts and scientists, including, among others, acting member of the Crimean Academy of Science Aleksander Khloptsev, during 2022, the peninsula is almost certain to start experiencing massive droughts anew, meaning that more water will be required.[99] For now, however, it is unclear how Russia is planning to solve these issues.

Second, Donbas—to be more specific, the part that Moscow had *de facto* transformed into a "grey zone"—is rapidly turning into an ecological time bomb as well, threatening regional areas well beyond Ukraine's borders. And while the local environmental

---

[98] Sevryugin, "'Dlya voyennykh baz vody hvatayet,'
[99] Aleksandr Yankovskiy and Inna Annitova, "Po chetnym – zasukha: zhdat li Krymu dozhdya v 20211 godu," [On Even – Drought: Should Crimea Wait for Rain in 2022], *Krym.Realii*, June 11, 2021, https://ru.krymr.com/a/krym-sezonnye-perepady-opresneniye-vody-eksperty-zasukha/31302961.html.

Water Crises and Looming Ecological Catastrophe | 169

situation is rapidly deteriorating, Russia and its "separatist" proxies are doing almost nothing to mitigate the looming ecological catastrophe. If this trend continues, contamination— including of the local groundwater aquifers—could spread beyond Donbas, affecting the Sea of Azov and ultimately the entire Black Sea basin.

If one day Ukraine manages to take back Crimea and eastern Donbas, solving the water issues and ecological problems in these territories will necessitate diverting massive financial resources. But no definitive estimates of those total costs can be made, in part because neither Ukrainian nor Western specialists can gain full access to these Russian-occupied areas. According to some Ukrainian experts, the restoration of the NCC alone will require at least $1 million.[100] Others posit that if Ukraine manages to retake Crimea, new hydraulic structures will have to be built.[101] The international community will need to address the issue seriously, since the impact will not be confined to these areas nor Ukraine alone.

---

[100] Ihor Tokar, " 'Krymskaya pustynya': reki peresokhli, a kanal rushytsya," ["Crimean Desert": Rivers Dried up, and the Canal Collapsed], *Krym.Realii*, September 11, 2020, https://ru.krymr.com/a/krymskaya-pustynya-obostreniye-problemy-vodosnabzheniya/30821282.html.

[101] "Professor obyasnil, pochemu nelzya vosstanovit rabotu Severo-Krymskogo kanala," *Propozytsiya*, October 9, 2020, https://propozitsiya.com/profesor-poyasniv-chomu-ne-mozhna-vidnoviti-robotu-pivnichno-krimskogo-kanalu.

6.

Vulnerable Arteries: Severe Challenges to the Security of Ukraine's Internal Waterways

Andrii Ryzhenko

March 8, 2022

On December 3, 2020, Ukrainian President Volodymyr Zelenskyy signed the law "On Inland Water Transport." This legislation permits business activities in and access to Ukrainian rivers for foreign vessels (article 27), with the exception of ships and water craft flying the flag of a state aggressor or owned by a person or company from a state aggressor (article 45). Crucially, however, no restrictions exist for crew members who hold citizenship from a state-aggressor country.[1]

The Ukrainian parliament and government hoped that this law would jump-start the reform of river transportation in Ukraine— by some measures, the cheapest and most environmentally friendly method of delivering goods—turning the Dnipro into a major international transport artery. Resuming the use of effective inland waterways was also one of the priority tasks set by the president and is part of Ukraine's commitments in the framework of European integration aimed at eventual accession

---

[1] Ukrainian Rada, "About Inland Water Transport, December 3, 2020, https://zakon.rada.gov.ua/laws/show/1054-20#Tex.

to the European Union.[2] The law includes the implementation of five main European directives and is designed to bring Ukraine in line with European legislation.[3]

The legislative draft underwent much controversy and long-term discussions before being adopted in parliament. Ukrainian private businesses expressed some concerns over unfair conditions, mostly related to the fact that foreign vessels would be excluded from the payment of a value-added tax (VAT) for fuel used within Ukraine's inland waters. In July 2020, the costs for one ton of fuel would have been $720 for Ukrainian vessels and $408 for foreign ships. But from the other side, some Ukrainian and European politicians outlined the importance of this law for Ukraine's European integration process.[4] The pros and cons of the law's economic and political outcomes were actively debated in Ukrainian media.

But it seems that its security consequences were not discussed at all, at least publicly. Thus, access to critical Ukrainian infrastructure by river routes certainly represents a new opportunity for Russia. Sabotage and diversions are well-known techniques for Russian Special Operations Forces (SOF) and private military companies (PMC), as demonstrated in Crimea,

---

[2] On February 28, 2022, in the midst of Russia's large-scale re-invasion of Ukraine, Kyiv formally submitted its request to join the European Union as a full member. The EU is expected to discuss Ukraine's application, in light of the Russian war of aggression, during a summit scheduled for March 10.

[3] Ukrainian Government, "Law 'On Inland Water Transport' Has Been Adopted, Aays Vladyslav Kryklii," December 3, 2020, https://www.kmu.gov.ua/en/news/zakon-pro-vnutrishnij-vodnij-transport-prijnyato-vladislav-kriklij.

[4] AgriPolit.com, "Закон №1054-IX «Про внутрішній водний транспорт»: кінець українського судноплавства чи перехід на міжнародні стандарти?, [Law 541054-IX "On Inland Water Transport": The End of Ukrainian Shipping or the Transition to International Standards?]," December 31, 2020, https://agropolit.com/agrodebaty/4-zakon-11821-d-pro-vnutrishniy-vodniy-transport-kinets-ukrayinskogo-sudnoplavstva-chi-perehid-na-mijnarodni-standarti.

172 | BLACK SEA BATTLEGROUND

Donbas, Syria and Libya. Over the past two decades, Moscow has tailored its SOF, a tool of Russian power politics (subordinated to the General Staff), to be fully commensurate with the realities of nonlinear ("hybrid") warfare. Designed as a force capable of performing "reconnaissance, sabotage, subversion, counter-terrorism, counter-sabotage, counter-intelligence, guerrilla, anti-partisan and other actions," the SOF can collaborate with locals. [5]

Since February 24, 2022, Ukraine has faced an existential war of aggression launched by Russia. Regular battles, heavy shelling, Russia's indiscriminate bombing of population centers, and targeted missile strikes of strategic sites are presently daily challenges for Ukrainian Armed Forces to defend against. But with the Russian war machine seeing its momentum blocked and hostilities dragging on, Moscow is increasingly turning to tactics designed to terrorize the Ukrainian nation into submission. Pitched battles and Russian military maneuvers around sensitive and dangerous sites like the Zaporizhzhia nuclear power plant or in the Chernobyl exclusion zone (both located on the vital Dnipro River or its tributaries)[6], underscore this increasingly desperate strategy by Moscow. And if the advance of Russian combat forces can be entirely bogged down or even reversed, Moscow may choose to more systematically employ sabotage activities up and down Ukraine's internal waterways to bring about maximum civilian deaths and ecological damage.

If the war ends with Russian forces (at least mostly) withdrawing and Ukrainian sovereignty preserved, the pre-war plans to open the country's rivers for foreign vessels may end up being

---

[5] Sergey Sukhankin, "Unleashing the PMCs and Irregulars in Ukraine: Crimea and Donbas," September 3, 2019, https://jamestown.org/program/unleashing-the-pmcs-and-irregulars-in-ukraine-crimea-and-donbas/.

[6] "Russian forces are firing at the Zaporizhzhia Nuclear Power Station in Enerhodar," *Kyiv Independent*, March 4, 2022, https://kyivindependent.com/uncategorized/russian-forces-are-firing-at-the-zaporizhzhia-nuclear-power-station-in-enerhodar/; "Russian military control of Ukraine nuclear plants cause for grave concern, nuclear energy agency warns," *United Nations*, March 6, 2022, https://news.un.org/en/story/2022/03/1113382.

exploited by Russia to deploy and deliver sabotage teams onto government-controlled Ukrainian territory. Russia will be able to employ personnel or passenger vessels as cover. And any such vessels could store and carry substantial quantities of weapons, explosives, or poisonous materials deep into Ukrainian territory. Obviously, in peacetime, the Russians will ensure all necessary inspection documents and legends are in order, and they will be able to "legally" deliver their subversive personnel and cargo to Ukraine's numerous riparian industrial objects, where sabotage operations could result in significant damage to the economy, ecology and populations living nearby or downstream. Such activities could be designed to pressure and destabilize the government in Kyiv as well as intimidate Ukraine's Western partners into further concessions.

Russian Aggression in Ukraine

Since the beginning of the Russian aggression against Donbas in 2014, several sabotage and diversionary activities were recorded in different parts of Ukraine: the explosion of a natural gas pipeline (Poltava region); the destruction of railway bridges (Luhansk region), the disruption of military ammunition warehouses (eastern, northern and central Ukraine); as well as attempted and successful assassinations of Ukrainian military personnel and supporters (Kyiv, Odesa, Kherson, Mykolaiv and Mariupol).[7] The Ukrainian Armed Forces and the Security Service of Ukraine have detained hundreds of persons associated with intelligence or saboteur groups of Russia-backed separatists or the regular Russian military.[8] In some cases, Russian agents

---

[7] ArmyInform, "Російські диверсії та теракти на території України (2014-2018) [Russian Sabotage and Terrorist Attacks on the Territory of Ukraine (2014-2018)]," August 12 , 2019, https://armyinform.com.ua/2019/08/rosijski-dyversiyi-ta-terakty-na-terytoriyi-ukrayiny-2014-2018/.
[8] Roger McDermott, "Russian Spetsnaz Personnel Detained in Ukraine," *Eurasia Daily Monitor* 12, no. 94 (May 2015), https://jamestown.org/program/russian-spetsnaz-personnel-detained-in-ukraine/.

174 | BLACK SEA BATTLEGROUND

infiltrated areas far from the front line to collect information on Ukrainian combat units. On February 16, 2021, the Ukrainian Security Service detained in Odesa a man alleged to be the leader of an intelligence group of Moscow-backed separatists in eastern Ukraine. This man traveled 900 kilometers from Luhansk to the Black Sea to carry out his intelligence mission.[9] So the level of Russia's sabotage, intelligence and diversionary activities in Ukraine remained high all the way up until the massive re-invasion in February 2022. And the opportunity to use free river access may have already been exploited.

Major Man-Made Disasters and Sabotage in Ukraine

The most tragic anthropogenic calamity in Ukraine's recent history happened during World War II. On August 18, 1941, the Dnipro hydroelectric plant (*Dniproges*), located on the Dnipro River in Zaporizhzhia, was destroyed, and its dam blown up. In its retreat from invading Nazi Germany forces, the Soviet military disabled the *Dniproges'* equipment in a simple and remarkable way: by switching off the lubricant distributor while the turbines were operating at full speed. Deprived of lubrication, the turbines heated up and literally devoured themselves, turning into a pile of unusable scrap metal. It was an uncomplicated but effective means of destruction—a turn of the handle by one person.

The operational goal was to flood the German troops who were still on the right bank of the Dnipro. However, no one was warned about the planned explosion on the dam itself, along which Soviet military transports and troops were moving. Also, Soviet military units located down from Zaporizhzhia in the Dnipro floodplains were not told of the plans either, even though the telephone connection on the left bank was functioning normally.[10] As result of the explosion, a 30-meter water wave from the broken dam

---

[9] Radio Free Europe/Radio Liberty, "Ukraine Detains Man Accused Of Leading Sabotage Group For Russia-Backed Separatists," February 16, 2021, https://www.rferl.org/a/ukraine-detains-man-accused-of-leading-sabotage-group-for-russia-backed-separatists/31105833.html.

[10] http://www.cawater-info.net/review/dneproges_accident.htm

washed over many villages around Zaporizhzhia and killed around 120,000 people, civilians and military.[11]

Also worth mentioning is the well-known accident at the fourth power unit of the Chernobyl nuclear power plant on April 26, 1986. This facility is located on the banks of the Pripyat River, a tributary to the Dnipro, the waters of which filled the power plant's large (22 square kilometers) cooling reservoir. The cause of the accident was negligence during routine maintenance—not a deliberate act of sabotage.

It took about 30 years to take control of the accident-damaged nuclear reactor, covering it with a sarcophagus that cost about $2 billion. The 30-kilometer exclusion zone around the nuclear power plant is still closed, and people are not allowed to stay there. But since 2014, various intelligence sources have indicated Russian SOF interest in potentially using riverways to covertly reach the Chernobyl nuclear power plant in order to sabotage it with explosive. In November 2016, the Security Service of Ukraine detained several people who were preparing to sabotage another nuclear facility, in Zaporizhzhia, the most powerful nuclear power plant in Europe.[12] In late February 2022, Russian military forces invading from the north marched through the Chernobyl exclusion zone to reach Kyiv, they shelled the area, and continue to occupy the radioactive site as of March 8, 2022.[13]

---

[11] UA Info, "В 1941 г. убегающая Красная Армия взорвала плотину ДнепроГЭСа, убив 100 000 украинцев [In 1941, the Fleeing Red Army Blew up the Dnieper Hydroelectric Power Station Dam, Killing 100,000 Ukrainians]." https://uainfo.org/blognews/435920-v-1941-g-ubegayuschaya-krasnaya-armiya-vzorvala-plotinu-dneprogesa-ubiv-100-000-ukraincev-video.html.

[12] Depo, "На Запорізькій АЕС викрили держзраду: готували диверсії для зупинки 'атомки' [At the Zaporozhye NPP Exposed Treason: Prepared Diversions for a Stop of 'Atomichttps]," November 23, 2016, zp.depo.ua/ukr/zp/na-zaporizkiy-aes-vikrili-derzhradu-gotuvali-diversiyi-23112016144800.

[13] "Russian forces seize Chernobyl nuclear power plant," *BBC News*, February 25, 2022, https://www.bbc.com/news/world-us-canada-60514228.

176 | BLACK SEA BATTLEGROUND

In the eight years prior to Russia's 2022 re-invasion, there were at least a dozen explosions at Ukrainian arms warehouses and arsenals—mainly in the country's northern and eastern regions. Notably, several of them were near navigable Ukrainian rivers. In every case, the investigation into the incident pointed to deliberate sabotage, although the extent of the damage caused by the explosions made it nearly impossible to prove provenance. Some of these targets were located close to populated areas and industrial sites. Tens of thousands of people were evacuated during rescue operations. And about 210,000 tons of ammunition were destroyed in the explosions and fire. For a sense of scale, during this same time period, the Ukrainian military engaged on the front line used only 70,000 tons of ammunition.[14]

A particularly destructive incident of sabotage happened on October 9, 2018, in which Ukraine lost numerous shells and other artillery ammunitions, including 122-millimeter Grad rockets, due to a fire at an ammunition depot near Ichnya, in Chernihiv region. The ammunition's detonation led to the fire and destruction of buildings and facilities in Ichnya. The electricity and natural gas supply were reportedly cut off in the affected area. The local railway service also was suspended. About 20,000 local residents had to be evacuated.[15]

The cause of the fire, according to the General Staff of the Armed Forces of Ukraine, was four explosions in different parts of the arsenal. "According to the data we have at the moment, there were two explosions at the same time, and then at the other end of the arsenal there were two more explosions. These explosions caused a fire," said the deputy chief of the Ukrainian General Staff.

---

[14] Radio Svoboda, "Explosions at Military Depots: How Are They Being Investigated and What Conclusions Have Been Drawn," May 13, 2019, https://www.radiosvoboda.org/a/donbass-realii/29937425.html.
[15] Unian, "Ukraine Loses Heavy Artillery Ammunition in Recent Ammo Depot Explosion in Chernihiv Region," October 9, 2018, https://www.unian.info/society/10292025-ukraine-loses-heavy-artillery-ammunition-in-recent-ammo-depot-explosion-in-chernihiv-region.html.

He noted that the most likely cause was sabotage.[16] Interestingly, the explosion happened one day before the birthday of the Ukrainian chief of defense, General Viktor Muzhenko. One year earlier, on September 27, 2017, the day after then-president Petro Poroshenko's birthday, a similar explosion badly damaged a military ammunition depot in his native Vinnitsa region. This coincidence in time and place is very much in line with the spirit of Russian special operations to enhance the psychological effect on enemy officials.

All these cases confirm Ukraine's high vulnerability to sabotage and diversionary threats. And the open access to main river arteries can significantly simplify the deployment to such facilities and enable the delivery of special equipment and personnel to a target even during peace time.

Sabotage-Related Industrial Disasters Along International Rivers

Rivers are among the cheapest means of transporting goods and producing electricity. Today about 60,000 fresh-water reservoirs and 45,000 dams of all types exist in the world. But as a rule, the construction of hydraulic structures in densely populated areas has always caused certain challenges, the most important of which being to ensure the reliability of construction and secure the safety of the nearby population. Over the past 80 years, there have been more than a thousand accidents involving large hydraulic structures (dams) globally. Several recent accidents at hydroelectric power plants are worth noting because, although they occurred due to technical problems during operation, similar disastrous effects can be deliberately instigated through military strikes or sabotage.

On August 17, 2009, a turbine of the Sayano-Shushenskaya hydroelectric power station, located near the city of Sayanogorsk, in Russia, failed catastrophically. Breakage of the turbo generator cover bolts flooded the whole operational building, killing 75

---

[16] Tatiana Popova, "Explosions in Ichnia: The First Versions and Possible Consequences," Radio Svoboda, October 9, 2018, https://www.radiosvoboda.org/a/29533936.html.

178 | BLACK SEA BATTLEGROUND

people. Power generation from the station ceased completely following the incident, leaving the nearby area without electricity for two days. Three of the plant's ten turbines were completely destroyed, and five others were seriously damaged. During the accident, water immediately flooded the engine and turbine rooms, causing the transformer to explode. That resulted in an oil spill, releasing at least 40 tons of transformer oil, which spread over 80 kilometer down the Yenisei River.[17] Restoration work to resume full operations at the Sayano-Shushenskaya hydroelectric power station took five years and cost Russia more than a $1.3 billion. The work was finally completed in 2017.[18]

The accident at Sayano-Shushenskaya was repeated less than a year later on July 21, 2010, at the Baksan hydroelectric power station (Kabardino-Balkaria, Russia), when a series of explosions damaged the facility's operating room. But here, the cause was clearly sabotage. Nine unknown persons entered the hydroelectric plant, killing two guards. After setting up explosives, they escaped (though were later detained and jailed). The sappers who arrived at the scene managed to prevent another detonation by clearing one of the planted bombs.[19]

Another interesting case is the international dispute over the construction of Ethiopia's $4.2 billion hydroelectric dam, which would be Africa's largest. The construction of the Grand Ethiopian Renaissance Dam has been going on since 2011 and should be finished sometime in 2022. Egypt, in the past, has threatened to go to war over its "historic rights" to the Nile River. Ethiopia's decision to construct the dam challenged a colonial-era agreement that gave Egypt and Sudan rights to Nile water, with

---

[17] Kommersant, "Три года спустя воду [Three Years Later Water]," August 17, 2021, https://www.kommersant.ru/doc/2003048.

[18] RBC.ru, "RusHydro Fully Restored the Sayano-Shushenskaya HPP After Accident," November 21, 2017, https://www.rbc.ru/rbcfreenews/5a1434329a79474190011cf2

[19] RBC.ru, "Terrorist Attack at the Baksan Hydroelectric Power Station: Four Explosions Thundered," July 21, 2010, https://www.rbc.ru/society/21/07/2010/5703dc319a79470ab5022e e7.

Egypt taking 55.5 billion cubic meters and Sudan 18.5 billion cubic meters of the overall 84 billion cubic meters capacity, with 10 billion being lost to evaporation. Ethiopia's intention to block the Nile and much of its waters provoked strong reactions in Egypt, especially from Islamist party leaders, who publicly supported Ethiopian insurgents in sabotaging the dam. They said that Cairo made a "strategic mistake" when it did not derail the dam's construction.[20] Tensions among Egypt, Sudan and Ethiopia over the Grand Ethiopian Renaissance Dam escalated in August 2020, after Ethiopia announced that it started filling the dam reservoir, contrary to Egypt's mandate.[21] And amidst Russia's sharp military escalation on Ukraine's border, in February 2022, just days before Russian forces began their wide-scale attack on the country, the conflict over the Ethiopian dam heated up as well. Ethiopia announced, on February 20, that it would begin partial power generation for the first time, a move harshly condemned by both Egypt and Sudan.[22]

A different accident took place on February 7, 2021, in northern India, after a Himalayan glacier broke and swept away a small hydroelectric dam. Around 125 people were reported missing, with 32 confirmed dead. India suspected China may have remotely set off explosives in a glacial lake. But a Chinese expert refuted these suspicions, arguing that the main reason for the glacier's break was Indian military construction. The dispute is

---

[20] Hamza Hendawi, "Egyptian Politicians: Sabotage Ethiopia's New Dam," June 3, 2013,
https://apnews.com/article/72049ba7e3164ee6a24ef157f71215e5.
[21] John Mukum Mbaku, "The Controversy of the Grand Ethiopian Renaissance Dam," August 5, 2020,
https://www.brookings.edu/blog/africa-in-focus/2020/08/05/the-controversy-over-the-grand-ethiopian-renaissance-dam/.
[22] Mohamed Saied, "With world attention on Ukraine, Nile dam conflict escalates," *Al-Monitor*, March 2, 2022, https://www.al-monitor.com/originals/2022/03/world-attention-ukraine-nile-dam-conflict-escalates.

180 | BLACK SEA BATTLEGROUND

still ongoing, with extensive discussions beyond these two countries.[23]

Generally, when an average-sized dam breaks, significant areas downstream become flooded within 15–30 minutes under a layer of water 0.5–10 meters deep. The affected territory can remain under water from several hours to several days. A breakthrough wave moving along the riverbed causes colossal damage to inhabited areas and the local economy.[24]

Thus, the most likely course of sabotage against objects located on or close to riverways include:

- Destroying dams for the purpose of flooding and damaging large areas with significant casualties, destroying economic sites, agriculture and infrastructure facilities;
- Deliberately damaging the turbine mechanism of generator and electrical equipment of a hydroelectric power plant to block energy supplies and bring significant economic and ecological damage;
- Blowing up any strategically important riparian object resulting in significant political, military, economic or psychological injury; and
- Harming the ecology or environment, particularly fresh-water resources and river ecosystems through, in the worst-case scenario, the release of chemical, radiological or nuclear materials into the atmosphere or water.

In all cases, the delivery of a group of saboteurs with equipment and explosives is possible on board a merchant vessel. It might assist potential sabotage activities against a significant number of economic objects located on the banks of Ukraine's main waterways: the Dnipro and Bug rivers.

---

[23] Xu Yelu, "Chinese Expert Refutes China Suspicions in India Glacier Break," February 13, 2021, https://www.globaltimes.cn/page/202102/1215587.shtml.
[24] Lyapichev, Gidrologicheskaya i tekhnicheskay bezopasnost gidrosooruzheniy: Uchebnoe posobie. – M.:*RUDN*, 2008. P.37.

Possible Consequences of Sabotage on Power Plants and Dams

In total, about 32,000 rivers or streams flow into the Dnipro basin, including 89 rivers with a length of more than 100 kilometers. All major cities situated on Ukrainian rivers—Dnipro, Zaporizhzhia, Kremenchug, Kherson, Mykolaiv, Cherkasy and Kyiv—have significant amounts of strategically vital industrial and infrastructure objects.

The largest river in Ukraine with the status of inland waters is the Dnipro. It provides fresh water not only to consumers within its basin but also to large industrial centers in Ukraine's south and southeast. More than 30 million people use the Dnipro's waters. In Ukraine alone, the river supplies 50 large cities, about 10,000 industrial enterprises, 2,200 rural communities and 50 large irrigation systems.[25] Six big reservoirs (from 410 to 2,250 square kilometers in size) were built on the Dnipro to support the functioning of hydroelectric plants up and down the river: Kyiv, Kaniv, Kremenchug, Middle Dnipro, Dnipro and Kakhovka.

The most powerful and oldest hydroelectric power plant on the Dnipro River is *Dniproges*, built in 1932, and producing 1,569 megawatts of electricity yearly. Kyiv's hydroelectric power plant is the first in the Dnipro's cascade. Whereas the Kremenchug and Kakhovka hydroelectric plants have the biggest water reservoirs.[26] Besides that, both the Zaporizhzhia nuclear power plant and the deactivated Chernobyl nuclear power plant are located near the Dnipro's banks.[27] As a rule, all power plants and industrial sites located on navigable rivers are vulnerable to sabotage.

---

[25] Suchasnyy stan , problemy ta perspektivy rozvitku gidroenergetiki Ukrainy. Analitychna dopovid. *NISD,* 2014.

[26] Ira Samosvat, "Six of the Most Powerful Hydroelectric Power Plants in Ukraine," Shotam.info, April 12, 2020, https://shotam.info/shist-naypotuzhnishykh-hidroelektrostantsiy-ukrainy/.

[27] The decommissioned Chernobyl nuclear power plant is located on the Pripyat River, near where the Pripyat flows into the Dnieper.

182 | BLACK SEA BATTLEGROUND

The protection of the hydroelectric and nuclear power plants on the Dnipro, thus, creates a serious challenge for Ukraine's security. The first difficulty arises from the age and deficient condition of the equipment. The protective hydraulic structures, pumps and compressor stations on the Dnipro's reservoirs, on average, have operated for more than 50 years, under heavy loads. Significant effort and funds are required to maintain this machinery in operable technical condition.

The second problem pertains to this network's inherent susceptibility to sabotage. The physical protection of riverine energy infrastructure is regulated at the departmental levels of the state enterprise Ukrainian Hydraulic Energy (*Ukrgidroenergo*), with minimum coordination with other national security and defense structures. Moreover, the protection of particularly important facilities is primarily carried out by separate paramilitary guards in a reactive manner and in accordance with agreements concluded with the respective enterprises. The protection of nuclear power plants was ensured by the Ukrainian National Guard only prior to the outbreak of the 2022 war.[28]

Since 2014, the Ukrainian authorities have identified a number of vulnerabilities in the system to protect Ukraine's hydroelectric plants. Real or simulated setting up of explosive charges, aerial reconnaissance, penetration of divers and vessels within the restricted area, unauthorized stops and vehicles left in restricted areas, as well as other provocative acts to test the vulnerabilities in the security system were all recorded by *Ukrgidroenergo* guards over the years. Additional security measures were initiated and carried out at the Dniester cascade in Chernivtsi region and at the *Dniproges*, which is located close to the (pre-February 24, 2022) Donbas front line. Between 2016 and 2017, the paramilitary guards of *Ukrgidroenergo* detained and handed

---

[28] Ukrainian Rada, "About the National Guard of Ukraine," https://zakon.rada.gov.ua/laws/show/876-18#Text.

over to the police 132 trespassers of hydroelectric power plant exclusion zones.[29]

The State Emergency Service of Ukraine has conducted calculations and wargaming of possible consequences caused by natural or man-made disasters on rivers. A few possible scenarios of catastrophic flooding caused by damage to Ukrainian dams is worth considering, particularly in light of the Russian military's assaults on and occupation of key Ukrainian hydroelectric sites since February 24.

In the case of a breakthrough at the Kyiv hydroelectric power plant, the Ukrainian government estimated that the falling water would next overwhelm and destroy the Kaniy hydroelectric power plant, located 43 kilometers (26.7 miles) downstream on the Dnipro. The breakthrough flood would then enter the Kremenchug reservoir, raising the water level by 2.1 meters and possibly cause flooding in the areas of Chernihiv, Kyiv, Cherkasy and Kirovohrad. An entire, or even partial, destruction of the Kyiv dam would produce a wave with an initial speed of 50–70 kilometers per hour and height of around 10–12 meters. This wave would reach the Kaniv hydroelectric power plant in four hours and the Kremenchug hydroelectric power plant in 31.

The destruction of the Kremenchug hydroelectric power station could have the most serious consequences. Overflow of this dam's reservoir would destroy the Middle Dnipro, including the *Dniproges*. Parts of the territory of Kirovohrad, Poltava and Dnipropetrovsk could be flooded. The breakthrough flood would be delayed in the Kakhovka reservoir, but would cause flooding of part of the Dnipropetrovsk region and a number of other regions in southern Ukraine. In total, an area of 7,000 square kilometers (2,700 square miles), covering eight Ukrainian regions, would be under threat of potential catastrophic flooding. The flood zone could include up to 495 settlements; 19 cities, including Kyiv, Kremenchug, Dnipro, Zaporizhzhia, Nikopol and

---

[29] Liga 360, "ПОЯСНЮВАЛЬНА ЗАПИСКА," July 10, 2017, https://ips.ligazakon.net/document/view/gh55i00a?an=9&ed=2017 0 7 10.

184 | BLACK SEA BATTLEGROUND

Kherson; and 353 Ukrainian industrial sites. As many as around 11.5 million people might need to be evacuated from flooded areas. Navigation on the Dnipro would likely be disrupted as the breakthrough wave would probably destroy all bridges and a large number of water transport facilities along the river.[30]

Acts of sabotage or artillery and aerial strikes could well have the consequences described here. To create a gigantic wave or severely damage dam structures, a significant amount of explosives is required. For example, 20 tons of explosives were used to breach *Dniproges* in August 1941.

In this regard, the role of Ukraine's special services in conducting proactive control over such sites, including in cooperation with local civilian partners, is crucial. The practical interaction of all components of the Ukrainian security and defense sector was never wholly worked out to deal with full-scale disasters such as this.

Danger of Ecological and Chemical Sabotage

Another vulnerability of Ukraine's internal waterways is the possibility of ecological and chemical sabotage. Riverine cargo vessels are capable of carrying hundreds or thousands of tons of liquid and bulk supplies in their holds. The intentional unloading of harmful chemicals into a river would cause extensive toxic effects on the regional ecology and wildlife. Given the fact that rivers are the main source of drinking water for most of the Ukrainian population, this challenge is dangerous and could cause significant harm to both the Ukrainians themselves and the ecosystem.

Small-size ecological accidents happened now and again in Ukraine prior to the total war Russia launched in late February 2022, and they required considerable management efforts. In June 2019, a truck carrying one ton of chemical insecticides

---

[30] State Emergency Service of Ukraine, https://www.dsns.gov.ua/files/prognoz/weekly/DirectivaZatoplenya/Басейни/Дніпро1.pdf

overturned into the small Ros River (Vinnitsa region). The accident was reported to the Bila Tserkva district state administration and police. During three days of rescue operations, the water supply to nearby cities and villages with a combined population of about 150,000 stopped.[31] This relatively small accident was fortunately quickly localized.

The chemical industry is one of the principal sectors of the Ukrainian economy and includes over 1,600 enterprises. In 2019, Ukraine's chemical industry output reached $2.8 billion.[32] Many of these enterprises are located in cities on or close to the Dnipro and other Ukrainian rivers, such as Rivno, Cherkasy, Zaporizhzhia, Dnipro, Kyiv, Kherson, Mykolaiv and Odesa. Many of the products or chemical additives they manufacture are highly flammable and explosive. Of particular note are fertilizers such as ammonium nitrate, the accidental detonation of which has repeatedly led to tragedies. In Ukraine, 1.8 million tons of ammonium nitrate are produced annually, most of which is used by the domestic agricultural sector.

An illustrative example is the disaster that occurred at the Port of Beirut in Lebanon. On August 4, 2020, a huge explosion rocked the Lebanese capital, shattering glass and causing extensive damage to buildings and infrastructure within a 3-kilometer radius. The blast occurred because of the accidental ignition of 2,750 tons of ammonium nitrate, which had been stored in the Beirut Port area for years under wholly inadequate conditions. Two hundred people were killed, and 6,000 suffered injuries. Three hundred thousand people were displaced due to damaged and destroyed homes across the metropolitan area. The impact of this unprecedented explosion, which registered as a 3.3 magnitude earthquake, was felt as far away as Cyprus. One primary concern immediately following the disaster was the potentially toxic plume released by the explosion and subsequent fires. Chemical protection teams and environmental experts were

---

[31] "Chemicals," *Ukraine Invest*, accessed April 6, 2021, https://ukraineinvest.gov.ua/industries/chemicals/.
[32] "Environmental Accident: A Ton of Chemicals Hit Russia," *BBC News*, June 9, 2019, https://www.bbc.com/ukrainian/news-48573546.

immediately deployed to assess the situation.[33] This tragedy had large international resonance and became a lesson for many countries, including Ukraine.

In addition to its own production facilities, Ukraine imports ammonium nitrate from abroad. The statistics of storage and transshipment of imported ammonium nitrate in Ukraine is striking: 100,000–150,000 tons imported from Georgia, Bulgaria, Turkey and Romania is stored and transshipped monthly via Ukrainian maritime and river ports in the Mykolaiv, Kherson and Odesa regions. Since this fertilizer is actively used on Ukrainian farms, supply volumes traditionally increase on the eve of and during sowing campaigns. According to various estimates, there are more than 600 such warehouses with ammonium nitrate in the country.

Immediately after the tragedy in Beirut, President Zelenskyy tasked the Cabinet of Ministers with figuring out whether such a situation could repeat itself in Kherson or Mykolaiv, where tens of thousands of tons of explosive substances flow through sea and river routes every month. He called on the government to study how these products are transported across Ukraine, who controls the respective manufacturers and traders; how transshipment and transportation are carried out, and what is the level of risk of explosions or sabotage at Ukrainian warehouses that store such volatile substances.

However, the quantity of ammonium nitrate warehoused inside Ukraine may never have been accurately calculated. Just days after the tragic explosion in Bierut, in the largest port of Ukraine, Pivdenny (Odesa region),[34] local residents discovered more than 10,000 tons of ammonium nitrate that was stored in the open air

---

[33] IFRC Technological & Biological Hazard Preparedness, *Case Study: Chemical Explosion Beirut Port: Technological and Biological (CBRN) Hazards*, 2020, https://media.ifrc.org/ifrc/wp-content/uploads/2020/12/CaseStudy_BeirutExplosion_TechBioHazardsweb.pdf.

[34] Pivdenny Port, located in the city of Yuzhny, 33 kilometers northeast of Odesa, handled 62 million tons of cargo in 2020.

without any observance of safety or security rules. This triggered protests by the area population.[35] Also in August 2020, the media reported that local residents identified 3,200 tons of ammonium nitrate in the Port of Mykolaiv. Apparently, it was unloaded from an arrested ship in 2018; but the port's authorities falsely claimed that all ammonium nitrate had been shipped out of Mykolaiv in 2019.[36]

These facts illustrate the vulnerability and high level of potential danger for inhabitants living near or downstream from critical chemical-sector infrastructure in the riparian areas of Ukraine. The Russian war of aggression naturally places these objects under threat from shelling, bombings and air strikes; but if the Russian invasion can be reversed or if the Russian military believes it cannot win the conflict on the battlefield, then such a situation may sharply raise the risk of sabotage directed against Ukraine's chemical industry. Large loads of fertilizer loaded onto riverine merchant vessels or stored in port areas can easily be turned into a tool of widescale destruction. Explosions may be set up ashore or on the water, during a vessel's voyage. The initial detonation does not require a particularly significant amount of explosives to, for example, blow up a dam. Committing such an act of sabotage may not even necessitate special military training and could be carried out by a single person who works in a port or an industrial facility or is a riverboat crew member. In short, the challenge of preventing such diversionary activities on Ukrainian rivers will call for a well-resourced and coordinated response by multiple elements of the country's military, security and civil defense services.

---

[35] Andrey Miselyuk, "Why Ammonium Nitrate in the Port Yuzhny Is the Tip of the Iceberg," RBC.ua, August 12, 2020, https://daily.rbc.ua/rus/show/pochemu-ammiachnaya-selitra-portu-yuzhnyy-1597209199.html.
[36] https://hromadske.ua/ru/posts/v-nikolaevskom-portu-dva-goda-nazad-hranili-ammiachnuyu-selitru-govoryat-chto-ee-uzhe-ubral

Conclusion

The possibility of military strikes on or acts of sabotage against critical economic infrastructure along Ukraine's internal waterways is severe. Particularly if the Kremlin's war of aggression, launched on February 24, 2022, continues to drag on or fails to go Moscow's way, Russia may turn back to sabotage as an asymmetric and cost-effective tactical tool with strategic impact to undermine Ukraine in its political, military, economic and social spheres. The aforementioned series of tragic accidents in Ukraine and around the world over the past eight years confirm how destructive such acts of sabotage could be.

The law "On Inland Water Transport," when it was passed in December 2020, did not provide for any systematic security measures to prevent and respond to possible acts of sabotage along Ukrainian riverways, making riparian industrial and critical infrastructure sites—as well as nearby or downstream populations—potentially even more vulnerable. Although the legislation only opens up navigable Ukrainian rivers to foreign vessels not registered to foreign aggressor states (first and foremost, Russia), it leaves a loophole that permits vessels crewed by individuals holding Russian citizenship. Once the active war situation dies down enough to allow for it, Ukraine should immediately conduct a comprehensive review of internal security systems for their ability to prevent, monitor, identify and respond to acts of sabotage and manmade and natural disasters on Ukrainian rivers. The National Security and Defense Council of Ukraine will need to lead this process and prepare relevant and clear recommendations to be approved and immediately released by the head of state.

Based on this assessment, Ukraine should implement regulatory means and work out the practical cooperation among all structures of its security and defense sector to minimize the risks and respond rapidly to acts of sabotage on riverways. Importantly, the Ukrainian state should generate additional military and law enforcement capabilities to secure major navigable rivers as well as improve collected intelligence to prevent such acts of sabotage, which may again become more appealing to Russia should its mass invasion falter or be reversed. It is expedient to develop and widened contacts with Ukraine's main strategic partners in order to exchange relevant intelligence as well as coordinate combined measures to combat this potential state-sponsored sabotage against Ukrainian internal waterways.

The Ukranian Cabinet of Ministers has to plan and allocate funds in the short term for the renovation and repair of hydraulic river structures that were damaged in the war or that were already in worn-out conditions. The poor shape of Ukraine's network of hydraulic structures invites acts of sabotage and can seriously worsen the consequences of such irregular warfare attacks. Following the war, Ukraine should actively consider applying for foreign loans and EU grants to modernize its riverine infrastructure. Finally, it will be critical to inspect all Ukrainian industrial and agricultural storage sites for their safety conditions and to accurately catalog where (and whether properly) large amounts of explosive and combustible cargo is stored along rivers, in sea ports, and in watershed areas. Post-war remedial actions will likely be immediately necessary to minimize risks of further loss of life or ecological disasters.

7.

Neutrality With No Guarantees: The Evolution of Moldova's Defense and Security

Dumitru Minzarari

April 1, 2022

Defense and security policies have always been an elite endeavor in the Republic of Moldova. The general population does not consider these issues salient enough to confront the authorities over them in case of disagreement. Partially, this is due to a widespread belief, shared by both the majority of voters and mainstream politicians, that defense and security issues, in their current state, have little impact on the country's economic outcomes and welfare. And it is the economy that is of most concern to Moldova's ruling elites—for kleptocrats, in order to maximize the base for their rent-seeking; for liberal politicians, to improve the economic prosperity of citizens in order to be reelected. In fact, historically, defense and security matters have been vastly ignored by all of Moldova's ruling elites since the country received its independence in 1992. If this is to change, it will only be due to a significant national security crisis, or if the thinking of the Moldovan ruling elites evolve toward a more accurate understanding of the impact of defense and security on the economic welfare of the country.

The July 11, 2021, parliamentary elections that brought to power the Party of Action and Solidarity (PAS) can, therefore, be expected to have important bearing on determining the role of defense and security issues in wider governmental policy over the next four years. Following the election results, which gave PAS a comfortable majority in the legislature, with 63 out of 101 seats, the ruling party took control of not only the parliament but also the government and the presidency. The latter is due to the fact that the former leader of PAS, Maia Sandu, won the nationwide presidential elections in November 2020. Even though she is not formally a member of PAS anymore—due to legal provisions demanding that the head of state not have any formal political affiliation—she retains significant influence over the party. The success of PAS in the last parliamentary elections was largely possible thanks to Sandu's political authority among the population, which served as a driving force for PAS in the 2021 campaign. Moreover, even though Moldova is a parliamentary republic, in which the president holds mostly symbolic functions, the position is important in the context of the country's defense and security policies, as the commander-in-chief of the Armed Forces. Finally, because the president is elected by popular vote, instead of being nominated by the parliament, this office can wield significant political influence if the incumbent is willing to exercise it.

Given this significant governing power and political influence, PAS can effectively reshape and remodel many dimensions of Moldova's domestic and foreign policies. Besides the new administration's rhetoric and initial policy steps, the ruling party's cabinet nominations can serve as a useful indicator of how defense and security issues rank in the list of its governance preferences and priorities. And as of February 2022, those above-mentioned signs suggest that, so far, PAS may be no different from previous administrations in terms of how it views the role of defense and security issues in overall governance. In fact, these two issues seem to be at the bottom of the PAS administration's priorities. One notable data point has been the nomination of a minister of defense with no political clout and, therefore, no ability to push for or make substantial changes in the areas under his management. Another bit of evidence has been the decision to

192 | BLACK SEA BATTLEGROUND

keep the head of the Intelligence and Security Service, who was appointed before PAS had full control of the parliament. If the PAS administration had the ambition and knowledge to use the national intelligence service effectively, it would likely not have opted to preserve the leadership nominated by a previous government that PAS has staunchly fought to oust. These, in addition to a number of other factors touched upon later in the text, indicate that the new government does not understand the role and importance of defense and security for the Republic of Moldova.

However, this challenge has not haunted solely this government. It is an issue related to Moldova's wider strategic culture— specifically, the way political elites understand the role of the armed forces in national policies.[1] Arguably, three factors have most strongly influenced and led to the emergence of a disdainful view of national defense and security matters among Moldova's political class. These are 1) the perceived failure of the military approach to effectively address Russia's proxy war against the Republic of Moldova in Transnistria in 1992; 2) the 1996 governance crisis involving a conflict between the civilian authorities, in which the military leadership took sides; and finally, 3) the salience of the economics domain and, respectively, the complete demotion of the defense and security sectors to consumers rather than suppliers of resources. Altogether, these factors have impelled and accustomed Moldova's political elites to pay only superficial attention to defense and security areas. The respective state agencies in this space have, for decades, been mostly symbolic elements of governance.

The following chapter provides further details on the three aforementioned factors that have distorted the strategic culture of Moldova's political elites. This is followed by an effort to produce an accurate threat assessment for the country, shedding light on the security threats that Moldova has confronted and how they have evolved. Accordingly, it will examine the ways that

---

[1] For a detailed explanation of this analytic concept, see Alastair Iain Johnston, "Thinking about Strategic Culture." *International Security* 19 (4), 1995: pp. 32–64.

different Moldovan governments attempted to deal with these threats, including the policies that were adopted and the funding that authorities provided in support of these policies. Finally, the analysis will build upon the presented material to offer scenarios along which Moldova's defense and security policies are most likely to develop as well as their consequences.

A Historical Roadmap

When the Soviet Union collapsed, the effective leadership of the newly independent Republic of Moldova was taken over by the national members of the Soviet Communist *nomenklatura*. However, unlike their peers in Moscow, who were involved in managing strategic issues—including by interacting with the state's defense and security agencies—the local elites in Moldova had never before faced issues demanding the use of armed force in either overt or covert ways.

Thus, it is little wonder that Moldova's political leadership was caught by surprise by a wave of incidents during 1990–1992, in which armed individuals, by threat or force, took over local governmental buildings, police stations and intelligence agency offices in the administrative districts on the left bank of the Nistru River (Camenca, Ribnita, Dubasari, Grigoriopol and Slobozia—the area today referred to as the Transnistrian region of the Republic of Moldova).

In many respects, the sequence of events leading up to and during the Transnistrian conflict mechanics closely mirror the process that prepared and triggered the Russian proxy war in Ukraine's Donbas more than 20 years later.[2] Most references about the process of "squeezing out" the Moldovan authorities from the region point to a series of incidents between November and December 1990, including one in which the Dubasari district administration was surrounded by armed individuals and its staff

[2] For these similarities, see: "Kak Rossija otkryvala Donbas: Top-5 priznanii," *Radio Svoboda*, January 26, 2021, https://www.radiosvoboda.org/a/31069837.html.

194 | BLACK SEA BATTLEGROUND

forced to leave the building.[3] However, there is an important gap in the understanding of the micro-dynamics of this historical process, given most publicly available sources are of Russian origin and deliberately aim to create a picture favorable to the official Russian version of the conflict. Nevertheless, even the Russian sources recognize the creation of paramilitary structures by the "leadership of the Transnistrian Moldovan Republic"—a Russian government proxy—starting as early as 1990.[4] And Russian sources also note these units were supplied with weapons and personnel by the 14th (Soviet) Army, which operated under Moscow's command during this entire time.[5]

The Moldovan authorities treated the situation as a criminal issue and used police units to deal with a militarily equipped and trained opponent. To their credit, the authorities subsequently came to understand the importance of the military dimension. In September 1990, they created the State Department for Military Issues, and—after declaring independence on August 27, 1991— started to build the Moldovan National Army in September 1991.

---

[3] Elena Zamura, "Adevaruri despre razboiul din Transnistria (1990– 1992,." Interview with Ion Costas, former Minister of Interior and Minister of Defense of the Republic of Moldova. *Curentul International*, March 5, 2010, http://curentul.net/2010/03/05/adevaruri-despre-razboiul-din-transnistria-1990-1992. See also: Marius Vahl and Michael Emerson, "Moldova and the Transnistrian Conflict," *Journal of Ethnopolitics and Minority Issues in Europe*, vol. 1, p. 6, 2004, https://d-nb.info/1190973456/34.

[4] See: "Vozniknovenije I razvitije vooruzhennogo konflikta v Pridenstrovskom regione Respubliki Moldova," Ministry of Defense of the Russian Federation, https://structure.mil.ru/mission/peacekeeping_operations/more.htm?id=10336232@cmsArticle, accessed on September 10, 2021.

[5] See Mihail Bergman, "Vozhd' v chuzhoj stae," *Lenin.ru*, 2004, http://web.archive.org/web/20110727001814/http://www.lindex.le nin.ru/Lindex4/Text/9220.htm. The source needs to be read with caution as it represents the memoirs of the former military commandant of Tiraspol, the administrative center of the Transnistrian region. Nonetheless, it does contain several important confirmations of the Russian military's role in the conflict.

Neutrality With No Guarantees | 195

However, the personal accounts of combat participants reveal that the operation on the Moldovan side was chaotic, poorly organized and equipped, often without central operational guidance, leaving various units to fight based on their own initiative. An incident near the Tighina (Bender) fortress, for example, characterized such poor planning, resulting in multiple casualties on the Moldovan side. As Moldova's combatants were transported to the line of contact in buses, without weapons, which were moved separately, they were ambushed by pro-Russian paramilitaries and were unable to fight back.[6] In another instance, the Moldovan leadership authorized a clandestine operation to capture Igor Smirnov—the leader of the self-proclaimed regime in Tiraspol—in Ukraine, following Kyiv's refusal to cooperate and extradite him. The operation was conducted successfully: Smirnov was taken to Chisinau and a criminal investigation was launched against him. And yet the Moldovan leadership released him shortly thereafter, allegedly under pressure from Moscow.[7]

Following the war in Transnistria, the Moldovan authorities have generally been timid when it came to defending national security interests against the Russian Federation. The first three administrations in Chisinau were run by former senior functionaries of Soviet Moldova's Communist *nomenklatura*.[8] Either due to an inferiority complex toward Moscow, or for other reasons—including a lack of qualified advisors—Moldovan defense and security policies during that time were marked by

---

[6] Ziarul de Garda, "Ion Costas: 'Zile de eclipsa. Cronica unui razboi nedeclarat,' " *ZDG*, April 21, 2011, https://www.zdg.md/reporter-special/oameni/ion-costas-zile-de-eclipsa-cronica-unui-razboi-nedeclarat.

[7] Ala Coica, "Operatiunea de capturare a lui Igor Smirnov: 'Destinul Moldovei este sa se uneasca cu Romania,' " *Timpul*, March 3, 2014, https://www.timpul.md/articol/operaiunea-de-capturarea-a-lui-igor-smirnov-destinul-moldovei-este-sa-se-uneasca-cu-romania-55874.html.

[8] These were Mircea Snegur (president during 1991–1997), Petru Lucinschi (president during 1997–2001), and Vladimir Voronin (president during 2001–2009). They effectively had control over the executive power in Moldova, unlike their successors.

significant and costly errors. Those early officials in Chisinau were either ignorant of or only softly addressed crucial issues like the Tiraspol regime's installation of "customs" or "border guard" checkpoints at the administrative border with Moldovan government–controlled territory, in violations of the existing agreements.[9] The strongest visible responses were often banal statements reflecting "deep regrets." Any more resolute responses, themselves a rare occurrence, were almost always rolled back, similar to what happened in the Smirnov detention case.[10] From a security perspective, one can therefore characterize the period of 1991–2009 as one of strategic timidity.

Civil-Military Tensions

Civilian control over the armed forces has historically been strong in the Republic of Moldova, mainly an inheritance from the Soviet Union, which had a tradition of tight control over the defense and security sectors by the political leadership. However, in 1996, a conflict emerged between then-incumbent president Mircea Snegur and his competitor in the forthcoming presidential elections, parliamanetary speaker Petru Lucinschi. The conflict involved, by proxy, the minister of defense, General Pavel Creanga, whom Snegur wanted to dismiss and replace with the deputy defense minister, General Tudor Dabija.[11] Creanga refused to accept the presidential decree, asserting that the procedure was incomplete. He was supported by the prime minister, Andrei Sangheli, and the parliament, led by Luchinschi. However, General Dabija reportedly attempted to implement the presidential decree, by mobilizing support at the Ministry of Defense and the General Staff of the National Army, leading to an internal conflict

---

[9] Ion Stavila and Gheorghe Balan, "Conflictul transnistrean: esecul reglementarii unui conflict care poate fi solutionat," *Revista Militara* 2 (4), 2010: p. 9, https://ibn.idsi.md/sites/default/files/imag_file/Conflictul%20transni strean.pdf.

[10] The only exception was the refusal of Moldova's then-president Vladimir Voronin to sign the notorious Kozak Memorandum in 2003.

[11] Valentina Basiul, "1996: Politicienii preocupati maim ult de prezidentiale decat de problem," *Radio Europa Libera Moldova*, August 6, 2016, https://moldova.europalibera.org/a/27901942.html.

Figure 1: Moldova's Military Budget (Percentage of GDP)

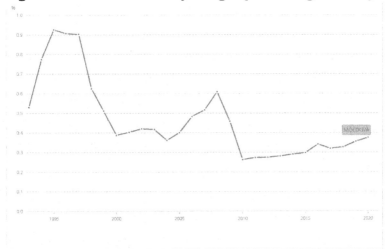

(Source: World Bank)

within the defense structures. Witnesses described the events as a major unfolding crisis, with numerous people (highly unusually) seen carrying rifles on the premises of the defense ministry.[12]

As a result of the parliament's formal inquiry with the Constitutional Court, Snegur's decree was found to be unconstitutional, by violating the principle of separation of powers. However, the consequent actions of Petru Lucinschi, who won the 1996 presidential election, suggest that he grew concerned about the power of the military. He replaced Creanga with his confidant, Valeriu Pasat, who was recalled from his duty as ambassador to the Russian Federation. The new president also removed General Dabija from his post as deputy defense minister shortly thereafter. As **Figure 1** shows, the defense budget dropped during his tenure from 0.903 percent of GDP in 1997 (one of the highest in Moldova's history) to 0.387 percent in 2000.

---

[12] Author's discussions with former military officers who witnessed this crisis.

198 | BLACK SEA BATTLEGROUND

The Oligarchization of the Defense and Security Sectors

Following the first three presidents, who constitutionally enjoyed effective executive power in the Republic of Moldova, their successors were largely reduced to symbolic roles. During 2009–2015, Moldova entered a period of rule by a series of parliamentary coalitions,[13] with prime ministers who wielded varying degrees of power. This period saw the rise to power of notorious oligarch Vlad Plahotniuc as well as the fall of Prime Minister Vladimir Filat, another Moldovan tycoon. The defense budget underwent its most significant drop during this time— from 0.609 percent of GDP in 2008 to 0.263 percent in 2010. Since then, Moldova's defense budget grew, reaching 0.375 percent of GDP in 2020 insignificantly (see **Figure 1**).[14]

The period between 2009 and 2015 can be described as one of increasing "oligarchization," in which defense and security sectors were treated according to their perceived economic value. That situation worsened during 2015–2019, when Plahotniuc *de facto* ruled Moldova, treating it as his personal fiefdom. The authorities during this time largely considered the defense and security sectors of insignificant importance, due to their limited ability to produce rents or be monetized. The only exception were the Ministry of Interior and, to a lesser extent, the Intelligence and Security Service, which largely acquired the functions of internal police, helping Plahotniuc to coerce his opposition, civil society, business competitors and vociferous citizens.

A vivid example of that kind of attitude toward the defense and security sector occurred in 2017, when Moldova expelled five Russian diplomats, including the Russian military attaché and his

---

[13] The coalitions, with the misleading name Alliance for European Integration, were among the most corrupt governmental regimes in the history of Moldova.

[14] "Military Expenditure (% of GDP) - Moldova," World Bank, 1993–2020, https://data.worldbank.org/indicator/MS.MIL.XPND.GD.ZS?locations= MD.

deputy, for alleged espionage.[15] The measure came in response to evidence collected by Moldova's intelligence agency that the Russian deputy military attaché, a military intelligence officer, recruited former parliamentarian Iurie Bolboceanu into revealing state secrets in exchange for money.[16] This was probably the boldest action against Russia that Moldovan authorities ever undertook. And while there is nothing unusual about expelling diplomats over espionage charges, it is surprising that Moldova had never done this before with regard to Russia, even though it repeatedly had the necessary evidence to do so. In fact, authorization for this bold action was most likely not informed primarily by national security concerns but rather seemed to be designed to send a warning signal from Vlad Plahotniuc to the Russian authorities, which had initiated a series of criminal investigations, including on money laundering charges, against him.[17]

Another case in point was the Moldovan parliament's passage of the "Anti-Propaganda Law" in December 2017, while the legislature was under the *de facto* control of Plahotniuc. The text of the law aimed to reduce the influence of Russian media in Moldova's informational space.[18] Yet the actual motivations for the law's passage—to create the threat of costs for Russia in Moldova, presumably in retribution for Moscow's legal attacks on

---

[15] "Intr-o singura luna, cinci diplomati rusi au fost declarati 'persona non grata' in Republica Moldova," *Publica.md*, August 2, 2017, https://www.publika.md/intr-o-singura-luna-cinci-diplomati-rusi-au-fost-declarati-persona-non-grata-in-republica-moldova_2976491.html.
[16] Iurii Botnarenco, "Ex-deputatul Iurie Bolbocanu, anterior condamnat pentru spionaj in favoarea Rusiei, a fost achitat de Curtea de Apel," *Adevarul.ro*, June 19, 2019, https://adevarul.ro/moldova/politica/ex-deputatul-iurie-bolboceanu-condamnat-spionaj-favoarea-rusiei-fost-achitat-curtea-apel-1_5d0a9075892c0bb0c68edf50/index.html.
[17] "Zaversheno rassledovanie dela o vyvode Plahotnjukom iz RF 500 mlrd. rub," *Interfax*, August 31, 2020, https://www.interfax.ru/world/723942.
[18] Diana Preasca, "Legea anti-propaganda a fost votata in Parlament," *Moldova.org*, December 7, 2017, https://www.moldova.org/legea-anti-propaganda-fost-votata-parlament.

200 | BLACK SEA BATTLEGROUND

Plahotniuc—is supported by the fact that the legislation was never effectively implemented.

In a final illustrative example of how defense and security issues were exploited by the Plahotniuc regime for personal benefit, in 2018, his office put pressure on the Moldovan Ministry of Defense to withdraw its objection to accrediting a new Russian military attaché of questionable background for this diplomatic post.[19] Russia's Foreign Minister Sergei Lavrov demanded, in a meeting with his Moldovan counterpart at the 2018 Munich Security Conference, that Chisinau accept the accreditation of the new military attaché as a precondition for the restoration of bilateral relations.[20] At the same time, Moscow projected this pressure through Western diplomats, conditioning the unblocking of routine procedures in the Joint Control Commission (JCC)[21] on the return of the Russian military attaché and his deputies. That Russian-instigated Western pressure proved instrumental in resolving the impasse; but it was ultimately accepted by the Moldovan side because it notably contained incentives favorable to the Plahotniuc regime, which was then interested in building personal relations in the European Union and the United States.

The Period of Strategic Vulnerability

In 2019, Plahotniuc was removed from power by a peculiar Russian-European-US-brokered situational coalition of Socialist and pro-European forces. Subsequently, effective control over the

---

[19] Author's observations during his time working at the Moldovan Ministry of Defense during January–June 2018.

[20] Vasile Kojocari, "Lavrov nazval uslovija dlja poteplenija moldavsko-rossijskih otnoshenii," *Deschide.md*, February 23, 2018, https://deschide.md/ru/russian_news/politic_ru/26835.

[21] Author's observations during his time working at the Moldovan Ministry of Defense during January–June 2018. The JCC is an element of the Russia-imposed conflict resolution mechanism, formed of representatives of the Republic of Moldova, the Russian Federation, the Russia-backed Tiraspol regime, and Ukraine. The body is responsible for the monitoring of ceasefire violations and security incidents in the Security Zone. For more details see https://gov.md/ro/content/actele-de-baza-ale-cuc.

country was gradually transferred to Igor Dodon, Moldova's president during 2016–2020 and the leader of the Socialist Party, which formed the largest faction in the parliament until July 2021. Dodon acquired unlimited political control in Moldova after November 2019, following the dismissal of Prime Minister Maia Sandu over their disagreement about the substance of judicial reforms.[22]

Given Dodon's subordinate relations with Moscow,[23] the defense and security sectors of Moldova after November 2019 became vulnerable to Russian influence. For instance, immediately after Plahotniuc fled Moldova and Dodon started to take over his rent-seeking network, including the corrupt judicial system, the Moldovan Court of Appeals released Iurie Bolboceanu. It did so two years after he started to serve his 14-year espionage sentence, based on "procedural fallacy" of the prosecutors.[24] Bolboceanu was finally acquitted after prosecutors withdrew the accusation of "state treason" against him.[25]

Dodon was vocal about the espionage case from the very beginning, publicly questioning the government's decision from

---

[22] Dumitru Minzarari. 2019. "The Socialist Party Tries to Derail Justice Reform in Moldova, Topples the Government". *Eurasia Daily Monitor* 16 (158), 12 November. https://jamestown.org/program/the-socialist-party-tries-to-derail-justice-reform-in-moldova-topples-the-government.

[23] For details see Dumitru Minzarari. 2019. "The New Wave of Russia's surreptitious Offensive in Eastern Europe." *Eurasia Daily Monitor* 16 (132), 26 September. https://jamestown.org/program/the-new-wave-of-russias-surreptitious-offensive-in-eastern-europe.

[24] Stela Mihailovici. 2019. "Avocatul lui Iurie Bolboceanu ofera detalii. Ce decizie a luat de fapt Curtea de Apel si de ce ii nemultumeste. #Ceurmeaza". TV8.md, 20 June. https://tv8.md/2019/06/20/avocatul-lui-iurie-bolboceanu-ofera-detalii-ce-decizie-a-luat-de-fapt-curtea-de-apel-si-de-ce-ii-nemultumeste.

[25] Stela Untila, "Fostul deputat Iurie Bolboceanu a fost achitat de Judecatoria Chisinau, in dosarul privind 'tradare de patrie,' " *NewsMaker.md*, October 16, 2020, https://newsmaker.md/ro/fostul-deputat-iurie-bolboceanu-a-fost-achitat-de-judecatoria-chisinau-in-dosarul-privind-tradare-de-patrie.

his presidential perch and claiming there was not enough evidence to prove the case. Besides his official statements, he called a Supreme Security Council meeting to discuss the case and then demanded that the Moldovan intelligence services provide information on known violations by all foreign diplomats, hinting that Western diplomats may also deserve to be expelled.[26] All defense ministers appointed by Dodon, including the one in the Maia Sandu cabinet—Pavel Voicu—had quickly made connections with their Russian counterpart, actively participated in Russia-led political-military events in the Commonwealth of Independent States (CIS) framework, and advanced "political-military cooperation" with Russia.[27] This had rarely happened before, if at all, given that Moldova's participation in CIS structures and events formally excludes participation in the political-military dimension. Therefore, Dodon's short but total control over Moldova's government institutions could be seen as a period of strategic vulnerability for Moldova's defense and security sectors.

Signals of Strategic Ignorance

With PAS's overwhelming victory in the July 2021 parliamentary elections, the situation around Moldova's defense and security sectors changed compared to Dodon's period of rule. At a minimum, the new government halted the incipient trend of inhibiting effective cooperation with the West in military and security areas on the one hand, while strengthening such ties with Russia on the other hand. Nevertheless, the PAS government's

---

[26] Maxim Andreev, " 'Skazki pro belogo bychka': Dodona ne ubedili argumenty spetssluzhb o vydvorenii rossijskih diplomatov," *NewsMaker.md*, June 7, 2017, https://newsmaker.md/rus/novosti/skazki-pro-belogo-bychka-dodona-ne-ubedili-argumenty-spetssluzhb-o-vydvorenii-ross-31791.

[27] For instance, see "Victor Gaiciuc, interest de strategia 'impotriva implicarii SUA in treburile interne' ale altor tari," *Deschide.md*, December 19, 2019, https://deschide.md/ro/stiri/politic/58520/Victor-Gaiciuc-interesat-de-strategia-%E2%80%9E%C3%AEmpotriva-implic%C4%83rii-SUA-%C3%AEn-treburile-interne%E2%80%9D-ale-altor-%C8%9B%C4%83ri.htm.

first signals in the defense and security sphere did not considerably differ from Moldovan policies and approaches before 2019 (including those implemented during the Plahotniuc regime)—albeit for different reasons. This situation is due to the artificial separation of Moldova's anti-corruption and rule of law reforms—the key drivers of Sandu's and PAS's governing program[28]—from the national security dimension. This governing strategy ignores the increasing trend of corruption being weaponized by states[29] in their attempts to influence other countries, making it an important national security issue. Russia has been particularly keen and active in weaponizing corruption, using it as "a tool of statecraft to interfere with, co-opt, weaken, and destabilize democratic institutions and processes"[30] in the post-Soviet area. For instance, as soon as the PAS government started to effectively dismantle the corrupt legal system built by Plahotniuc, which Dodon consequently acquired control over, Russia used a number of actors and sources to attack these efforts. This included falsely invoking the Gagauz ethnic background of the demoted general prosecutor, Alexandru Stoianoglo, in the obvious attempt to draw condemnation and pressure from the West.[31]

Another example of strategic ignorance involves dealing with Russia based on what the new authorities in Chisinau refer to as

---

[28] Vitalie Calugareanu, "UE Sprijina Presedentia in lupta contra clanurilor corupte coordinate din Parlament," *DWRomania*, March 1, 2021, https://p.dw.com/p/3q3cu.

[29] Philip Zelikov, Eric Edelman, Kristofer Harrison, and Celeste Ward Gventer, "The Rise of Strategic Corruption: How States Weaponize Graft," *Foreign Affairs* (July/August 2020.).

[30] Matthew H. Murray, Alexander Vindman, Dominic Cruz Bustillos, "Perspectives: Assessing the Threat of Weaponized Corruption," *EurasiaNet*, July 12, 2021, https://eurasianet.org/perspectives-assessing-the-threat-of-weaponized-corruption.

[31] For an example see "Moldovan Socialists Preparing Rally Against Prosecutor General's Detention," *Interfax*, October 6, 2021, https://interfax.com/newsroom/top-stories/72831.

"pragmatic dialogue."[32] This approach presupposes that trade issues, the status of Moldovan workers in Russia, the removal of ammunition and armaments from the Transnistrian region, as well as the withdrawal of Russian troops there can be discussed with Moscow based on a positive-sum logic. However, the Russian vision of pragmatic relations with Moldova are built on a zero-sum logic: for Russia, pragmatism in this context is when "Moldovan authorities can decide for themselves, without any steering from outside."[33] In other words, Russia understands that without the support of its Western partners, Moldova would be unable to balance Russian pressure and influence, and would instead end up bandwagoning with Russia,[34] becoming a *de facto* satellite state.

As Russia does not view Moldova purely through an economic lens, Moscow does not perceive its relations with Chisinau through a positive-sum logical framework. It is this rationale that has been totally ignored by the new Moldovan government—a fact that has vividly emerged during its negotiations with Russia on natural gas imports, on the sidelines of the larger energy crisis in Europe. Moldova's deputy prime minister responsible for infrastructure and regional development, Andrei Spanu, after a few rounds of negotiations with various high-level Russian officials and the Gazprom leadership, admitted that Russia's demanded price for a new natural gas contract was unfair for Moldova's citizens, containing "both financial and non-financial conditions."[35]

---

[32] Julia-Sabina Joja, "Voice of Freedom: Interview with Moldovan President Maia Sandu," *American Purpose*, July 28, 2021, https://www.americanpurpose.com/articles/voice-of-freedom.
[33] "Lavrov: SShA preamo zapreshajut Sandu govorit' o stremlenii razvivat' otnosheniya s Rossiyei," *TASS*, October, 13, 2021, https://tass.ru/politika/12648073.
[34] On balancing and bandwagoning strategies, see Stephen M. Walt, "Alliance Formation and the Balance of World Power," *International Security*, 9 (4), 1985: pp. 3–43.
[35] "Andrei Spinu: Oferta propusa de Gazprom nu este in avatanjul R.Moldova. Pretul cerut include conditii financiare si nefinanciare," *Deschide.md*, October 23, 2021, https://deschide.md/ro/stiri/economic/94117.

The "non-financial conditions" are linked to Russian stipulations that Chisinau delay its implementation of the EU Third Energy Package,[36] legislation that, once put into effect, would diminish Russian influence on Moldova's energy system and consequently on Moldovan politics. These conditions are also likely referring to Russia linking the issue of natural gas exports with Moldova's concessions on other bilateral issues, including the Transnistrian conflict negotiations. This is consistent with the apparent preference of Russian officials to negotiate on Transnistria with Moldova's Deputy Prime Minister for Reintegration Vlad Kulminski.[37]

Moldova was the first to fall into the "linkage trap," when it initially decided to send Kulminski to Moscow to negotiate both the gas contract and issues related to the Transnistrian conflict.[38] This was a major diplomatic error that could have been avoided; Chisinau should have been resolute about keeping the two matters separated in bilateral discussions, avoiding Kulminski's involvement in the gas talks. These examples reflect just some of the indicative signals that the PAS-led government is still unaware of the important effects of security and defense issues on many domestic and foreign policy objectives of Moldova.

Besides the prioritization of the economic and rule of law dimensions of governance, PAS also seems to have a poor opinion of the ability of the Moldovan Armed Forces to fulfil their duty of national defense and deterrence of armed aggression. The current authorities have basically no expertise in defense and security, which makes them extremely risk-averse on these issues. Moreover, the PAS authorities put a lot of emphasis on personal

---

[36] Tatjana Djatel and Vladimir Solovjev, "Bez gazu nedelja," October 24, 2021, https://www.kommersant.ru/doc/5049852.

[37] Vladimir Solovjev and Tatjana Djatel, "Moldavia stolknulas' s trubnosteami," October 19, 2021, https://www.kommersant.ru/doc/5040294.

[38] "Vizita viceprim-ministrului Kulminski la Moscova: Ce a discutat cu Andrei Rudenko, Dmitrii Kozak si Grigorii Karasin," *Jurnal.md*, October 8, 2021, https://www.jurnal.md/ro/news/1e5b8895177bc8f3/vizita-viceprim-ministrului-kulminski-la-moscova-ce-a-discutat-cu-andrei-rudenko-dmitrii-kozak-si-grigorii-karasin.html.

206 | BLACK SEA BATTLEGROUND

trust in recruiting people, and they significantly resist accepting expertise from outside the party's inner circle. These feelings were likely aggravated by the veiled threats of conflict escalation in Transnistria, issued by Russian officials both publicly[39] and in closed talks, which have aimed to deter the PAS government from promoting what Russian officials call "anti-Russian" policies.[40] President Sandu has made efforts to avoid irritating Russia—for instance, during her January 2021 visit to Brussels, she specifically chose not to visit NATO Headquarters. Moreover, Prime Minister Natalia Gavrilita attended the virtual gathering of the CIS chiefs of state on October 15, 2021—a conspicuous departure from the practice of the last decade, when Moldova tried to avoid such events. The only exception was the period between 2019 and 2021, when the pro-Russian president Igor Dodon had control over the government.

Moldova's Threat Assessment

Moldova faces a range of defense and security threats that are mostly the results of its unique geographic location and historical legacy, partially attributed to the post-Soviet choices made by its political elites. Following the armed escalations of all "frozen" or latent conflicts in the post-Soviet area where Russian troops were present—namely (besides Moldova) Georgia, Ukraine and Karabakh[41]—a military escalation of the Transnistrian conflict is

---

[39] "Maia Sandu vorbeste, in presa rusa, despre o discutie cu Putin in care sa-I ceara retragerea trupelor rusesti din Transnistria," PROTV Chisinau, July 20, 2021, https://protv.md/international/maia-sandu-vorbeste-in-presa-rusa-despre-o-discutie-cu-putin-in-care-sa-i-ceara-retragerea-trupelor-rusesti-din-transnistria---2573975.html.

[40] The label "anti-Russian" is applied by the Russian officials to any policy that aims to move Moldova closer to the West, or weaken the existing leverages that Russia has built in Moldova, including in the energy sector, economy, social domain, media and communications, etc.

[41] For an assessment on the Russian role in the 2020 Azerbaijan-Armenian war in Nagorno-Karabakh, see Dumitru Minzarari, "Russia's Stake in the Nagorno-Karabakh War: Accident or Design?" *Point of*

quite plausible. This risk has tremendously increased after Russia launched its full-scale re-invasion of Ukraine in February 2022, indicating that Moscow's threshold for direct military escalation against its neighbors is significantly lower than it was presumed to be. The proper questions to ask are under what conditions such an escalation in Transnistria could happen, and what costs would need to be imposed on Russia in order to deter it?

As part of its conventional war against Ukraine, Russia has been trying to acquire control of the Ukrainian coastal region around Odesa via a joint amphibious and land attack, which would physically connect Russian forces in occupied Crimea with Moldova's Transnistrian region. Such an outcome, if successful, would be a likely trigger to subsequently threaten Moldova with a military invasion. The alternative for Chisinau would be accepting the demands of an ultimatum, similar to the one Kyiv received from Moscow, involving federalization and an effective mechanism giving the Kremlin total political control over Chisinau.

Besides the risk of a conventional attack, an assessment of Russian actions in the region over the past decade and a half indicate that both conventional (Georgia 2008 scenario) and proxy-type (Ukraine 2014) aggressive actions are possible. What ultimately occurs depends on the particular goals Russia may wish to advance and the related costs it may deem acceptable. For instance, if it wants to send a particularly powerful message to the West and claim strong resolve, it could orchestrate a conventional type of invasion even without conquering the Odesa region.

Moldova's Transnistrian region offers a favorable platform for launching such a conventional invasion, as the population would not actively resist. For one thing, Russia has applied a complete passportization policy in Transnistria, having distributed Russian passports to local inhabitants since the 1990s. It also has military forces stationed in this separatist Moldovan region—including

---

View, Stiftung Wissenschaft und Politik, November 12, 2020, https://www.swp-berlin.org/en/publication/russias-stake-in-the-nagorno-karabakh-war-accident-or-design.

208 | BLACK SEA BATTLEGROUND

troops deployed under the title of "peacekeepers" as well as a military contingent designated to secure the ammunition depot at Cobasna. Furthermore, it practically commands all the armed units of the secessionist region. Therefore, it can explore a range of options for invoking a *casus belli*, including by conducting false flag operations.

However, as the Ukraine case revealed, Russia also intitiates military aggression without any real justification. In case additional troops or reinforcements are needed, Russia could use the airports in Tighina, Chisinau and Marculesti, first dropping a small assault force that would take over the airport infrastructure and then accept incoming Russian military cargo aircraft with these troops. Russia's similar attempt to take over Kyiv at the start of its conventional aggression against Ukraine in February 2022 would indicate the high plausibility of this scenario. While operationally challenging, Russia could also try to first deploy helicopters at low altitude using nap-of-the-earth (NOE) flying techniques to avoid detection, and then send in troops from its bases in Crimea into the Transnistrian region; from there, they could be moved further inside the Republic of Moldova, as needed.

Given that Moldova has basically no military airspace radar capabilities, such a scenario is highly plausible. However, the costs for such an operation—both material and reputational, and in case Moldova were to resist militarily—would be significant for the Kremlin, notwithstanding Russia's already seriously damaged international position as a consequence of its 2022 war against Ukraine. The cost of an invasion against Moldova would undermine Russia's argument that Ukraine is a unique case and once more strongly underscore Russia's revanchist ambitions.

However, since cost calculations for aggression are based on *ex ante* perceptions of the expected gains and losses that a military operation would bring, open aggression against Moldova would depend on Russia perceiving either extremely high costs from inaction, or significantly low costs as a result of its military action. Before Russia invaded Ukraine in February 2022, the only likely *casus belli* for Russia to invade Moldova would have been an attempt by Moldovan Armed Forces attempting to recover (purportedly or truly) control over Transnistria. This presumption is no longer valid. Based on the observed actions of Russia, it is highly likely that the Kremlin would instead confront Moldova with an ultimatum, either publicly or via diplomatic channels. Based on the timid response of the Moldovan government to Russia's invasion of Ukraine,[42] Chisinau's most likely response—which Russian analysts would readily perceive—would be to give in to Russian demands and give up military resistance. Therefore, contrary to how the PAS government seems to perceive the current situation, its policy of openly indicating it is afraid to confront Russia is actually increasing the risk of receiving such a military ultimatum from Moscow.

It is useful to understand the evolution of Russian incentives for war before and after it launched its full-scale conventional war against Ukraine. Prior to the February 2022 Russian re-invasion of Ukraine, the risk of war for Moldova was much lower, as Moscow's costs calculations were perceived to be different. For instance, the most likely—though still low-risk—scenario for Moldova would have been for Russia to apply the 2014 Donbas model to Transnistria, operationalizing the principles of a proxy war and escalating militarily. Russia actually resorted to this very model in 1990, when it initiated the Transnistrian conflict. Before February 2022, the rationale of trading its "peacekeeping" operation for violent conflict was questionable. On the contrary, Russia had hailed its operation in Transnistria as a successful endeavor and used it as a model for its interventions in post-Soviet area. An escalation of the Transnistrian conflict back into a violent phase would hurt the interests of the local political elites in this separatist quasi-statelet, which, over the last few decades, acquired broad economic interests extending into the right bank of the Nistru River and even the EU. Currently, it is much easier for the Russian government to ignore these interests, given that it revealed a complete shift in the paradigm that directed its foreign

---

[42] "Hitrovyverennaya pozitsiy," *Kommersant*, March 25, 2022, https://www.kommersant.ru/doc/5272303?fbclid=IwAR3MbaleAezM ZYbFuirQujcS-gZn5isnZ9o8s4Ifezjw-76y4rnyehV-jnk.

and security policy toward the post-Soviet area. Russia is clearly ready to use its military to conquer by force the former republics, an attitude only likely to change if it suffers a significant defeat in Ukraine.

As part of the potential Russian ultimatum, the likeliest change in the *status quo* in the Transnistrian conflict would be for Russian forces to expel the Moldovan authorities from the small pockets of territory it controls on the left bank of the Nistru, as well as from the town of Bender. This would bring some tactical and operational advantages to the Russian military were it to decide to strengthen its position and put additional pressure on the Moldovan government, particularly since the stakes in negotiations suddenly increased following the February invasion.

Yet, Russia has other options with which to put pressure on the Moldovan government, short of a conventional invasion. A likely Russian action affecting Moldova's defense and security would be for Moscow to use the Gagauzia region of Moldova to launch a proxy-style (Donbas scenario) operation. Gagauzia is strongly pro-Russian and has a degree of autonomy that, technically, would permit elements of the local elite to covertly prepare (with Russian help) a group of trained personnel to operate as a local "militia." As seen in its earlier operations, the Russian military is known to utilize local groups of "rebels" that serve as a smokescreen for Russian military detachments and that do the heavy lifting to acquire physical and administrative control over the target territory. According to Moldovan governmental sources, Russian military intelligence has been recruiting fighters for Donbas both in Gagauzia but also among Moldovan citizens working in Russia.[43] That fact makes this threat scenario that much more realistic and feasible to implement. Given the size of the Gagauz region, as well as the poor preparation of the Moldovan defense and security agencies, it would be highly

---

[43] "Moldovenii au ajuns mercenary pentru rusi in Siria si Donbas. Guvernul de la Chisinau a declansat o ancheta oficiala," *PROTV.ro*, July 16, 2017, https://stirileprotv.ro/stiri/international/moldovenii-au-ajuns-mercenari-pentru-rusi-in-siria-si-donbas-guvernul-de-la-chisinau-a-declansat-o-ancheta-oficiala.html.

possible for them to miss such an operation at its incipient stages, while it is still most vulnerable to governmental counteractions. Furthermore, the strategic ignorance indicator discussed earlier, along with the strategic timidity of the Moldovan government, would likely prevent Chisinau from taking effective and prompt actions, even if it were informed in time. The fact that the Russian side well understands the strategic culture traits of the Moldovan authorities makes this risk even more possible.

Along with using Gagauzia as a focal point for any future proxy aggression, such an operation would probably trigger a range of activities meant to distract governmental attention, resources and efforts toward a set of artificial crises. To reduce the probability that Moldova's government would decide to militarily resist, Russia may employ a range of threatening actions. These might include protests in other areas of the country, acts of sabotage against critical public infrastructure or units of the Ministry of Defense and Ministry of Interior, as well as actions to inhibit the security and defense forces from deploying or freely operating on Moldovan territory, such as blocking roads and key intersections. Some of these measures were successfully employed in Crimea and Donbas and, previously, in Transnistria in the early 1990s. Given the experience in Ukraine and other conflicts, Russia could also use unmanned aerial vehicles (UAV) to set fire to Moldovan ammunition depots or other critical targets.[44] Under these conditions, it is critically important for the security services to recognize the threat, deploy response units quickly, and effectively identify and address the challenges, by lethal force if necessary. This is the main vulnerability of the Moldovan side. As mentioned earlier, the strategic culture of Moldova's ruling elites would likely result in hesitation, refusing to allow the use of lethal force until the last moment and being overtaken by the opponent's surprise action. After the opponent creates new facts on the ground, the recovery of administrative control over the lost territory would end up being quite costly and

---

[44] Russia has been operating UAVs from its base in the Transnistrian region to monitor the activities and installations of the Moldovan military in the proximity of the Security Zone.

likely require large-scale military operations to reverse the losses.

Nevertheless, this scenario would also most likely not be the first choice of the Russian Federation in an attempt to consolidate its influence over the Moldovan authorities. Given that Moldova is insulated from Russia by Ukraine, the logistical support for a military operation against Moldova—even a proxy one—could be quite challenging for Moscow, unless it manages to wrest control over Odesa and the surrounding Ukrainian territories in the ongoing war there. Moreover, while Russia could achieve its military objectives in Moldova, it may find it difficult to maintain the gains over an extended period of time. Furthermore, even a proxy type of operation using Gagauzia, where Russia could present it as a local "ethnic rebellion" to avoid damage to its international reputation, would nevertheless generate additional economic and political costs for Russia. And the Kremlin's attempts to sow confusion and spread misinformation about its designs for Ukraine ahead of as well as during the war have further undermined Russian credibility on the international stage. This makes it more difficult for Russia to invoke justifications for its aggression that the West would turn a blind eye to. A least costly scenario would be the utilization of the strongest advantages Russia acquired in Moldova, compared to other post-Soviet countries. This includes control over a rather large and still quite influential political party that has seats in the parliament, namely the Socialist Party under the leadership of Igor Dodon.

This strategy is also likely to be put into action, under certain conditions. On the one hand, Russia already applies economic and political pressure on Moldova, aiming to degrade the well-being of voters while trying to blame the PAS government. This is quite visible under the ongoing (2021–2022) energy crisis that has affected Europe generally but hit Moldova quite hard in particular, due to the latter's scarce economic resources and lack

Neutrality With No Guarantees | 213

of energy alternatives.[45] At the same time, Russia is preparing to bring the Socialist Party back into power by exploiting the crisis to erode the popular support of PAS. In parallel, Moscow can be expected to channel some of its resources through the Socialists to address critical popular needs and use the large media network that it controls or is able to access in Moldova[46] to transfer these actions into political influence. A potential indicator pointing to the probability of this course of action is Dodon's declaration in the fall of 2021 that he will give up his member of parliament mandate and instead lead the "Moldovan-Russian Business Association," recently created by the Russian business association "*Delovaja Rossija*" (Business Russia).[47] The organization is presented as a public entity; but given its significant financial clout, it is surely operating as a cover for the Russian government.[48]

Dodon could use this new platform to avoid prosecution by the Moldovan legal authorities, as he could operate safely from Russia. Yet, he could also still participate in the process of ruling the Socialist Party, similarly to how Ilan Shor—a fugitive oligarch—leads his party that entered the parliament in the July

---

[45] "Moldova Declares State of Emergency Over Gas Crisis," *Al Jazeera*, October 22, 2021, https://www.aljazeera.com/news/2021/10/22/moldova-declares-state-of-emergency-over-gas-crisis.

[46] As a representative description of the media space in Moldova see "Monitorizarea mass-mediei in campania electorala pentru alegerile parlamentare anticipate din 11 iulie 2021," *MediaAzi*, Raport nr. 5 (July 2–10, 2021), http://media-azi.md/ro/publicatii/monitorizarea-mass-mediei-%C3%AEn-campania-electoral%C4%83-pentru-alegerile-parlamentare-anticipa-3. That monitoring of ten major mass media (TV) outlets during elections suggested that there is a significant potential to use them in orchestrating an anti-PAS communication campaign.

[47] "Noua misiune a lui Igor Dodon: lasa mandatul de deputat pentrua fi sef la o asociatie de afaceri," *Moldstreet*, October 18, 2021, https://www.mold-street.com/?go=news&n=12859.

[48] See the organization's official web-site: https://www.deloros.ru/about-us1.html.

214 | BLACK SEA BATTLEGROUND

2021 elections.[49] Most importantly, in this position, Dodon would be able to channel Russian funding into Moldova in ways that would be difficult to detect by the Moldovan authorities or to link to the Socialist Party. This model of Russia's financial assistance of the Socialist Party—which would serve as an economic and political proxy—would be an effective approach to weaponize corruption and consolidate Russia's economic interests and influence in Moldova. It would allow the Russian Federation to directly participate, similar to a Moldovan political actor, in influencing Moldova's domestic and foreign policies to the extent the Socialist Party will be able to affect them. This effectively represents a strategy of interstate aggression—though of a more subtle nature—because it effectively undermines Moldova's sovereignty, while permitting Russia to potentially achieve goals that traditionally would have been advanced via military operations. As such, it is an approach Moscow will attempt to explore first, before military coercion. And that option is made all the more feasible thanks to the current PAS government's position toward Russia, revealing weakness and a lack of resolve: It includes publicly refusing to join the EU sanctions against Russia following the latter's attack on Ukraine; having all high-level officials place exaggerated emphasis on the neutrality status of Moldova in their public statements; and making obvious efforts not to irritate Russia, which has even been noticed by the Russian media.

Moldovan Responses to Defense and Security Challenges: The Sacred Cow of Neutrality

The way the various Moldovan governments perceived and assessed the impact of defense and security threats confronted by the country since gaining independence in 1991 have naturally affected their response policies. During the period described by "strategic timidity," there was a variation in the degree, if not the substance, of implemented policies. Under the presidential tenure of Mircea Snegur (1990–1997), the Moldovan ruling elites learned an extremely tough lesson, following their defeat at the

---

[49] Sor Party obtained 6 out of 101 seats in the parliament.

hands of the Russian 14th Army, which openly sided with the Tiraspol paramilitaries, following an extended period of covert support. This first major military defeat of Moldova's nascent Armed Forces, together with the passive reaction Moldova received in response to its multiple pledges to various international bodies, including the United Nations, impelled the country's leadership to bandwagon with Russia. It yielded to Russian pressure and included in its 1994 Constitution the provision of permanent neutrality. The intention was to address the voiced Russian concern about a potential re-unification of Moldova with Romania, and trade neutrality in exchange for the withdrawal of Russian troops.

The error was that Moldovan authorities included the neutrality provision in the Constitution, which is highly difficult to change, and therefore lost a potential bargaining chip with Russia by making this change. As a result, the Russian Federation does not have any incentive to withdraw its military forces from Transnistria. It has been challenging for one single political party to achieve a constitutional majority in the parliament. Moreover, there was always a political force in the legislature that has been receptive to Russian demands. In time, the Moldovan population became more favorable to the idea of neutrality, in part thanks to the Moldovan authorities' continual confirmation of that policy over the years. Therefore, popular support for neutrality has become an obstacle in its own right, making it difficult for any government to quickly reverse the policy. Altogether, this has given Russia confidence that the policy of neutrality will persist, and Moscow has never felt the need to make concessions with regard to the withdrawal of forces and armaments from the Transnistrian region.

Neutrality today remains the sacred cow of Moldova's security policy, and it is included in all national security and defense doctrinal documents. The 2008 National Security Concept, for example, begins with an introductory section containing the phrase "the permanent neutrality represents the basic principle, the foundation of the national security concept."[50] Not a single government or ruling coalition in Moldova has dared to take effective steps toward either slowly adjusting or changing that policy. This is despite the fact that a significant majority of the Moldovan population supports Moldova's course toward European integration. Although these figures have fluctuated up and down over the years, in June 2021, over 65 percent of respondents of a nationwide public opinion poll declared that they would vote for Moldova's integration into the European Union, while only 25.7 percent stated they were against such a move.[51]

Presumably, with a skillfully developed and implemented strategic communication campaign, the popularity of the EU among the population could likely be extended to NATO—particularly since most NATO members are also EU members or countries that Moldovan citizens are positively predisposed toward. The hesitancy or resistance of Moldovan authorities to embark upon this path is explained by their timidity toward the Russian Federation and concerns about Russian responses. While the latter are not clearly understood by most Moldovan politicians, when it comes to bilateral relations with Russia their risk-averse nature has always prevailed.

Besides the questionable logic of neutrality, Moldovan authorities have never developed or articulated any strategic vision about how to address the major defense and security threats that the country confronts. This has been reflected in Moldova routinely accepting other parties' agendas when it comes to Transnistrian negotiations—namely those of Russia, the Organization for Security and Co-operation in Europe (OSCE) or the EU—instead of attempting to drive the agenda itself. Over the years, Moldovan authorities have been criticized by Western diplomats for being unable to come up with a national vision about how to resolve the

---

[50] Conceptia Securiatatii Nationale a Republicii Moldova, May 22, 2008, https://www.legis.md/cautare/getResults?doc_id=24400&lang=ro.
[51] "Barometrul Opiniei Publice," Moldovan Institute for Public Policies, June 2021, https://ipp.md/wp-content/uploads/2021/07/Raport-BOP-2021_.pdf.

Transnistrian conflict. This has been a fair accusation for some time, but it is not completely justifiable any longer. President Sandu and other dignitaries have pointed out that Moldova's policy toward the conflict is grounded in the goal of withdrawing the Russian military and ammunitions from the region, changing the militarized "peacekeeping" mission into a civilian one, and creating economic incentives to attract the support of Moldovan citizens living in Transnistria.

This view, while clear, lacks an implementation strategy. Successive Moldovan governments have never gone beyond political statements or incipient efforts to build international support for the idea. Given that the conflict is listed in many of Moldova's official documents as one of the greatest national security threats, the lack of progress in building an effective implementation strategy may seem puzzling. However, this is entirely consistent with the traits of Moldova's strategic culture described earlier, and it is an expected behavior in this regard.

By viewing the military tool of the state as ineffective, and under economic pressure, Moldovan officials have largely ignored the National Army. With one of the smallest defense budgets in Europe, Moldovan military forces have degraded in training, equipment and quantitative indicators. For instance, some recent available data indicates that Moldova recruited 1,250 conscript soldiers during the recruiting season of April–June 2021. It intended to recruit another 1,050 conscript soldiers during the recruiting season of October 2021–January 2022.[52] These

---

[52] See: "Government of Moldova decree nr. 153-IX, 8 September 2021," Monitorul Oficial al Republicii Moldova, Nr. 219–225, art. 251, 2021, https://gov.md/sites/default/files/document/attachments/subiect_13 _-_329_ma_2021.pdf.

numbers have been consistent over the past few years,[53] but overall, it is possible to see a generally decreasing trend.[54]

The length of Moldovan conscript service is one year, which makes it difficult to provide high-quality military training for the recruits, especially given the scarce resources available for training activities. While the Moldovan military is not enthusiastic about providing figures to the public, data from 2015 shows that over 62 percent of the annual defense budget was spent on salaries, while another 35 percent went toward maintaining military infrastructure.[55] That left little for operational costs and training. Provided that the defense budget has not evolved, it is quite likely that the cost structure remains the same today.

The scarce data made available by the Moldovan Defense Ministry suggests that some of the operational and equipment costs are covered by military assistance that Moldova receives from its Western partners, especially from the United States. In September 2021, for example, Moldova obtained unspecified equipment from the US in the amount of $5 million, toward which Moldova reportedly contributed $1 million of its own funding.[56]

---

[53] Maxim Stratan, "In perioada aprilie-iulie, aproximativ 1210 reruit vor fi incorporate pentru indeplinirea serviciului militar in termen," *NewsMaker.md*, May 14, 2020, https://newsmaker.md/ro/in-perioada-aprilie-iulie-aproximativ-1-210-recruti-vor-fi-incorporati-pentru-indeplinirea-serviciului-militar-in-termen.

[54] Data shows a drop from over 3,000 recruits per recruiting season in 2002 to some 1,200 per recruiting season in 2020. See Veaceslav Berbeca and Sergiu Lipcean, "Armata Nationala: Intre interese de grup si dezvoltare strategica," *Moldovan Institute for Public Policies*, p. 23, 2020, https://ipp.md/wp-content/uploads/2020/06/Armata-Nationala-intre-interese-de-grup-si-dezvotare-strategica1.pdf.

[55] Anatolie Esanu and Victor Mosneag, "Armata Nationala: Cifre sumbre si secrete de stat," *Ziarul de Garda*, April 19, 2017, https://www.zdg.md/reporter-special/reportaje/armata-nationala-cifre-sumbre-si-secrete-de-stat.

[56] "Echipamente militare oferite de SUA pentru Armata Nationala a Republicii Moldova," *Radio Europa Libera Moldova*, September 27, 2021, https://moldova.europalibera.org/a/echipamente-militare-

The equipment came as part of the implementation of the Defense Capacity Building Initiative (DCBI) program run by NATO, which Moldova has benefited from as of 2015. According to NATO public data, Moldova's DCBI assistance covers areas such as strategic planning, non-commissioned officer (NCO) corps development, Special Operations Forces development, intelligence-sharing and communications, as well as the physical security of ammunition and stockpile management, among others.[57]

It also appears that Moldova manages to compensate somewhat for its insufficient training costs by sending its troops to NATO and Partnership for Peace (PfP) exercises. For instance, in 2019, some 663 Moldovan military personnel participated in 20 NATO military exercises.[58] However, while this training helps, it is by no means sufficient. Given the available data on funding and activities, it is clear that the Moldovan military conducts inadequate drills to maintain even a minimal level of combat readiness.

The Moldovan side has also made poor use of the available military assistance that its Western partners could provide. It tended to accept anything it was offered, without making objective calculations of its strategic needs, or attempting to address them by actively engaging its partners. The Russian war against Ukraine indicated that a large part of the assistance Moldova received from NATO—via programs such as "Building Integrity" or "Women, Peace and Security"—are good only during peace time and are poor substitutes for much-needed combat training or modern equipment. While it is true that shifting away

---

oferite-de-sua-pentru-armata-na%C8%9Bional%C4%83-a-republicii-moldova/31480112.html.

[57] "Defence and Related Security Capacity Building Initiative," NATO, June 9, 2021, https://www.nato.int/cps/en/natohq/topics_132756.htm.

[58] "Parteneriat si cooperare. Cum este sustinuta Moldova de NATO in solutionarea problemelor de securitate, ecologie si apararea drepturilor," *NewsMaker.md*, December 16, 2020, https://newsmaker.md/ro/parteneriat-si-cooperare-cum-este-sustinuta-moldova-de-nato-in-solutionarea-problemelor-de-securitate-ecologie-si-apararea-drepturilor.

from the assistance programs of limited use for national defense was challenging, it is also a fact that the Moldovan authorities invested little thinking into deriving true top priorities or into efforts to convince Western partners to help address these.

In contrast to the serious funding and functioning challenges faced by the Moldovan military, the Ministry of Internal Affairs (MAI) and the Security and Intelligence Service have fared much better. In particular, the MAI has received almost 3.3 times more funding than the Ministry of Defense for 2021. That has been a consistent trend over the years. It is mainly due to the fact that previous oligarchic governments viewed the MAI as a tool for their protection but also coercion against domestic opponents and competitors. It is both indicative and surprising for a country that has foreign troops on its territory against its will and is unable to exert its sovereignty over 12 percent of its territory.

Conclusion

A historical overview suggests that following the violent phase of the Transnistrian conflict, in particular after 1997, the Moldovan authorities *de facto* stopped seeing the Russian military presence on Moldova's territory as a major security threat. Instead, gradually, successive governments focused on issues of internal security. They elevated the funding and status of the MAI while progressively decreasing resources for the Moldovan military.

A combination of explanations can clarify this trend, which evolved over the years. Initially, facing a military defeat from the Russian 14th Army in Transnistria, the Moldovan authorities viewed the national defense forces as ineffective for addressing the conflict. And as oligarchic interests began to prevail in Moldova after 2009, the value of the defense ministry—a resource consumer, rather than a resource provider—further dropped. Furthermore, Moldova's weak economic development also contributed to the lower position of defense and security issues on the preference rankings of both the population and the governing authorities.

It is perhaps surprising in retrospect how relatively quickly Moldova's population became used to the Russian military presence. But as such, the electorate has not operated as a pressure mechanism on the ruling elites: voters do not penalize governments for inaction or create any incentives to adjust the country's defense and security policies. Instead, the domain of defense and security issues is widely perceived in Moldova as an elitist and, in some ways, inconsequential agenda.

The Russian large-scale re-invasion of Ukraine indicates that Moscow's threshold for war is lower than it was believed to be. This demands a review and reassessment of the level of security risks that Moldovan policy was based on until recently. It was only due to heavy combat and economic costs as a result of its war that Russia eventually withdrew many of its initial demands toward Ukraine and has started to shown hesitancy in advancing militarily beyond Donbas. This turnaround was mainly possible due to the modern training that Ukrainian combat forces received, the military equipment assistance it obtained from Western partners, as well as the strong resolve of the Ukrainian population to resist, which had solidified and consolidated since 2014.

The Moldovan authorities lack the strategic culture to understand this and draw lessons for its own defense and security organizations. Should Moscow threaten Chisinau, the most likely outcome would be for the Moldovan government to bandwagon with rather than seek to balance against Russia, even if military resistance would be feasible and permit Moldova to retain its sovereignty. Moldova needs its Western partners, in particular the US, to assist review and rebuild Moldovan strategic culture, as well as to encourage Chisinau to invest more in qualitative and quantitative terms into its own defense. This is critical, since Moldova lacks strategic depth; if it does not organize and enact a strong resistance to a Russian invasion—which should actually be feasible given the limited combat forces Russia could readily bring to bear in Moldova assuming Odesa does not fall—Chisinau will have nothing left than capitulate. Moldova's total capitulation would have significant effects not only for itself, but for NATO as well. Given its proximity to NATO borders, and shared language

222 | BLACK SEA BATTLEGROUND

and culture with EU and NATO member Romania, Moldova would likely become a highly effective operational hub for Russia's further strategic actions against the Euro-Atlantic alliance's southeastern front.

8.

Referee and Goalkeeper of the Turkish Straits: The Relevance and Strategic Implications of the Montreux Convention for Conflict in the Black Sea

John C. K. Daly

May 10, 2022

On February 24, 2022, in an early-morning televised address at 5:55 Moscow time, Russian President Vladimir Putin announced a "special military operation" to "demilitarize" and "denazify" Ukraine, which began minutes later. The massive assault caught Western politicians by surprise and immediately raised questions about how the North Atlantic Treaty Organization (NATO) might assist Ukraine, even though the latter is not yet a member of the 30-country alliance. It was almost immediately realized that navigation issues pertaining to the Black Sea basin—on the one hand, freedom of access to this body of water for Ukraine's Euro-Atlantic partners, and on the other hand, blocking the Russian navy's comings and goings—would be a crucial pillar of this Western support to Kyiv.

224 | BLACK SEA BATTLEGROUND

The sole maritime passage between the Black Sea and the Mediterranean is collectively known as the Turkish Straits, a 164-nautical-mile channel consisting of the Bosporus and Dardanelles straits and the inland Sea of Marmara, which lies between them. NATO member Turkey exercises total sovereignty over the Straits, but its ability to regulate maritime traffic across them is conscribed and defined by the 1936 Montreux Convention Regarding the Regime of the Straits, frequently referred to simply as the Montreux Convention. The Montreux Convention's articles clearly differentiate between commercial shipping and warships; in peace time, the former are allowed unhindered free passage, while the latter are subjected to numerous restrictions, including whether the naval vessels belong to Black Sea riparian countries or are foreign. The Montreux Convention is weighted heavily in favor of the fleets of Black Sea riparian nations.

In the new regional maritime environment of the Russian-Ukrainian conflict, earlier calls for reconsideration and possible modification of the 86-year-old treaty, including surprisingly from some Turkish politicians, have reemerged. Yet, more immediately, days after Russia began its "special military operation" against Ukraine, the Turkish government chose to exercise its treaty right to unilaterally close the Straits to naval traffic. And that decision has had critical implications for the further course of the war.

A Brief History of Conflict in and Around the Turkish Straits

The Eastern Mediterranean and the Turkish Straits have been fought over for millennia, with the Montreux Convention representing an early 20th-century diplomatic effort to constrain such conflicts. One of Europe's first great literary works, *The Iliad*, written down around the 8th century BCE and credited to the Greek oral poet Homer, tells how King Agamemnon of Mycenae led an alliance of Greek city-states to undertake a decade-long siege of Troy, a prosperous walled city situated in Asia Minor at the entrance to the Dardanelles. Long thought to be fiction, an artificial mound at Hisarlık, now roughly 4 miles (6.5 kilometers) equidistant from the Aegean and the Dardanelles, which was first excavated in the mid-19th century by amateur archeologist Heinrich Schliemann, has been put forward as the historical site of Troy. Though debate on this topic continues to rage on in the academic literature.

Three centuries after the chronicling of *The Illiad*, in 492 BC, Persian king Darius the Great launched his empire's first invasion of Greece, intended to punish the city-states of Athens and Eretria for supporting Ionian cities against Persian rule. The Greek historian Herodotus in his *Histories* recounts how Darius' military engineers constructed a half-mile floating bridge across the Bosporus to permit his troops to cross from Anatolia into Thrace to begin their march on Greece. Herodotus subsequently notes that in 480 BC, Darius' son Xerxes I prepared for the second Persian invasion of Greece by ordering two pontoon bridges built across the Hellespont (Dardanelles) to allow his army similar passage.

Two millennia later, control of both the Dardanelles and Bosporus would prove crucial in the Ottoman campaigns, first to capture Constantinople and subsequently to invade Eastern Europe and the Balkans. In the mid-14th century, during the civil war over Byzantine succession, claimant John Kantakouzenos (later Byzantine Emperor John VI) concluded an agreement with Ottoman Beylik ruler Orhan Ghazi for military support. Orhan subsequently crossed the Dardanelles and ravaged Thrace, permanently establishing an Ottoman military presence in Europe, despite Emperor John VI's subsequent requests that he withdraw.

On May 29, 1453, troops of Ottoman Sultan Mehmet II, subsequently known as *Fatih* ("the Conqueror"), stormed and captured Constantinople, extinguishing the Byzantine Empire and establishing a permanent Turkish presence in Europe. Prior to besieging Constantinople's land walls, Mehmet had his

226 | BLACK SEA BATTLEGROUND

engineers construct fortifications at Rumeli Hisarı, just north of the great city on the western shore of the Bosporus Strait.[1]

The Rumeli Hisar was deliberately built next to the Strait's narrowest point, only 2,170 feet (660 meters) across. Also known in Turkish as Boğazkesen ("cut-throat,"), the epithet emphasized the military structure's tactical importance for closing the channel, as its enfilading artillery's field of fire interlinked with its opposite, Anadolu Hisarı. The latter, eastern fort was built in 1393–1394 by Ottoman Sultan Bayezit I, in preparation for his own, failed siege on Constantinople; it is the oldest surviving Turkish architectural structure built in Istanbul on the Bosporus' Anatolian coast.[2]

In 1453, the two completed fortifications' interlocking artillery fire effectively closed the channel to incoming assistance for Constantinople from Genoa's Black Sea colonies. Mehmet's victory reverberated throughout Christendom and began a period of Ottoman domination of the Turkish Straits that would survive until the end of World War I and the fall of the Ottoman Empire. Two decades after the Ottoman capture of Constantinople, in 1477, Gedik Ahmet Pasha conquered the Crimean Peninsula, which would effectively turn the Black Sea into an Ottoman lake for more than two centuries, until Russia became strong enough to contest Turkish suzerainty there.

Even prior to building Rumeli Hisarı, Sultan Mehmet further sought to tighten Ottoman nautical control of the Straits and isolate Constantinople by constructing the Kilidülbahir fort on the European shore of the Dardanelles in 1452. But this stronghold's Anatolian counterpart, Seddulbahir, was only erected two

---

[1] "Mimarlık Müzesi koleksiyonunda Rumeli Hisarı," Mimarlık Müzesi, İstanbul, [n.d.],
https://web.archive.org/web/20060118093405/http://www.mimarli
kmuzesi.org/biyografi.asp?id=10075.
[2] "Mimarlık Müzesi koleksiyonunda Anadolu Hisarı," Mimarlık Müzesi, İstanbul, [n.d.],
https://web.archive.org/web/20060118084123/http://www.mimarli
kmuzesi.org/biyografi.asp?id=10016.

Referee and Goalkeeper of the Turkish Straits | 227

centuries later, in 1659, in response to the rival Venetians occupying the Eastern Mediterranean islands of Lemnos and Tenedos, at the entrance to the Dardanelles, three years earlier.

In 1695, geopolitical concerns led Russian Tsar Peter I (later given the epithet "the Great") to attack the Ottoman fortress at Azov, on the Don River, which flowed into the Sea of Azov, the northeastern appanage of the Black Sea. While the assault failed, the tsar returned the following year with a hastily constructed galley fleet; the date is commemorated as the beginning of the Russian navy. Even though the 1696 assault captured Azov, the Russians had to return it in the subsequent peace settlement. The Azov campaign represented the first of the Russian Empire's eventual 11 conflicts with the Ottoman Empire, which ended only when World War I destroyed them both. It fell to Peter's successor, Empress Catherine II (also later called "the Great"), to make Russia a Black Sea power. Her victories during her war with the Ottomans, 1768–1774, allowed Russia to gain access to the Black Sea by annexing what is now southern Ukraine, where her government founded Odesa, Mikolaiv and Kherson. Centuries later, these settlements became key front-line cities in the Kremlin's 2022 attack on Ukraine.

Catherine II's war against the Ottoman Empire ended with the 1774 Treaty of Küçük Kaynarca, whose favorable terms for Russia included territory encompassing Azov, Kerch, Yenikale, Kinburn and the Black Sea coast delineated between the Dnipro and Bug rivers. The Russian victory also ended restrictions on its naval and merchant shipping in the Sea of Azov, granted Russia the right to petition on behalf of Orthodox Christians under Ottoman rule and, lastly, made the Crimea Peninsula a Russian protectorate. Tsarina Catherine dropped all pretense, however, and annexed Crimea nine years later, the same year in which the future Black Sea Fleet base of Sevastopol was founded in the finest deep-water port on the Black Sea.

Russian influence over the Ottoman Empire would reach its zenith with the bilateral Treaty of Hünkâr İskelesi. Signed on July 8, 1833, the document rewarded Russia for having dispatched its Black Sea Fleet and troops to defend Constantinople from an

228 | BLACK SEA BATTLEGROUND

Egyptian army threatening to overthrow the Ottoman Empire. When government officials questioned the Sultan as to why he accepted assistance from his Empire's traditional enemy, Mahmud II reportedly replied, "A drowning man will clutch at a serpent." Under the terms of the treaty, valid for eight years, both the Bosporus and Dardanelles could be closed to foreign warships if Russia requested it. Superseded by the July 1841 London Straits Convention, signed by Russia, the United Kingdom, France, Austria and Prussia, the new treaty reaffirmed the "ancient rule" of the Ottoman Empire by closing the Turkish Straits to all warships during wartime except those of the Ottoman sultan's allies. Efforts around that time by Tsar Nicholas I to achieve a European consensus over the "Eastern Question"—what to do if the Ottoman Empire, the "sick man of Europe," declined further— were rebuffed.

The new diplomatic pact failed to dispel the cloud of suspicion surrounding the aforementioned 1833 Hünkâr İskelesi agreement when the Crimean War erupted in October 1853, after the Ottoman Empire declared war on Russia. Five months earlier, in May 1853, with armed conflict seemingly inevitable, commander of Russia's Black Sea Fleet, Admiral Vladimir Kornilov, had drawn up a "cruising program between the Bosporus and Sevastopol" and advocated for a preemptive strike on the Bosporus. In the wake of Russia's November 1853 naval victory at Sinop, on Turkey's Black Sea coast, the British and the French fleets entered the Black Sea in January 1854 to forestall a seemingly likely Ottoman collapse. By September, the Anglo-French fleet landed troops in Crimea to besiege Sevastopol and destroy the Black Sea Fleet. Kornilov had vociferously argued for sending the Black Sea Fleet to attack the Anglo-French at sea but was overruled by his superior, Prince Alexander Menshikov, who called for scuttling Russian naval force in Sevastopol to defend the harbor. The Western European powers' siege of Sevastopol lasted 349 days, until the city's capture shortly before the war ended in March 1856, with the Treaty of Paris.

The victors imposed a harsh peace on the Russians; the treaty proclaimed the Black Sea as neutral, closing it to all warships and prohibiting coastal fortifications, which effectively neutralized

Russia's Black Sea naval efforts since the time of Peter the Great. With Russia forbidden to have a naval presence in the Black Sea basin, the treaty thus nullified the strategic importance of Sevastopol as a naval port. Russia would chafe under the terms of the treaty until France's defeat in the 1870–1871 Franco-Prussian War, when diplomatic support from the new German Empire, combined with a more moderate diplomatic approach by a humbled France, allowed Russia to denounce the Treaty of Paris restrictions and begin to rebuild its Black Sea naval presence.

Naval events in the Straits at the outset of World War I were instrumental in persuading the initially neutral Ottoman Empire to join the German and Austro-Hungarian side. On August 3, 1914, after war was declared, the German Kaiserliche Marine Mediterranean Division's Moltke-class battlecruiser SMS *Goeben* and Magdeburg-class light cruiser SMS *Breslau*, then at the Austrian Navy's Adriatic Pola base, dropped plans to return to Germany and instead set sail for Constantinople; the decision followed secret German negotiations with Ottoman War Minister Enver Paşa. After the elderly and outgunned British 1st Cruiser Squadron declined to engage the German pair, they arrived at the Dardanelles on August 10. As the Ottoman Empire was still officially neutral, to circumvent neutrality regulations, the German government generously offered to "gift" the ships to the Ottoman Navy. On August 16, renamed *Yavuz Sultan Selim*, SMS *Goeben* became the flagship of the Ottoman Navy and SMS *Breslau* became *Midilli*.[3]

Swapping out their German uniforms for Ottoman ones and fezes, in November 1914, both ships' crews led a squadron across the Black Sea to bombard the Russian fleet and Russian Black Sea ports, resulting in British and Russian declarations of war on the Ottoman Empire.

---

[3] Ersan Bas, *Muavenet-i Milliye ve Goliath'in Batirilişi*, İstanbul Deniz Müzesi, [n.n.], pp.12.
https://denizmuzesi.dzkk.tsk.tr/dmk/upload/files/201611/58353023 88c7a-1479880739.pdf.

230 | BLACK SEA BATTLEGROUND

The next year opened with a disastrous British naval campaign designed to knock the Ottoman Empire out of the war, hinging on the Royal Navy forcing the Dardanelles open and capturing Constantinople. On March 18, 1915, a combined Anglo-French squadron entered the Dardanelles, only to retreat due to heavy artillery fire and mines, which sank three battleships and heavily damaged three more. Even though the incursion alerted the Ottoman government to Allied intentions, the United Kingdom two months later launched the ill-fated Gallipoli campaign, nearly within sight of the fabled ruins of Troy. By the time the British withdrew after eight months, the bloody land campaign had claimed over a third of a million men, either killed or wounded.[4]

When the Armistice ended World War I in November 1918, four European empires had been destroyed: the Austro-Hungarian, German, Ottoman and Russian, with hastily assembled new nation-states arising from the rubble. The Paris Peace Conference produced both the 1919 Treaty of Versailles and the 1920 League of Nations, followed by the 1922 Washington Naval Treaty, all intended to produce a more just postwar world and diminish the chances for yet another global conflagration. Complicating these laudable intentions, the next two decades would see the rise of fascism in Italy and Germany as well as a redrawn map of the Middle East, with the UK and France establishing protectorates there even as a new Republic of Turkey was being forged in a nationalist war to repel foreign occupiers.

Antecedents of the Montreux Convention: The Sèvres and Lausanne Treaties

After World War I, international concerns over the Turkish Straits entwined with Turkish nationalists fighting foreign occupation. The Ottoman Empire began to fracture, assisted by the victorious

---

[4] "Çanakkale Savaşı 1915–1916," Tarihi Olaylar, [n.d.].
https://www.tarihiolaylar.com/tarihi-olaylar/canakkale-savasi-1915-1916-826#:~:text=%C3%87anakkale%20Sava%C5%9F%C4%B1%20(1915%2D1916).

Allies' plans for partitioning the "sick man of Europe." In August 1920, Ottoman government official signed the Treaty of Sèvres, which not only created occupation zones in the Empire but also directly ceded significant territories to the UK, France, Italy and Greece. The treaty also established a Zone of the Straits, under the control of the League of Nations' International Straits Commission, which would internationalize the Bosporus, Sea of Marmara and Dardanelles by permitting full navigation to warships and merchantmen of all countries in both peace- and wartime.

The Treaty of Sèvres, not surprisingly, outraged Turkish public opinion and ignited Turkish nationalists against both the decrepit Ottoman government and the foreign occupiers arriving under the treaty terms. A hero from the Gallipoli campaign, Mustafa Kemal Atatürk, led Turkish nationalists to defeat the Ottoman reactionaries and the foreign invaders during what came to be known as the Turkish War of Independence. Three years later, the 1923 Treaty of Lausanne modified or removed the most noxious terms of the Treaty of Sèvres. It created the internationally recognized sovereign Republic of Turkey on most of the Ottoman Empire's Anatolian territory populated by ethnic Turks, as well as restored the Straits to Turkish control under the condition that Turkey keep them demilitarized and allow all foreign warships and commercial shipping free passage.

The last condition angered Turkish patriots, and the new nationalist Turkish government under Atatürk, in developing a national security strategy, eventually rejected the noxious terms of the Treaty of Lausanne. Turkey subsequently remilitarized the Straits area over the following decade, much as the Russians in the previous century had repudiated the more onerous terms of 1856 Treaty of Paris, which had ended the Crimean War by abolishing Russian sea power in the Black Sea.

232 | BLACK SEA BATTLEGROUND

The Montreux Convention Regarding the Regime of the Turkish Straits

After protracted diplomatic negotiations between the World War I victors and the vanquished, full Turkish sovereignty over the Straits was formalized on July 20, 1936, in the Montreux Convention Regarding the Regime of the Turkish Straits. The conference was attended by the Union of Soviet Socialist Republics (USSR), Turkey, the United Kingdom, France, Bulgaria, Romania, Greece, Yugoslavia, Australia and Japan. The conference was convened at the suggestion of Turkey to revise the Convention on the Black Sea Straits, approved by the 1922–1923 Lausanne Conference. The United States was also invited to the conference that preceded the signing of the Convention but declined to participate and, consequently, was not a signatory.[5]

Three important positions needed to be balanced: the competing agendas of Turkey, the Soviet Union and the UK. Turkey, as the country with the longest Black Sea coastline, wanted to remilitarize the area and gain as much control over the Straits as possible; the USSR wanted unrestricted passage so that its Black Sea Fleet could access the Mediterranean; while the UK, ever concerned about the Suez Canal, its lifeline to India, in turn, wanted some limitations placed on potential Soviet influence in the Mediterranean. Not surprisingly, the accord ended up being a compromise between the three positions. The Soviet Union and a number of other states had not been able to agree to the terms of the Lausanne Conference and not only never ratified it, but continued to fight against it. For the opponents of the Lausanne Conference, the best element of the Montreux Convention was that it terminated the detested International Straits Commission, imposed by the Treaty of Sèvres.

Briefly put, Montreux, signed by the UK, Bulgaria, France, Greece, Japan, Romania, Turkey, the USSR and Yugoslavia, placed the Straits under sovereign Turkish control. The Convention treats the Straits as an international shipping lane, completely open to

---

[5] Devrim Yaylalı, "The Montreux Convention Regarding The Regime Of The Straits: A Turkish Perspective," *Turkishnavy.net*, April 27, 2014, https://turkishnavy.net/?s=Montreux.

commercial vessels, all the while delineating the rights of Black Sea riparian countries and their naval forces but allowing Turkey the right to restrict the naval traffic of non-Black Sea states.[6]

The Convention contains 29 articles, four annexes and one protocol. While Articles 2–7 cover the passage of merchant ships transiting the Turkish Straits, over half of the Conventions Articles 8–22, concern the passage of warships, separating them into Black Sea riparian and foreign vessels, giving the former significant rights and privileges. In peacetime, the Convention broadly guarantees the general right of warships of all countries to transit the Straits but with a bias toward the Black Sea riparian states of Turkey, Bulgaria, Romania and the Soviet Union. Foreign warships seeking passage may not have a displacement greater than 15,000 tons and may not remain in the Black Sea longer than 21 days, whereas Black Sea navies are exempt from those restrictions.

Three articles specifically modify the peace-time rules safeguarding warships' rights to transit during times of war: Articles 19, 20 and 21, all of which have garnered much attention since Putin began his assault on Ukraine.

Article 19 specifically regulates the passage of warships of belligerent powers through the Bosporus, Sea of Marmara and Dardanelles when Turkey is not a party to the war. Article 19 states that, at such times, "warships [not belonging to any of the respective warring parties] shall enjoy complete freedom of transit and navigation through the Straits" under the normal peacetime rules. However, the warships of belligerent states "shall not [...] pass through the Straits" except if a) one of the belligerents is acting under lawful collective defense rights obligations that Turkey is also a party to or b) any belligerent warship must pass through the Straits to return to its base.

---

[6] *1936 Convention regarding the Regime of the Straits*, Montreux, Switzerland, July 20, 1936, pp. 19, https://cil.nus.edu.sg/wp-content/uploads/formidable/18/1936-Convention-Regarding-the-Regime-of-the-Straits.pdf.

During the present Russo-Ukrainian conflict then, Russian Black Sea Fleet warships currently deployed outside the Black Sea could return northward through the Straits while Russian non-Black Sea Fleet warships currently operating in the Black Sea, such as the Baltic and Northern Fleet amphibious landing ships that arrived in early February 2022, could depart. However, no further transfers of Russian warships through the Straits would subsequently be permitted until the end of hostilities.

Article 20 applies when Turkey itself is involved in the conflict. In such cases, Turkey has complete discretion over all warship navigation through the Straits, and no state, whether Black Sea or non–Black Sea, then enjoys freedom of transit or navigation through the Straits without the Turkish government's express approval.

Article 21 applies a constrained interpretation of Turkey's Article 20 powers when Turkey "considers itself to be threatened with imminent danger of war." As with Article 20, such a circumstance would suspend operational peace-time regulations on a warship's passage. Unlike Article 20, Article 21 stipulates that warships separated from their bases by the Straits must generally be allowed to transit to return home. Furthermore, if Turkey invokes Article 21, it must notify other High Contracting Parties. As originally written in the 1936 text, if two-thirds of the "Council of the League of Nations" and half of the High Contracting Parties reject Turkey's measures as unjustified, Turkey's Article 21 invocation is suspended.

Finally, under Article 24 of the Montreux Convention, Turkey is required to supervise "the execution of all the provisions ... relating to the passage of vessels of war through the Straits."

Unlike in World War I, which it entered at the conflict's outset, Turkey remained neutral in World War II, until it declared war on February 23, 1945. It had strictly interpreted the Montreux Convention as affecting Nazi German warships, thus largely preserving the Black Sea as a low-grade theater of operations during the life-and-death struggle. Following its declaration of war on Germany, Turkey for the first time invoked the Montreux

Convention's Articles 5 and 20 and declared a "state of war," thus allowing it to ban German and Italian warships from using the Turkish Straits to gain access to the Black Sea. Despite this, the USSR in March 1945 denounced the 1925 Soviet-Turkish Treaty of Friendship and Neutrality, believing that Turkey had violated the Montreux Convention in May-June 1944 by surreptitiously allowing 13 Kriegsmarine auxiliary warships through the Straits under the guise of civilian ships after their armaments were partially removed before the passage and returned after it.[7]

In June and July 1945, following the Allied victory over Germany, the always opportunistic Joseph Stalin had Soviet Foreign Minister Viacheslav Molotov give the Turkish ambassador, Selim Sarper, a list of conditions he expected to be fulfilled. These included joint Turkish-Soviet control over the Straits, the provision of military bases in the Bosporus and Dardanelles to the Soviets, and the return of Kars and Ardahan districts to the USSR.[8]

Stalin also raised the question of the return of "territories legally belonging to the Soviet Union" as well as revising the Montreux Convention's terms during the "Big Three" Potsdam conference in Berlin in July–August 1945, in discussions with US President Harry Truman and British Prime Minister Winston Churchill. Stalin remarked,

> For the position of such a large state as Russia, the question of the Straits is of great importance. The Montreux Convention is wholly directed against Russia, it is a treaty hostile to Russia. Turkey has been granted the right to close the strait to our navigation, not only when there is a war, but also when it seems to Turkey that there is a threat of war, and the question of when this threat arises is decided by Turkey itself. Impossible position!

---

[7] " 'Lishit' Turtsiyu fakticheskogo kontrolya,' " *Kommersant*, June 19, 2021, https://www.kommersant.ru/doc/4866474.

[8] Роман Иванов, "Крест на Святую Софию. От Александра Освободителя до Иосифа Виссарионовича," *Военное обозрение*, 24 августа 2021, https://topwar.ru/186094-krest-na-svjatuju-sofiju-ot-aleksandra-osvoboditelja-do-iosifa-vissarionovicha.html.

Turkey can always feel that there is some kind of threat, and it can always close the Straits. [...] You think that a naval base in the Straits is unacceptable. Well, then give us some other base where the Russian fleet could be repaired, equipped and where it could, together with its allies, defend the rights of Russia. Here is how it goes. But to leave the situation as it is now is ridiculous. I finished.[9]

The British and Russian representatives agreed to look into the possibility of revising the Montreux Convention, perceived as not meeting the conditions of the time, through bilateral negotiations with the Turkish government; but Stalin had overreached.[10] Even as they verbally agreed on the need to review the Montreux Convention, Churchill and Truman diplomatically rejected all of the USSR's demands for bases in the Straits, along with Soviet claims to Turkish territory.

Stalin's imperious behavior at Potsdam, his aggressive pressure on Turkey, along with violations of the promises he made to his allies during the war, would eventually backfire in a spectacular manner. Within four years, Turkey would enter the North Atlantic Alliance. The enlargement of NATO subsequently led to the 1955 creation of its Eastern bloc counterpart, the Warsaw Pact. The deepening Cold War would, in turn, increase pressure on all Alliance members, particularly Turkey, that shared maritime and

---

[9] "Берлинская конференция. 17 июля – 2 августа 1945 г. Запись седьмого заседания глав правительств, 23 июля 1945 г., 17 час. 10 мин, Другие материалы Берлинской конференции, Советский Союз на международных конференциях периода Великой Отечественной войны 1941–1945 гг.: Сборник документов. Том VI. Берлинская конференция руководителей трех союзных держав – СССР, США и Великобритании [17 июля – 2 августа 1945 г.], Москва, Издательство политической литературы, 1984, pp.145–158, https://www-hist-msu-ru.translate.goog/ER/Etext/War_Conf/berlin08.htm?_x_tr_sch=http&_x_tr_sl=ru&_x_tr_tl=en&_x_tr_hl=en&_x_tr_pto=op,sc.
[10] Вадим Кулинченко, "Как Конвенция Монтрё определила порядок прохода судов и кораблей через черноморские проливы," Аргументы недели, 13 июля 2021, https://argumenti.ru/opinion/2021/07/730034.

land frontiers with the Soviet Union. Two months after Stalin's death, on May 30, 1953, the Soviet government, in a diplomatic note, renounced its former territorial claims on Turkey and demands on the Straits to strengthen "peace and security."[11]

The Cold War

Soviet naval developments in the 1960s began to raise Western concerns about the Montreux Convention's limitations on warships, particularly the potential transit through the Straits of Soviet aircraft carriers built at the USSR's most advanced naval shipyards in the Black Sea in Ukraine. In 1967, the Soviet navy commissioned what it termed to be not an aircraft carrier but an "anti-submarine cruiser" (*protivolodochnyy kreyser*), christened *Moskva*. Built in Ukraine's Nikolaev South (Shipyard No. 444) shipyard, *Moskva* and its sister ship *Leningrad* were not true aircraft carriers; instead of fixed-wing aircraft, they carried helicopters to detect submerged US and NATO submarines. While both vessels remained homeported in the Black Sea, the Turks allowed their deployment through the Straits a number of times, on the basis of their Soviet "cruiser" terminology, for voyages in the Mediterranean, the Atlantic and the Indian Ocean. The Soviet government made similar "cruiser" arguments in both 1976 and 1979, and in each instance, Turkey permitted the Soviet navy to pass several more advanced *Kiev*-class aircraft carriers through the Straits.

The Montreux Convention After the Dissolution of the USSR

The breakup of the Soviet Union devastated Moscow's Armed Forces, particularly the navy. Russian attempts to rebuild its naval forces were stymied by the fact that the Soviets' most advanced naval shipyards at Nikolaev (in Ukrainian, Mykolaiv) were now in

---

[11] Александр Самсонов, "Почему Сталин не взял Константинополь и Черноморские проливы,"
Военное обозрение, 19 апреля 2019), https://topwar.ru/156965-pochemu-stalin-ne-vzjal-konstantinopol-i-chernomorskie-prolivy.html.

a new country, Ukraine. Additional irritants in the newly evolving Russian-Ukrainian bilateral relationship quickly became the division of Black Sea warships among the pair and the future status of Sevastopol.

Ukraine became a party to the Montreux Convention in 1992.[12] Joining the treaty was not easy, as according to the Convention's Article 28, excepting the original signatories, it was open only to the accession of "any state that signed the Lausanne Peace Treaty of July 24, 1923." Kyiv eventually prevailed in breaking the deadlock by sending a diplomatic note to the government of the French Republic as the depositary of the Convention, stating that Ukraine, as a Black Sea riparian coastal state, considered itself a party to the 1936 Convention in accordance with international law on the basis of the institution of succession, a position ultimately accepted by the other signatories.

Soon thereafter, the 1994 United Nations Convention on the Law of the Sea (UNCLOS) prompted calls for a revision of the Montreux Convention. However, as Turkey is not a signatory to the UN treaty due to the Eastern Mediterranean country's longstanding dispute with Greece, the Montreux Convention has remained unaffected.[13]

In subsequent decades, as Russia's pressure on its neighbors grew, regional NATO aspirants Georgia and Ukraine heightened the Alliance's concerns about the security situation in the Black Sea. During the August 2008 Russian invasion of Georgia, Turkey briefly considered the size and number of US warships it would allow to enter the Black Sea through the Bosporus, when the George W. Bush administration requested the passage of hospital

---

[12] Сергій Мещеряк, "Про політико-правові інструменти," День, №182, 9 жовтня, 2018,
https://day.kyiv.ua/uk/article/podrobyci/pro-polityko-pravovi-instrumenty.

[13] "What does the Montreux accord say about closing Black Sea access to Russia?," TRT World, February 27, 2022,
https://www.trtworld.com/magazine/what-does-the-montreux-accord-say-about-closing-black-sea-access-to-russia-55083.

ships USNS *Comfort* and USNS *Mercy*, both converted oil tankers, displacing 69,360 tons apiece.[14]

Ankara quickly rejected the request under the terms of the Montreux Convention, as, even though they were hospital ships, USNS *Comfort* and USNS *Mercy* were US Navy vessels and, accordingly, would violate Montreux's size limits.[15] This was despite the fact that Turkey, as a NATO member, had supported Alliance programs to train and equip the Georgian Armed Forces. Georgia lost most of its fleet during the August 2008 war but has since provided its remaining bases for NATO ships to use.

The Istanbul Canal

The Istanbul Canal (*İstanbul Kanalı*) project, linking the Sea of Marmara and the Black Sea via a man-made route parallel to the Bosporus, introduced an element of uncertainty into Turkey's previously stalwart support for the Montreux Convention. The *İstanbul Kanalı* was initially described by Turkish President Recep Tayyip Erdoğan as his "crazy project," when he broached the concept on April 27, 2011, at the Istanbul Congress Center.[16] After letting it stay dormant for seven years, Erdoğan revived the project in 2018. Earlier, remarks by Erdoğan that the Istanbul Canal had "nothing to do with Montreux Convention," raised concerns in some quarters that Turkey was abandoning the treaty

---

[14] John C. K. Daly, "Analysis: Naval aspects of the South Ossetia confrontation," United Press International, August 21, 2008, https://www.upi.com/Energy-News/2008/08/21/Analysis-Naval-aspects-of-the-South-Ossetia-confrontation/52431219349503/.

[15] Sedat Ergin, "Türkiye'yi Karadeniz'de ABD ile Rusya arasında zorlu bir sınama bekliyor," *Hürriyet Gazeteci*, March 14, 2022, https://www.hurriyet.com.tr/yazarlar/sedat-ergin/turkiyeyi-karadenizde-abd-ile-rusya-arasinda-zorlu-bir-sinama-bekliyor-42015555.

[16] "İstanbul için 'çılgın'lık vakti!," *Habertürk Gazetesi*, 27.04.2011, https://www.haberturk.com/ekonomi/makro-ekonomi/haber/624917-istanbul-icin-cilginlik-vakti.

or somehow opening it up to revisions.[17] These anxieties have resurfaced periodically even though the construction of a canal adjacent to the Bosporus would do nothing to change the situation of the Dardanelles and the internal Sea of Marmara remaining un-bypassable choke points governed by Montreux.

The proposed Istanbul Canal, originally priced at $9.8 billion, would run to the west of the Bosporus, along a 28-mile (45-kilometer) route through the European part of the city. Despite Erdoğan's fervent support, the project has run into headwinds of rising and severe domestic opposition, along with the government's inability to find substantial investment, either domestic or foreign.

It is not a new idea: a canal connecting the Black Sea to the Sea of Marmara was first proposed in the 16th century during the reign of Sultan Suleiman the Magnificent, while in 1994, then–Prime Minister Bülent Ecevit announced a similar plan for a "second Bosporus."[18]

Resistance to Erdoğan's "crazy project" includes environmentalists who warn that building a canal could destroy local water supplies and the regional ecosystem, retired admirals concerned that the project would weaken Turkish sovereignty over the Straits as enshrined in the Montreux Convention and the liberal political opposition. Istanbul's popular Republican People's Party (CHP) mayor, Ekrem İmamoğlu, touted as a potential challenger to Erdoğan, is leading the campaign against the canal, criticizing it as an environmental catastrophe and a financial disaster. Its real cost, he notes, will be more than $75

---

[17] "Kanal Istanbul has nothing to do with Montreux Convention: Erdoğan," *Daily Sabah*, April 14, 2021, https://www.dailysabah.com/business/transportation/kanal-istanbul-has-nothing-to-do-with-montreux-convention-erdogan.
[18] John C. K. Daly, "Bosporus Bypass Canal - An Idea Whose Time Has Come?," oilprice.com, June 6, 2011, https://oilprice.com/Energy/Energy-General/Bosporus-Bypass-Canal-An-Idea-Whose-Time-Has-Come.html.

billion, not the $12.5 billion–15 billion assiduously promoted by Erdoğan.[19]

On April 1, 2021, 126 retired Turkish ambassadors released a statement castigating the project, warning that it could jeopardize the Montreux Convention and negatively affect Turkey's "absolute sovereignty" over the waterways.

> The Istanbul Canal will open the Montreux Convention for discussion. Atatürk's Turkey's greatest diplomatic success after the Treaty of Lausanne, the Montreux Convention, if opened to discussion, would lead to the loss of Turkey's absolute sovereignty over the Istanbul–Çanakkale [fort city guarding the Mediterranean Sea–side entrance to the Dardanelles] Straits and the Sea of Marmara. [...] Our ally, the USA, which is not a party to the Montreux Convention and sees the Convention as an obstacle to its entry to the Black Sea as it wishes, has been trying for years to eliminate Montreux or to make a new contract to which it will be a party. The Istanbul Canal [...] will serve the USA's purpose of opening Montreux to discussion. Opening the Montreux Convention for discussion will lead to Turkey imperiling its vital sovereignty and security advantages from the treaty, in short, a real survival problem, which may cause Turkey to lose all these gains. The Istanbul Canal, which will serve the interests of states with various ambitions on the Republic of Turkey, should be abandoned.[20]

Worse was yet to come: Three days after the retired ambassadors' declaration, an open letter appeared, signed by 104 retired

---

[19] Dorian Jones, "Controversy Growing in Turkey Over Erdogan's Massive Canal Project," *Voice of America*, January 15, 2020, https://www.voanews.com/a/europe_controversy-growing-turkey-over-erdogans-massive-canal-project/6182662.html.

[20] "126 emekli büyükelçiden Kanal İstanbul'a karşı bildiri!" *Haber7*, 01.04.2021, https://www.haber7.com/guncel/haber/3083587-126-emekli-buyukelciden-kanal-istanbula-karsi-bildiri.

admirals, further criticizing Erdoğan's megaproject for its alleged threat to the Montreux Convention. The admirals wrote,

> The Turkish Straits are one of the most important waterways in the world and have been managed according to multinational agreements throughout history. Montreux, which is the last of these treaties, protects Turkey's rights in the best way: It is not only a contract regulating the passage through the Turkish Straits but also a great diplomatic victory that completes the Lausanne Peace Treaty, which restored Turkey's full sovereignty over Istanbul, Çanakkale, the Sea of Marmara and the Straits. Montreux is the basic document of the security of the Black Sea riparian countries and is the convention that makes the Black Sea a sea of peace.
>
> Montreux is a convention that prevents Turkey from unintentionally entering the war on the side of one of the warring parties in any war. Montreux enabled Turkey to maintain its neutrality in World War II. For these and similar reasons, we believe that all kinds of discourses and actions that may cause the Montreux Convention, which has an important place in Turkey's survival, to be discussed/to be brought to the table, should be avoided.[21]

The admirals' mutiny caused an uproar among Justice and Development Party (AKP) government officials, who said it harkened back to coup times of Turkey's past; as such, several signatories were subsequently arrested. Nevertheless, the opposition seems to have had an effect, as the day after the admirals' letter appeared, as part of his ongoing efforts to drum up foreign investment for his Istanbul Canal project, Erdoğan remarked, "Turkey does not currently intend to withdraw from the Montreux Convention," adding that his government would

---

[21] "103 emekli amiralden Montrö ve Atatürk devrimleri bildirisi," *Cumhuriyet Gazetesi*, 4 Nisan 2022, https://www.cumhuriyet.com.tr/haber/103-amiralden-montro-ve-ataturk-devrimleri-bildirisi-1825515.

continue to implement the agreement until it found an opportunity to "improve" it.[22]

Erdoğan's bland assurances about Montreux Convention did not convince Putin. Five days after Erdoğan promoted his Istanbul Canal project, the Russian president had a telephone conversation with him, during which Putin remarked that, despite Turkey's intention to build the Istanbul Canal, it was critical to preserve the 1936 Montreux Convention Regarding the Regime of the Straits, as it was integral to ensuring regional stability and security.[23]

Seemingly oblivious to domestic and international criticism, on June 26, 2021, Erdoğan officially inaugurated the *İstanbul Kanalı* venture, whose projected cost had now risen to an estimated $15 billion. The success of Erdoğan's latest mega-project currently seems problematic at best. He has launched it at a time when the Turkish economy faces many challenges. Turkey's tensions with the European Union and the United States as well as its record-high levels of foreign debt have so far deterred most Turkish and foreign lenders from the project.

Russian Invasion of Ukraine and the Role of the Straits in 2022

"It is a wide road that leads to war, but only a narrow path leads home again." – Russian proverb

---

[22] "Туреччина поки не має наміру виходити з конвенції Монтре," Ірфакс-Україна інформаційне Агентство, 05.04.2021, https://interfax.com.ua/news/general/735416.html.
[23] "Телефонный разговор с Президентом Турции Реджепом Тайипом Эрдоганом," События, 9 апреля 2021 года, Администрация Президента России 2022 год, http://kremlin.ru/events/president/news/65338.

244 | BLACK SEA BATTLEGROUND

The Run-Up to the War

With 20/20 hindsight, perhaps the most startling aspect of Putin's February 24, 2022, assault on Ukraine was how foreign intelligence, particularly those in the US, the UK and NATO, all reported on the months-long buildup of Russian forces on its territory with Ukraine, as well as naval deployments to the Black Sea region. Government officials and analysts even had access to commercial satellite imagery that tracked the seemingly relentless massing of Russian forces. Putin and Russian Defense Minister Sergei Shoigu repeatedly dismissed Western concerns by stating that the military buildup was only in preparation for long-planned military exercises. A further element downplaying the intelligence was that the expected day for the beginning of Russia's military operation was repeatedly delayed.

Continuing its policy of *maskirovka* about Putin's true intentions, the Russian Ministry of Defense announced on January 20 the start of a series of naval maneuvers involving more than 140 ships and vessels and over 10,000 military personnel. The exercises, under the general supervision of the commander-in-chief of the Russian Military-Maritime Fleet (*Voyenno-Morskoy Flot*—VMF), Nikolai Evmenov, would be held in waters adjacent to Russian territory as well as operationally important ocean areas, including the Mediterranean, Arctic and Sea of Okhotsk, in the northeastern Atlantic and Pacific. Ten days later, the secretary of the Security Council of the Russian Federation, Nikolai Patrushev, repeated that Russia supposedly does not want to fight with Ukraine and that there was no threat from Moscow.[24]

Ironically, the week before the Russian Ministry of Defense announced its upcoming naval drills, a conference on planning the 2022 Ukrainian-US Sea Breeze exercise was held in Odesa.[25] The

---

[24] "Отряд десантных кораблей ВМФ РФ проследовал через Босфор в Черное море," *Интерфакс*, 9 февраля 2022, https://www.interfax.ru/world/820975.

[25] "Сі-Бриз-2022: прикордонники візьмуть участь у морській, сухопутній та авіаційній компонентах," Державна прикордонна

2021 iteration of these exercises was the largest in more than 20 years, involving 32 warships, 40 aircraft and 5,000 personnel from 17 NATO member states and partners. More than 60 countries and international organizations were invited to participate in the 2022 exercise.[26]

That said, prescient observers warned of the consequences before the conflict began. Four days before the outbreak of hostilities, Ukraine's ambassador to Turkey, Vasil Bodnar, observed that Russia's aggressive actions toward Ukraine since 2014 effectively destroyed regional cooperation in the Black Sea, in particular within the framework of the Organization of the Black Sea Economic Cooperation (BSEC) and the Black Sea Naval Cooperation Group (BLACKSEAFOR). Bodnar said,

> We had not only the BSEC, but also the BLACKSEAFOR format, which created a security environment in the region and created conditions for interaction and trust between the fleets. Since 2014, this has become impossible. We cannot take part in events where there is a Russian fleet. The situation is the same with Georgia, which does not recognize the Russian occupation and still has no diplomatic relations with Russia since 2008.[27]

Bodnar presciently concluded, "The situation in the region is already unstable, and decisive action must be taken to prevent it from escalating into an armed conflict."[28]

служба України, 13 січня 2022, https://dpsu.gov.ua/ua/news/si-briz-2022-prikordonniki-vizmut-uchast-u-morskiy-suhoputniy-ta-aviaciyniy-komponentah/.

[26] "Сі-Бриз-2022: прикордонники візьмуть участь у морській, сухопутній та авіаційній компонентах," Адміністрація Державної прикордонної служби України, 13 січня 2022, https://www.kmu.gov.ua/news/si-briz-2022-prikordonniki-vizmut-uchast-u-morskij-suhoputnij-ta-aviacijnij-komponentah.

[27] "Rosiya ahresyvnymy diyamy znyshchyla rehional'nu spivpratsyu u Chornomu mori – posol," *Ukrinform*, February 20, 2022, https://www.ukrinform.ua/rubric-world/3407854-elizaveta-ii-zarazilasa-koronavirusom.html.

[28] "Rosiya ahresyvnymy diyamy," *Ukrinform*, February 20, 2022.

246 | BLACK SEA BATTLEGROUND

On January 30, 2022, General (ret.) Benjamin Hodges, former commander of US Army Europe, stated during a UK-based *LBC* channel broadcast that rising tension between Russia and Ukraine had an "80 percent chance" of erupting into a full-blown conflict by the end of February. Hodges offered his views on changing the military dynamics in the Black Sea and the possible role that the Montreux Convention could play in ameliorating the violence, commenting, "Actually, there is a trump card that we can use against Russia, but we do not use. This is Turkey's control over the Straits. Turkey has legitimate reasons to close the straits to Russian military ships if we establish the right relationship with our Turkish allies to make sure they are not subject to Russian backlash." When queried if the issue had been raised with Turkey, Hodges replied, "I asked US National Security Advisor Jack Sullivan about this two weeks ago. As far as I understand, they are talking about this with our allies."[29]

The Turkish government, however, denied Hodges' observations as well as subsequent public assertions that Russia had violated the Montreux Convention by passing warships through the Straits; Ankara plainly rejected recommendations on social media that the Turks should close the Straits to Russian warships because of the purported infractions. Turkish diplomatic sources, meanwhile, strongly asserting that there were no negotiations with the US on the Montreux Convention, that all maritime passages through the Turkish Straits until then had strictly adhered to the Montreux Convention's stipulations and that Turkey's stance had not changed.[30]

With tensions rising, two days before the outbreak of war, Erdoğan offered to host a face-to-face summit between Putin and

---

[29] Aurora Bosotti, "Russia-Ukraine row in '80% chance' of erupting into all-out war 'Only Germany can stop it,'" *The Daily Express*, January 30, 2022, https://www.express.co.uk/news/world/1557787/Russia-Ukraine-war-warning-US-Army-Europe-Ben-Hodges-Germany-vn.
[30] Huseyin Hayatsever, "Rusya-Ukrayna gerilimiyle birlikte Batı, gözünü boğazlara çevirdi," *Cumhuriyet Gazetesi*, 15 Şubat 2022, https://www.cumhuriyet.com.tr/turkiye/rusya-ukrayna-gerilimiyle-birlikte-bati-gozunu-bogazlara-cevirdi-1908023.

his Ukrainian counterpart, President Volodymyr Zelenskyy, or a "technical meeting" between Ukrainian and Russian officials. Turkey's offer was perceived by some observers as no more than an image-building exercise for Erdoğan, whose domestic standing was deteriorating amid domestic economic turmoil. At the same time, Russia notably supplies nearly half of Turkey's natural gas and two-thirds of its wheat imports—surely an important consideration for Ankara.[31]

February 24—Putin's 'Special Military Operation' Begins

Despite being heavily outgunned, the Ukrainian Armed Forces were in a stronger position on the eve of Putin's declared invasion, on February 24, 2022, than they were in their initial encounter with Russia eight years earlier. Since its 2014 loss of Crimea to a Russian military invasion and subsequent occupation as well as annexation, Ukraine tripled its defense budget and strove to modernize its military, not only to defend against Russia but also to comply with NATO's entrance standards.[32]

On February 24, Ukraine sent Turkey an official request to implement the Montreux Convention. A number of media outlets mistakenly then reported that Turkey had acceded to the request.[33]

The Russian large-scale offensive elicited an immediate response the same day from NATO Secretary-General Jens Stoltenberg, who said that North American and European alliance members had already deployed thousands more troops to eastern NATO

---

[31] Nazlan Ertan, "Erdogan calls Russia's recognition of Ukrainian breakaways 'unacceptable,'" *Al-Monitor*, February 22, 2022, https://www.al-monitor.com/originals/2022/02/erdogan-calls-russias-recognition-ukrainian-breakaways-unacceptable.

[32] Frank Ledwidge, "The insurgency to come in Ukraine," *The Asia Times*, February 26, 2022. https://asiatimes.com/2022/02/the-insurgency-to-come-in-ukraine/.

[33] "Туреччина закриває Босфор і Дарданелли для військових кораблів," Укрінформ, 27.02.2022, https://www.ukrinform.ua/rubric-world/3415014-tureccina-zakrivae-bosfor-i-dardanelli-dla-vijskovih-korabliv.html.

248 | BLACK SEA BATTLEGROUND

member states and had placed more on standby, remarking: "We have over 100 jets [on] high alert protecting our airspace and more than 120 allied ships at sea from the high north to the Mediterranean. [...] We will continue to do whatever is necessary to shield the alliance from aggression."[34]

Despite Stoltenberg's forceful assertions, the reality is that, over the past several years, visits by NATO warships (from non-littoral member states' navies) to the Black Sea have been quite irregular. In 2019 and 2020, no NATO warships visited the Black Sea. In 2021 the number of NATO naval vessels visiting the Black Sea surged to 31, the same number as in 2014 and the highest annual level since Russia occupied Crimea. Ships from the US 6th Fleet, headquartered in Naples, accounted for 13 of this number, followed by Spain (5), the UK (3), Italy (3), Greece (3), France (3) and the Netherlands (1).[35]

Starting in November 2021 and continuing to the end of the year, there was an uptick in NATO activity in the Black Sea, as five non-littoral Alliance members' warships passed the Straits to operate there for 21 days under the Montreux Convention's terms—four from the US Navy's 6th Fleet and one French warship. These were the USS *Porter* (DDG 78) and USS *Arleigh Burke* (DDG 51) guided missile destroyers, the USS *John Lenthall* (T-AO-189) oiler, the 6th Fleet's flagship and command ship USS *Mount Whitney* (LLC 20), and the French Navy's FS *Auvergne* (D 654).[36]

---

[34] "Press briefing by NATO Secretary General Jens Stoltenberg following an extraordinary meeting of the North Atlantic Council," *NATO*, February 24, 2022, https://www.nato.int/cps/en/natohq/opinions_192408.htm.

[35] Тетяна Гучакова, Андрій Клименко, Ольга Корбут, "Перешкоди судноплавству в Азовському морі. Моніторинг утримання суден в Керченській протоці на 1 грудня 2021," Інститут Чорноморських стратегічних досліджень, 11.12.2021, https://www.blackseanews.net/read/182620.

[36] "Перебування військових кораблів нечорноморських країн НАТО в Чорному морі у листопаді–грудні 2021 року," Інститут Чорноморських стратегічних досліджень, 14.12.2021, https://www.blackseanews.net/read/182759.

Despite the rise in regional Russian-Ukrainian tensions, the departure of NATO's last non-local warship, FS *Auvergne* (D654), from the Black Sea, on January 2, 2022, led Ukraine's Institute for Black Sea Strategic Studies to observe: "At the time when the Russian military threat to Ukraine has dramatically escalated in January 2022, warships of the non–Black Sea NATO have been absent in the Black Sea for 21 days, obviously increasing the risk of aggression from the sea over the holidays."[37] The Institute's data shows that beginning with Russia's aggression against Ukraine in 2014, the largest contributor to NATO's subsequent Black Sea deployments was provided by the 6th Fleet, undertaking 76 out of NATO's 191 warship visits since then, roughly 40 percent.

NATO's torpor and relative inaction was matched by a lack of signaled resolve from Washington as to its willingness to remain physically involved. During a press conference in Romania on October 20 with Romanian Minister of Defense Nicolae-Ionel Ciucă, US Secretary of Defense Lloyd Austin was asked, "What is the US commitment to the Black Sea region?" The Pentagon head's reply underscored the importance of Black Sea security to US interests while, conspicuously, avoiding any mention of plans to boost or maintain US presence there:

> Security and stability of the Black Sea are in the U.S. national interest and are critical to the security of NATO's Eastern Flank. It goes without saying that the region is vulnerable to Russian aggression, and we have seen evidence of that by ongoing actions in Eastern Ukraine, occupation of parts of Georgia, militarization of the Black Sea, and provocative actions in the air and at sea. I would go further and say that Russia's destabilizing activities in and around the Black Sea reflect its ambitions to regain a dominant position in the region and to prevent the realization of a Europe that is whole, free and at peace.

---

[37] "Перебування військових кораблів нечорноморських країн НАТО в Чорному морі за 2021 та у січні 2022," Інститут Чорноморських стратегічних досліджень, 14.12.2021, https://www.blackseanews.net/en/read/184110.

And so, again, the Black Sea region is in the U.S. national interest, and we will stay focused on it, and we will continue to work with our partners in the region.[38]

Complicating matters for NATO was the fact that the possibility of providing potential maritime assistance to Ukraine remained uncertain until Turkey clarified its position on the war. Since the onset of the conflict, Turkey upheld strict neutrality, even though the government was in fact considering its options to close the Straits under the Convention's articles. Speaking to journalists on February 20, while attending the Munich Security Conference, just days before the outbreak of hostilities, Turkish Defense Minister Hulusi Akar hedged his bets and noted that Turkey successfully fulfills all its responsibilities within NATO. "It is our most sincere wish that the countries bordering the Black Sea live there in comfort, safety and prosperity. In this sense, we also express here that the Montreux Convention is important, the necessary support should be provided, and the order provided by the Montreux Convention is beneficial for all parties."[39]

While NATO waited on the Turkish government's decision about the Straits, it had other maritime assets in its Black Sea coastal members Bulgaria and Romania, whose improvement had been closely noted by Russia. In November 2020, for example, Russian Navy Captain 1st rank Vasily Dandykin observed, "Romania, although one of the poorest countries in Europe, pays great attention to the development of its navy. They receive new corvette-class ships. Its own shipbuilding industry is developing,

---

[38] "Secretary of Defense Lloyd J. Austin III's Remarks at Romanian Ministry of Defense Post-Bilat Joint Press Event," Bucharest, U.S. Embassy in Romania, October 20, 2022, https://ro.usembassy.gov/secretary-of-defense-lloyd-j-austin-iiis-remarks-at-romanian-ministry-of-defense-post-bilat-joint-press-event/.

[39] "Milli Savunma Bakanı Akar, Münih'te gazetecilere değerlendirmelerde bulundu," Demirören Haber Ajansı, 20.02.2022, https://www.haberler.com/milli-savunma-bakani-akar-munih-te-gazetecilere-14746473-haberi/.

Referee and Goalkeeper of the Turkish Straits | 251

in contrast to Ukraine's. That is, the Romanian fleet today is objectively more powerful than the Ukrainian or Bulgarian."[40]

The first indication that a shift on Montreux in Ankara was possible came on February 26, 2022, when Turkish Foreign Minister Mevlüt Çavuşoğlu publicly evaluated Ukraine's request for assistance under the terms of the Convention, stating,

> In this critical period, we will implement all the Montreux Convention's articles to the letter, just as we did before. [...] The provisions of the Montreux Convention are very clear and precise. If Turkey is in a war, all the passages subsequently are completely under the control of Turkey. If Turkey is not a party to a war and there are warring parties, Article 19 clearly states it. This applies to the ships of warring countries. It authorizes Turkey to close the passage through the Straits, but again, Article 19 gives an exception. This applies not only to Russia, but to all littoral countries. This also applies to Ukraine.[41]

The Ukrainian president immediately expressed his gratitude, tweeting, "I thank my friend Mr. President of TR @RTErdogan and the people of TR for their strong support. The ban on the passage of RU warships to the Black Sea and significant military and humanitarian support for UA are extremely important today. The people of UA will never forget that!"[42] Both the Russian and Ukrainian governments were well aware that the Turkish

---

[40] Сергей Вальченко, "Капитан оценил возможность войны за Крым с Украиной и Турцией," *Московский Комсомолец*, 26.11.2020, https://www.mk.ru/politics/2020/11/26/kapitan-ocenil-vozmozhnost-voyny-za-krym-s-ukrainoy-i-turciey.html.

[41] "Dışişleri Bakanı Çavuşoğlu: Montrö Anlaşması'nı tüm maddeleriyle beraber bu kritik süreçte uygulayacağız," T24 Bağımsız İnternet Gazetesi, 26 Şubat 2022, https://t24.com.tr/haber/disisleri-bakani-cavusoglu-ndan-ukrayna-daki-turkiye-cumhuriyeti-vatandaslarinin-tahliyesine-iliskin-aciklama,1017478.

[42] Володимир Зеленський @ ZelenskyyUa, Twitter, 2/26/22, 8:27 AM, https://twitter.com/ZelenskyyUa/status/1497564078897774598?ref_src=twsrc%5Egoogle%7Ctwcamp%5Enews%7Ctwgr%5Etweet.

implementation of the Montreux Convention's Article 19—forbidding the passage of the warring parties' (that is, specifically Russia's and Ukraine's) warships through the Straits, except for the one-time return of ships to their home ports—could significantly impact Russian force projection into and from the Mediterranean. By activating Article 19, Turkey had effectively bottled up Russia's Syrian squadron (*eskadra*) on the south side of the Straits, preventing it from actively assisting operations in the Black Sea if the restrictions lasted for even a few weeks.

Events now began to move quickly. The next day, Çavuşoğlu appeared live on *CNN Türk* and officially announced that Turkey would exercise its sovereignty under terms of the Montreux Convention and restrict the passage of Russian warships into the Black Sea due to its "war" in Ukraine. Çavuşoğlu said that since Russia's unprovoked military "operation" had turned into a "war … under these conditions, we will apply the Montreux Convention. Article 19 is quite clear. At first it was a Russian attack, and we assessed it with experts, soldiers, lawyers. Now it has turned into a war. It is not a military operation; it is officially a state of war."[43] As noted above, according to Article 19, warships of belligerent states are not allowed to pass through the Straits. Despite the ban on passage, warships of warring states, both coastal and non-coastal, separated from their bases, may return to these bases. Nevertheless, Çavuşoğlu added, without explaining his government's legal reasoning further, that the passage plan not only included Russian warships but also Black Sea littoral and foreign naval units as well.[44]

Some had a more expansive view of the role of the Montreux Convention. The same day that Çavuşoğlu spoke, the director of

---

[43] "Dışişleri Bakanı Çavuşoğlu CNN TÜRK'te: Temennimiz kalıcı ateşkes," CNN Türk, 17:06, 27.02.2022, https://www.cnnturk.com/dunya/son-dakika-rusyanin-saldirilarinda-son-durum-rus-heyeti-muzakereler-icin-belarusta.

[44] Servet Uzun, "Son Dakika: Bakan Çavuşoğlu'ndan Montrö açıklaması: Tüm ülkeleri boğazlardan savaş gemisi geçirmemesi konusunda uyardık," Dünya, 28.02.2022, https://www.haberler.com/son-dakika-bakan-cavusoglu-ndan-montro-14763965-haberi/.

Ukraine's Center for Army Studies, Conversion and Disarmament, Valentin Badrak, remarked that not everyone views Turkish actions under the Montreux Convention as neutral. To him, it was a precursor to the formation of an anti-Russian alliance. According to Badrak, "The West is imposing sanctions on Putin and his circle, including Gen. [Valery] Gerasimov [the Russian chief of the General Staff]. Turkey has closed off the Bosporus and Dardanelles and does not let Russian warship into the Black Sea. Effectively, we are watching an anti-Putin coalition being formed."[45]

Even as Turkey exercised its sovereign right under the Montreux Convention, on March 1, 2022, Erdoğan's spokesperson İbrahim Kalın said, during an interview with *CNN Türk*, "We must act with our country's priorities in mind. There must be a party capable of negotiating with Russia. Who will talk to Russia when everyone burns bridges? We do not plan to impose sanctions to keep this channel open."[46]

Ankara now put its sovereignty over the Straits into action; the same day that Kalın spoke, Çavuşoğlu told national broadcaster *Habertürk TV* that Turkey had asked Russia not to request sending its warships through the Straits even before the Turkish government labeled Russia's "special military operation" invasion of Ukraine a "war" and implemented Article 19 of the Montreux Convention. Çavuşoğlu said, "Russia said four of its ships would cross the Straits on February 27–28, three of which are not registered to bases in the Black Sea. We told Russia not to send these ships, and Russia said the vessels would not cross the Straits. Nobody should be offended by this, because the Montreux

---

[45] Валентин Бадрак, "Под Путиным зашаталось кресло, или Что свидетельствует о желании президента РФ выйти из игры," *Главред*, 27 февраля 2022, https://opinions.glavred.info/pod-putinym-zashatalos-kreslo-ili-chto-svidetelstvuet-o-zhelanii-prezidenta-rf-vyyti-iz-igry-10347734.html.

[46] "Ukrayna'ya Rusya işgalinde Türkiye hangi adımları atacak? İbrahim Kalın CNN TÜRK'te," CNN Türk, 01.03.2022, https://www.cnnturk.com/video/turkiye/ukraynaya-rusya-isgalinde-turkiye-hangi-adimlari-atacak-ibrahim-kalin-cnn-turkte.

254 | BLACK SEA BATTLEGROUND

Convention is valid today, yesterday and tomorrow, so we will implement it."[47]

One immediate result of Turkey invoking Article 19 was to effectively maroon the Russian naval units concentrated off the coast of Tartus, Syria, which were tasked with deterring US and NATO carrier groups in the Eastern Mediterranean. At the same time, those Russian *eskadra* vessels could not pass northward through the Straits and augment Russian naval units assisting ground operations against Ukraine. The stranded ships included the Slava-class cruisers RTS *Marshal Ustinov* (055) and RFS *Variag* (011), two Udaloi-class destroyers, two guided-missile frigates, two Kilo-class diesel-electric attack submarines, a Buian-class corvette, two assault boats and a various auxiliary vessels—all effectively sidelined from participating in Ukrainian operations by Turkey's actions.[48]

While the Russian government was undoubtedly disappointed by Turkey's rejection of its request to pass the aforementioned quartet of warships into the Black Sea, it nevertheless was mindful of the Montreux Convention's similarly prophylactic potential to prevent a NATO naval "surge" into the Black Sea beyond the Convention's restrictions on non–Black Sea powers, further bolstering Moscow's consistent support for the treaty. On March 2, Russia's ambassador to Ankara, Aleksei Erkhov, stated during a television interview, "I have to say that we appreciate [Turkey's] stance toward the protection and compliance of the Montreux Convention, which is an important international law document. I believe that together we can come to a situation where all our interests and all our desires can come true."[49]

---

[47] "Dışişleri Bakanı Mevlüt Çavuşoğlu: 3 Rus gemisine izin vermedik," Habertürk TV, 01.03.2022, https://www.haberturk.com/son-dakika-disisleri-bakani-cavusoglu-dan-haberturk-tv-de-aciklamalar-3361267.
[48] Sam LaGrone, "Russian Navy Masses 16 Warships Near Syria," *USNI News*, February 24, 2022, https://news.usni.org/2022/02/24/russian-navy-masses-16-warships-near-syria.
[49] "Rus Büyükelçi: Türkiye'yi Montrö tutumu nedeniyle takdir ediyoruz," Habertürk TV, 02.03.2022, https://www.haberturk.com/rus-buyukelciden-turkiye-ye-tesekkur-3362485.

The Russian Assault From the Sea and Naval Losses

While initial media coverage focused on the Russian military's aerial and ground assaults, the conflict has also had a notable naval component. On February 27, 2022, the General Staff of the Ukrainian Armed Forces reported that the Russian military was expanding its maritime operations, which included at least two attempts to land on Ukraine's Black Sea coast. All were successfully repulsed, during which the Russian navy lost two boats and ships.[50]

Nevertheless, the Russian re-invasion has included attacks from the sea on Ukraine's Black Sea cities of Odesa, Ochakov and Mariupol. One of the first casualties in the conflict was the flagship of the Ukrainian Navy, the 30-year-old *Krivak*-class frigate *Het'man Sagaidachnii*, scuttled at the Nibulon ship repair plant in Mikolaiv, on February 24, to avoid being captured by the Russians.[51] In Russia's 2014 Crimea operation, *Het'man Sagaidachnii* avoided capture by being out of the theater of operations, returning from an international anti-piracy deployment off Somalia. Subsequently homeported in Odesa, after Ukraine lost Sevastopol, the frigate ended up at the Nibulon facility on July 2021, in preparation for an extensive refit that the Ukrainian Navy hoped would have given the ship another decade of useful service.[52]

---

[50] "Україна відбила дві спроби морського десанту РФ - Генштаб ЗСУ," *Діфенс Експрес*, 27 лютого 2022, https://defence-ua.com/news/ukrajina_vidbila_dvi_sprobi_morskogo_desantu_rf_gensh tab_zsu-6229.html.

[51] Анна Шиканова, "'Так треба.' Флагман ВМС 'Сайгадачний' підтопили в Миколаєві в перший день війни," РБК-Україна, 03 Березня 2022, https://www.rbc.ua/ukr/news/tak-nuzhno-flagman-vms-saygadachnyy-podtopili-1646343826.html.

[52] " 'Гетьман Сагайдачний' може 'застрягти' на ремонті на невизначений період," *Діфенс Експрес*, 15 лютого 2022, https://defence-ua.com/people_and_company/getman_sagajdachnij_mozhe_zastrjagti_na_remonti_na_neviznachenij_period-6130.html.

256 | BLACK SEA BATTLEGROUND

The conflict has also created logistical problems for Russian VMF warships operating in the Eastern Mediterranean. On March 5, 2022, five Russian naval vessels attempting to access refueling facilities in Limassol, Cyprus, were refused entry because of Russia's attack on Ukraine. Cyprus, in solidarity with all other European Union members, banned Russian ships from entering their ports. The Cypriot Foreign Ministry in Nicosia informed Russia with a *note verbale* that, due to the ongoing conflict in Ukraine, their bilateral agreement on providing facilities and mooring permits would be suspended until further notice.[53]

Three weeks into the war, Ukraine struck a significant blow against the Russian navy. On April 13, a Ukrainian concealed coastal missile battery fired two Neptune subsonic sea-skimming cruise anti-ship missiles at the Russian Black Sea Fleet's flagship, the 39-year-old Slava-class cruiser *Moskva* patrolling around 60 nautical miles south of Odesa, in the vicinity of Snake Island. While Ukraine maintained that its missiles struck the *Moskva*, Russia insisted that the warship was heavily damaged by fire, not a Ukrainian missile strike, before it sank while under tow in rough seas.[54] Reportedly, other Russian naval vessels operating in the area quickly moved further away from the Odesa coast.[55]

Summing up the Russian VMF's position in the Black Sea after the loss of the *Moskva*, on April 28, the British Ministry of Defense tweeted: "Approximately 20 Russian Navy vessels are currently in the Black Sea operational zone, including submarines. *The Bosporus Strait remains closed to all non-Turkish warships,*

---

[53] Annie Charalambous, "Cyprus forbids mooring of five Russian navy ships this week due to Ukraine war," *Philenews*, March 5, 2022, https://in-cyprus.philenews.com/cyprus-forbids-mooring-of-five-russian-navy-ships-this-week-due-to-ukraine-war/.

[54] "Voyennyye moryaki uvideli misticheskiy sled v potere kreysera 'Moskva,'" *Moskovskiy Komsomolets*, April 15, 2022, https://www.mk.ru/politics/2022/04/15/voennye-moryaki-uvideli-misticheskiy-sled-v-potere-kreysera-moskva.html.

[55] Heather Mongilio, "UPDATED: Russia Says Damaged Cruiser Moskva Sank Under Tow Headed to Black Sea Homeport," *USNI News*, April 13, 2022, https://news.usni.org/2022/04/13/russian-navy-confirms-severe-damage-to-black-sea-cruiser-moskva-crew-abandoned-ship.

rendering Russia unable to replace its lost cruiser Moskva in the Black Sea [Emphasis added]. Despite the embarrassing losses of the landing ship *Saratov* and cruiser *Moskva*, Russia's Black Sea Fleet still retains the ability to strike Ukrainian and coastal targets."[56]

Conclusion

Codified by the 1936 Montreux Convention, Turkish sovereign control over the Straits continues to the present, though not without significant challenges, both internal and external.

Whatever the eventual outcome of the Russian-Ukrainian conflict, it is likely to increase calls to revise the Montreux Convention, both within Turkey and beyond. The CHP (Kemalist) opposition party's leader, Kemal Kılıçdaroğlu, two days before the Kremlin launched its massive assault, reaffirmed his faction's continuing stalwart support for the nearly 90-year agreement in its current form, remarking at a party conference: "To explain what a betrayal it is to open the Montreux Convention for discussion: Montreux has an extremely important meaning for the security of the world. If someone who does not know history or cannot read the world opens Montreux for discussion, they should know the consequences."[57]

Between the ultimate fate of the Istanbul Canal and the aftermath of the Russian-Ukrainian war, an additional potential element for consideration in any possible revision of the Montreux Convention's articles will be the singularly unique naval advantage that Russia currently maintains over the other five Black Sea littoral states—namely, Moscow's ability to quickly

---

[56] Kirstie McCrum, "Twenty Russian warships and submarines gather in Black Sea, MOD reports," *Wales Online*, April 28, 2022, https://www.walesonline.co.uk/news/world-news/twenty-russian-warships-submarines-gather-23808668.
[57] "CHP lideri Kılıçdaroğlu'ndan Montrö uyarısı," Habertürk, 22 Şubat 2022, https://www.haberturk.com/son-dakika-chp-lideri-kilicdaroglu-ndan-aciklamalar-3352835.

supplement its naval forces in the Black Sea by bringing elements of the Caspian Flotilla in via the Volga–Don Canal, classified under international maritime law as a Russian "internal waterway." Notably, in a show of strength a week prior to the re-invasion, on February 17, about 20 Caspian Flotilla warships departed from their home port in Makhachkala, Dagestan, to the Black Sea basin participate in the Russian navy's global "Training Plan for the Armed Forces of the Russian Federation for 2022," whose opening exercises began in January.[58]

This advantage was demonstrated again during the present Russo-Ukrainian war, when Caspian Flotilla vessels launched 3M-54 *Kalibr* cruise missiles to support operations in Ukraine.[59] With an estimated range of around 932–1,553 miles (1,500–2,500 km), the missile has become a mainstay in the Russian VMF's ground-strike capabilities. Since the Volga-Don Canal is internationally recognized as an "internal Russian waterway," the Caspian Flotilla's maritime assets remain beyond the range of non-Caspian littoral navies' surface assets while allowing its warships to become mobile missile strike platforms with little fear of retaliation, as first evidenced in the Flotilla's 2016 Syrian *Kalibr* missile attacks to those more recently launched against Ukrainian targets.

Since World War II, the United States increasingly came to believe that the Montreux Convention has given an unfair advantage to,

---

[58] "Разнородная группировка корабельных сил Каспийской флотилии вышла в море для участия в плановом учении," Новости, Министерство обороны Российской Федерации, 17.02.2022, https://function.mil.ru/news_page/country/more.htm?id=12409275 @egNews.

[59] "Оперативна інформація станом на 10.00 27 лютого 2022 року щодо російського вторгнення," Генеральний штаб ЗСУ, Twitter, 27 лютого 2022, https://www.facebook.com/GeneralStaff.ua/posts/260463059600113

.

particularly, Soviet/Russian Black Sea naval forces.[60] And this issue has risen to the forefront yet again, as NATO and the US have struggled to figure out how to sufficiently supply and support Ukraine in its war against Russia as well as protect maritime security in the Black Sea basin.

Even though the US was not a signatory to the Montreux Convention, amendments could be pursued under the international legal practice of *"clausula rebus sic stantibus,"* one of the oldest norms of customary international law, which provides for the unenforceability of an international convention, agreement or treaty due to fundamentally changed circumstances.[61] Indeed, a variant of this doctrine is codified in Article 62 of the Vienna Convention on the Law of Treaties and is generally contained as a provision in individual treaties. Bolstering the argument that such an option could apply in this case, two of the signatory states since the Montreux Convention was signed have disappeared, fracturing into smaller, independent, sovereign countries—the Soviet Union and Yugoslavia.

Unrest in the Black Sea seems likely to continue as long as neo-imperial Russia maintains the means to fiercely block Ukraine's pro-European and pro-democratic course, on the one hand, and the transatlantic community preserves its political will to keep backing Kyiv, on the other. All the while, the Montreux Convention continues to play its dual roles as both referee and goalkeeper.

---

[60] See Bulent Gokcicek, *The Montreux Convention regarding the Turkish Straits and its importance after the South Ossetia war*, Naval Postgraduate School, Monterey, California, Masters thesis, March 2008, pp. xvi, 77, https://apps.dtic.mil/sti/pdfs/ADA496759.pdf.

[61] Elihu Lauterpacht, *International Law: Disputes, War and Neutrality, pts. IX-XIV*, Cambridge: CambridUniversity Press, 2004, pp. 804.

9.

Arsenal of Empire: Russian Naval Construction in Crimea and Its Implications for Black Sea Security

Ihor Kabanenko

June 3, 2022

Since occupying Crimea in 2014, Moscow has turned the peninsula into an enormous military base—a so-called "unsinkable aircraft carrier"—facilitating the projection of Russian military forces throughout the Black Sea basin and into the Eastern Mediterranean. But perhaps just as importantly, occupied Crimea has been built up as a regional industrial center for warship construction.

Immediately after the annexation of Crimea, Russian Defense Minister Sergei Shoigu announced his intention to enlist the entire production capacity of the local arms industry into fulfilling the state defense order of the Russian Federation.[1] In mid-April 2014, the Ministry of Defense, thus, compiled a list of 23 Crimean enterprises, including 10 shipbuilding and ship-repair companies, that should be redirected to producing military arms

---

[1] "Shoigu: Minoborony organizuyet zagruzku predpriyatiy OPK Kryma dlya vypolneniya gosoboronzakaza," *TASS*, April 4, 2014, https://tass.ru/politika/1097156.

Arsenal of Empire | 261

and equipment for Russia. All of these enterprises were duly commandeered by Moscow in the first months after Crimea's illegal seizure.[2]

The following chapter analyzes the militarization of the shipbuilding industry in Crimea and identifies problems that Crimean shipyards have faced since the occupation began in 2014. Moreover, it assesses the outcome of the shift in production from commercial construction to naval projects at Crimean shipyards, executed to meet Moscow's regional naval strategy, which has included laying down new Russian warships. Finally, the study outlines the policy implications for Ukraine and the West of these Russian actions in Crimea, including their impact on Russian naval power projection capabilities in the Black Sea region and beyond.

Historical Background of Russian Shipbuilding in the Black Sea

Following the Russo-Turkish War (1768–1774) and the signing of the Peace Treaty of Küçük Kaynarca, the Black Sea coastal territories between the Dnipro and Southern Bug rivers became part of the Russian Empire. By gaining access to the Black Sea, Moscow soon undertook the task of creating a Black Sea Fleet and built new ships for this force. This led to the creation of the Kherson Admiralty on the Dnipro Estuary in 1778, the goal of which was specifically to build sailing warships.[3] This Admiralty included a shipyard, management and support services, workshops and warehouses. In the same year, the city of Kherson was founded on the site of a military fortification that protected the construction site of the harbor and shipyard.

---

[2] Ivan Safronov, "Crimean industry is included in the arms race," *Kommersant*, (in Russian), April 14, 2014, https://www.kommersant.ru/doc/2452032.
[3] "Foundation of Kherson", *Litopis Khersona*, (in Ukrainian), https://www.library.kherson.ua/young/tavrica/litopys/lit_1.htm.

262 | BLACK SEA BATTLEGROUND

In 1784, after Tsarist Russia's annexation of Crimea, the Akhtiarskoye (later Lazarevskoye) Admiralty was formed on Akhtiarska Bay (present-day Sevastopol Bay).[4] In the 20th century, this Admiralty was restructured exclusively to handle the Soviet Black Sea Fleet's warships and repair its auxiliary vessels.

In 1788, the Mykolaiv Admiralty was created on a plot of land along the Inhul River, at its confluence with the Southern Bug River. In 1790, the city of Mykolaiv was founded on this site, with the main purpose of ensuring the construction of large warships for the Russian Black Sea Fleet and hosting the fleet's headquarters.[5] However, despite the serious shipbuilding capabilities of the Mykolaiv Admiralty, its facilities still could not satisfy the growing ambitions of the Russian Empire on the eve of the Russo-Turkish War of 1828–1829; Russia needed ships of the line with more than a hundred guns on board, but the narrow Inhul River in Mykolaiv as well as the shallow Dnipro Estuary in Kherson did not permit the construction of such sizeable vessels. Instead, Russian authorities looked to the deep-water Bug Estuary of Mykolaiv to build larger warships. The Spassky Admiralty was consequently created there in 1826. The Kherson Admiralty's services, teams and shipyard equipment were transferred from to the Mykolaiv Admiralty in 1829.

Mykolaiv became the *de facto* center of naval shipbuilding in Tsarist Russia by the middle of the 19th century. The indicators of intensity for ship of the line construction at Mykolaiv far exceeded the expectations of the shipyards in St. Petersburg, founded by Peter the Great. The Mykolaiv yards commissioned six ships

---

[4] Larisa Levchenko, "History of the founding of Mykolaiv and Sevastopol military governorship", *State Archives of the Mykolaiv district*, (in Ukrainian), https://lib.chmnu.edu.ua/pdf/naukpraci/history/1999/2-1-3.pdf.
[5] "Museum of Shipbuilding and Navy", *Mykolaiv Pravda* (in Ukrainian), http://www.nikpravda.com.ua/muzej-sudnobuduvannya-i-flotu/.

annually, on average,[6] whereas St. Petersburg built almost half that number.[7] One of the main reasons for this gap in labor productivity was St. Petersburg's cold and humid climate. Researchers note that the working conditions at the St. Petersburg's shipyards were difficult, especially during severe winter frosts, which led to a high mortality among workers[8] and numerous cases of personnel fleeing the area—sometimes in massive numbers.[9]

The growing appetite of Tsarist Russia regarding the size and number of warships led to the creation, in 1897, of a new Mykolaiv shipyard facility on the deep-water part of the Southern Bug: the Naval Shipbuilding Plant (hereafter, the Black Sea Shipbuilding Plant).[10]

The advantages of southern shipyards over those located in the north became even more obvious beginning in the 1930s, with the introduction of manual arc welding to Soviet shipbuilding. This is due to the fact that low temperatures had a significantly negative effect on the welding process—namely, the formation of hot and cold cracks in the metal seam. Because of this defect, the welded seam of a vessel hull could collapse and the metal would break.[11] The influence of temperature on the quality of a ship's welded seam remains relevant to this day. For example, automated

---

[6] Yurii Kryuchkov, "Sailing shipbuilding in Mykolaiv (1790-865)," *Naval* (in Russian), 2018, https://www.korabelhobby.com.ua/drawings/russian-books/3150-parusnoe-sudostroenie-v-nikolaeve.html.

[7] "St. Petersburg – the capital of Russian shipbuilding" (in Russian), https://helpiks.org/9-33396.html.

[8] Luppov S.P., "The history of the construction of St. Petersburg in the first quarter of the 18th century", *Nauka* (in Russian), 1957.

[9] Bernadsky V.N., Suknovalov A.E., "Historical past of Leningrad," *Uchpedgiz* (in Russian), 1958. — 255 pgs.

[10] Bugaevska U.A., "From the history of Mykolaiv`s Naval shipyard," *Mykolaiv district`s archive* (in Ukrainian), http://mk.archives.gov.ua/pubonsite/314-z-istorii-vykolaivskogo-zavodu-naval.html.

[11] "The first welded structures in shipbuilding," *Biblioteka mashinostroitelya* (in Russian), https://lib-bkm.ru/publ/19-1-0-1880.

264 | BLACK SEA BATTLEGROUND

submerged arc welding of a large warship's hull made from heavy-plate low-alloy steel grades can be performed at temperatures no lower than –10 degrees Celsius (14 degrees Fahrenheit).[12]

Two new shipyards were built in Crimea in 1938: the Zaliv Shipyard in Kerch, specializing in the assembly of torpedo boats, minesweepers, tugs and fishing trawlers, as well as the Yuzhnaya Tochka shipyard in Theodosia, for the production of torpedo boats (later this shipyard was named the Theodosia Production Association "Sea").[13]

Yet Mykolaiv continued to strengthen its leadership position in the serial construction of large-tonnage warships for the Soviet navy, the Military Maritime Fleet (*Voyenno-Morskoy Flot*—VMF). By the middle of the 20th century, this city's shipyards complex included:

- The shipyard named after 61 Communards (now Mykolaiv Shipyard), which in terms of shipbuilding facilities was approximately equal to the Baltic Shipyard in Leningrad (today's St. Petersburg), and concentrated on the production of frigates, destroyers and cruisers;
- The Black Sea Shipbuilding Plant—a supergiant facility that began to build aircraft-carrying ships in the 1960s, constructed the VMF's first anti-submarine helicopter carriers and then built heavy aircraft-carrying cruisers. In the early 1990s, plans called for building nuclear-powered aircraft carriers at this plant. No analogues to this shipyard exist in modern-day Russia;
- The Southern Turbine Plant (now the Zorya-Mashproekt plant)—the only navy ship gas turbine

---

[12] Malyshev B.D., Melnik V.I. and Getiya I.G., "Manual arc welding," *Stroyisdat* (in Russian), 1990.

[13] "Zaliv shipyard, Kerch: history, production", *Novosti i obshestvo* (in Russian), https://autogear.ru/article/347/265/zavod-zaliv-kerch-istoriya-produktsiya/.

builder in the former Soviet Union. The Russian Federation also has no analogue for this production facility.

Meanwhile, Crimean shipyards were divided into several sectoral areas:

- Sevastopol would concentrate on carrying out all types of repairs of warships and auxiliary vessels;
- Kerch would be engaged in large-tonnage civil shipbuilding and became a pre-commissioning base for small warships destined for the Black Sea after being built at shipyards on the Volga River; it was expanded in 1970 to be able to construct several models of patrol ships (frigates);
- Theodosia would build high-speed warships and civilian vessels constructed from light alloys, including hydrofoils (1956) and an air cushion vessel (1980).

In general, the shipbuilding developments in and around the Black Sea that occurred at different times over the course of the Russian and Soviet empires were enabled by a number of favorable factors. First and foremost was the warm Black Sea climate, which is especially important for the construction of large surface warships with sophisticated electronics and also to meet the technical construction requirements in open areas (slipways). Second was the shipyards' proximity to the Mariupol factories producing metal for warship construction. The third key enabler was the deep-water area of the region's shipyards (except Theodosia), which allowed Moscow to build large-tonnage warships, including heavy aircraft carriers. And finally, the northern Black Sea coast had developed infrastructure for the training and accommodation of shipbuilding personnel. In short, the areas around and proximate to Crimea were for centuries the lifeblood of Russian ambitions to become a major naval power.

266 | BLACK SEA BATTLEGROUND

Moscow's Theft, Curatorship and Militarization of Ukrainian Shipbuilding Companies in Crimea

Moscow lost control of the shipbuilding facilities in Crimea and around the northern Black Sea littoral areas when the Soviet Union disintegrated in 1991 and Ukraine became independent. However, for the next two decades, the Ukrainian-controlled shipyards continued to supply the Russian Federation's naval arms producers with much-needed components, such as gas turbine engines. This arrangement lasted until the Ukrainian Revolution of Dignity (EuroMaidan), in 2013/2014.

Immediately after Russia annexed Crimea in early 2014, the peninsula was divided up into two "entities of the Russian Federation"—the Republic of Crimea and the federal city of Sevastopol—which were subordinated to the central power in Moscow. But over time, the status of occupied Crimea and Sevastopol were reduced and the Crimean Federal District was eliminated; instead, Russia reassigned all of Crimea to the Southern Federal District, administered by officials in Rostov-on-Don. This act, among others, unified the civilian structure on the peninsula with a regional military organizing structure—specifically, all elements of the Russian military forces in Crimea were included in the important Southern Military District, headquartered in Rostov-on-Don.

As part of this process, promoting the military industrialization of Crimea became the key aspect of Moscow's southeastern policy as well as the main driver of the peninsula's economy. And after eight years of occupation, the most striking Russian "success story" in Crimea is, therefore, the "military development" of its territory. This development has effectively meant building up Crimea into an extensive Russian military base, supported by reliable industrial, transport and logistics, energy and water infrastructure. Among of the central elements of this policy were the expropriation of Ukrainian shipbuilding enterprises in Crimea, their integration into the Russian military-industrial base, and the issuing of exclusive targeted military orders to enterprises on the peninsula.

Evidence of the general trend of the militarization of the Crimean economy is found in Russian economic activity code 84.22: "activities related to ensuring military security." For example, Sevastopol, the main base of the Russian Black Sea Fleet, has received up to $2.5 billion for military facilities development, equipment and weapons since 2014. Military activity, therefore, accounts for 70 percent of this Crimean port city's entire economy.[14]

In May 2015, the Russian Ministry of Industry and Trade introduced a so-called "curatorship" over the Crimean enterprises of the military-industrial complex. Under this system, the curators had to share orders with the Crimean shipyards and control their shipbuilding activities. Striking examples of such "curatorship" included:

- The Open Joint Stock Company Leningrad Shipyard Pella curating the Sea Shipyard (Theodosia), before the Pella yard changed its status to become a tenant of the Theodosia facility;[15]
- The Joint Stock Company Zelenodolsk Plant named after Gorky (Zeleinodolsk), part of the Ak Bars Shipbuilding Corporation, seizing the Zaliv Shipyard (Kerch) in August 2014 and then becoming the curator of this shipyard.

The curatorship scheme was officially suspended in August 2017, when the United Nations launched its Crimean package of sanctions. But it has continued *de facto* up to the present time in the form of the absorption of Crimean shipyards by Russian shipbuilding holdings. In the course of this transformation, the Zaliv Shipyard, for example, was "reorganized" into the

---

[14] "Back in the USSR. The Reverse Restructuring of the Crimean Economy," *BlackSeaNews*, August 28, 2020, https://www.blackseanews.net/en/read/169451.
[15] "The 'Trophy Economy' Militarization as a Factor of Industrial Growth," *BlackSeaNews*, October 25, 2020, https://www.blackseanews.net/en/read/169458.

268 | BLACK SEA BATTLEGROUND

Shipbuilding Plant named after B. E. Butomy[16] as part of the Ak Bars Shipbuilding Corporation. While, the Theodosia-based Sea Shipyard, initially operated by the Leningrad Shipyard Pella, eventually became part of the Joint Stock Company Kalashnikov Concern.[17] In 2018, it was subordinated to the Russian State Corporation Rostec and was later transferred to the United Shipbuilding Corporation of Russia.[18] It is important to note that, under occupation, the Crimean shipyards have no foreign shipbuilding orders—only Moscow's orders via Russian shipbuilding corporations are being commissioned.

According to the Russian state weapons program designed until 2027, 14 warships intended for Russia's Black Sea Fleet were laid down at Crimean shipyards in 2016–2020, including:

- Eight Project 22800 Karakurt-class missile corvettes (small missile ships in Russian classification), which are equipped with Kalibr long-range cruise missiles or Oniks (SS-N-25 Switchblade) anti-ship missiles. Three are being built at the Sea Shipyard, and three are still under construction at the Zaliv Shipyard, with one corvette commissioned in December 2021 and the final one still undergoing sea trials. This class of warships is intended to be a more seaworthy, blue water complement to the Buyan-M class corvettes, which had been designed for the

---

[16] "Kerch Zalyv Shipyard reorganized in the form of joining its beneficiary shipyard named by Butomy," *Interfax Russa* (in Russian), February 20, 2021, https://www.interfax-russia.ru/south-and-north-caucasus/news/kerchenskiy-zaliv-reorganizovan-v-forme-prisoedineniya-k-svoemu-beneficiaru-sudozavodu-im-butomy.

[17] "Russian concern 'Kalashnikov' assigned a resurrected shipyard in Ukraine in Feodosia," *Center for Investigative Journalism* (in Ukrainian), November 23, 2017, https://investigator.org.ua/ua/news-2/203738/.

[18] Anastasia Vedeneeva and Alexander Dremlyugin, "Rosteh to part with the Sea Shipyard which to be handed over to United Shipbuilding Corporation," *Kommersant* (in Russian), April 2, 2021, https://www.kommersant.ru/doc/4753274.

littoral zone and are currently serving in the Russian Black Sea Fleet.[19]

- Four Project 22160 patrol ships are under construction at the Zaliv Shipyard and capable of carrying various module armament as well as equipment packages tailored to different missions. This warship class is primarily intended for duties such as patrol, monitoring, and protection in open and closed seas.[20]
- Two Project 23900 amphibious assault ships (LHD), designed by the Zelenodolsk Bureau of Ak Bars Corporation. This class is intended to operate both in warm-water and northern seas, including in the frozen waters of the Arctic.[21]

Moscow is additionally building nine auxiliary vessels at the Crimean shipyards. Under construction at the Zaliv Shipyard are: *Volga* and *Vyatka*, twin Project 15310 icebreaker cable-laying vessels; two Project 23131 complex supply vessels; a Project MPSV07 rescue vessel; three Project 19910 small hydrographic vessels; and a Project CNF22 cargo ferry. The Sea Shipyard was involved in building different auxiliary boats in cooperation with the Yaroslavl Shipyard and the Nizhnenovgorodsky Teplohod Plant. Crimean enterprises belonging to Ukraine's armaments-production state concern Ukroboronprom became partners and suppliers of 59 enterprises of the Russian military-industrial complex after their illegal seizure by Russia in 2014. Those Crimean entities include, among others, Sea Shipyard

---

[19] Yuri Makarov and Alexander Mozgovoy, "Through thorns... to common sense," *National Defence* (in Russian), #11, November 2020, https://oborona.ru/includes/periodics/navy/2015/0730/153716373/detail.shtml.

[20] Evgeniy Damantsev, "Projects 22160 Corvettes: low-visible patrol ships with destroyer capabilities," *Voennoe Obozreniye* (in Russian), March 1, 2016, https://topwar.ru/91585-korvety-pr-22160-malozametnye-patrulnye-korabli-s-vozmozhnostyami-esminca-vsled-za-soobrazitelnym.html.

[21] Kirill Ryabov, "Project 23900 ships: universal amphibious ships developed by Russia," *Voennoe Obozreniye* (in Russian), July 22, 2020, https://topwar.ru/173342-korabli-proekta-23900-universalnye-desantnye-svoi.html.

(Theodosia), Zaliv Shipyard (Kerch), Design Technological Bureau Sudokomposit (Theodosia), Shipbuilding Enterprise Skloplastik (Theodosia) and Fiolent Plant (Simferopol). Crimean ship repair plants were also integrated into the Russian military-industrial complex; the Sevastopol Sea Plant, alone, as of January 2019, repaired 38 different Russian warships.[22]

How Russian Warship Construction Affects Black Sea Security

Russian naval officials first expressed interest in building amphibious assault ships, or LHDs, one year after the Russian-Georgian war of 2008. "If during last year's conflict with Georgia we had a Mistral-class [French-built amphibious-assault helicopter carrier] ship in the Black Sea Fleet, we would have completed the task in 40 minutes and would not have needed 26 hours, as was the case," Russia's then–Chief Admiral Vladimir Vysotsky said at the time.[23]

Russia signed a contract with France in 2011 for the supply of two Mistral-class amphibious assault ships at a cost of 1.2 billion euros (roughly $1.3 billion). The construction of these vessels, under the names *Sevastopol* and *Vladivostok*, began in 2012 and 2013, respectively. The transfer of the first of these to the Russian Federation was scheduled for October 2014, and the ships even completed several trials at sea as part of the on-site tests with Russian sailors on board. But after the annexation of Crimea in the spring of 2014 and a further imposition of Western sanctions against Russia, the agreement on the Mistrals was terminated; the ships were instead sold to Egypt.

---

[22] Andrii Klymenko, Tetiyana Guchakova and Olga Korbut, "Gray Zone" occupied Crimea: Violation of sanctions in 2018," *The Black Sea Institute of Strategic Studies*, Kyiv, 2019, https://www.blackseanews.net/en/read/169630.

[23] Kvyris Palitra and Irakli Alamashvil, "Vysotskiy: with 'Mistral' we would have grabbed the Georgian shore for 40 minutes," *Georgia Online* (in Russian), September 15, 2009, https://www.apsny.ge/articles/1253062679.php.

Arsenal of Empire | 271

After the collapse of the Mistral deal with France, Russian Deputy Defense Minister Yuri Borisov publicly announced (at the Heli Russia-2017 helicopter industry exhibition) that Moscow would unilaterally build its first-ever LHD helicopter carrier, which would be commissioned in 2022.[24] Notably, Russia only gained the ability to build such a warship following its annexation of Crimea, with the expropriation of the Kerch Zaliv Shipyard—one of Europe's largest shipbuilding docks (364 meters long and 60 meters wide).

No such analogues exist inside Russia.[23] Two of these advertised ships were laid down at the Zaliv shipyard on July 20, 2020, in a ceremony officiated by President Vladimir Putin. Though originally the pair of vessels was supposed to receive the names *Sevastopol* and *Vladivostok*—the names previously assigned to the Mistrals Russia never obtained[25]—in the end, they were christened *Ivan Rogov* and *Mytrofan Moskalenko.* According to sources in the Russian shipbuilding industry, the first of these helicopter carriers is expected to be commissioned in 2025, and the second in 2027.[26] According to a statement from the Zaliv shipyard's administration, both will be ready for operation in 2028.[27] The total price of the construction contract for these two

---

[24] Roman Skomorokhov, "The first Russian helicopters carrier will appear in 2022... Were you short of Mistrals?" *Voennoe Obozreniye* (in Russian), June 2, 2017, https://topwar.ru/117037-pervyy-rossiyskiy-vertoletonosec-poyavitsya-k-2022-godu-mistraley-ne-hvatilo.html.

[25] "The first two Russian helicopter carriers will be named from the Mistrals," *TASS* (in Russian), January 11, 2020, https://tass.ru/armiya-i-opk/7499381.

[26] "Russian LHDs will be built on modified projects," *Voennoe Obozreniye* (in Russian), August 14, 2020, https://topwar.ru/174106-rossijskie-udk-budut-stroitsja-po-dorabotannym-proektam.html.

[27] "Russia will build universal amphibious ships in Crimea for 8 years," *Novosti Kryma* (in Russian), March 15, 2021, https://news.allcrimea.net/news/2021/3/15/rossiya-8-let-budet-stroit-universalnye-desantnye-korabli-v-krymu-143962/.

272 | BLACK SEA BATTLEGROUND

amphibious assault vessels is reportedly 100 billion rubles ($1.4 billion).[28]

Each will presumably be able to carry up to 1,000 Russian marines and 75 combat vehicles, up to 20 helicopters, as well as unmanned aerial vehicles (strike and reconnaissance). Their sterns will be built with a well deck capable of transporting up to six Project 11770 Serna landing boats.[29] The LHDs' displacements will be up to 40,000 tons, and they will measure more than 220 meters in length. They will be designed to operate autonomously at sea for up to 60 days, and their planned top speed will be 22 knots. These warships are supposed to be equipped with missiles, artillery and anti-torpedo weapons; electronic warfare (EW) systems; as well as a "command, control, communications, computers, intelligence, surveillance and reconnaissance" (C4ISR) system to manage multiservice missions involving amphibious assault forces, combat ships, strike aviation and mechanized and other troops.[29] The Kremlin does not hide the fact that *Ivan Rogov* and *Mytrofan Moskalenko* are intended for expeditionary assault actions—a fact Russian media outlets themselves frequently refer to when describing the progress being made on the vessels' construction.[30]

The Kremlin does not publicly speak about the LHDs' destinations upon completion. One of these ships could be deployed to the Russian Northern Fleet, ensuring the ability to project

---

[28] "Source: Russia will spend 100 billion rubles on the first two helicopter carriers building," *TASS* (in Russian), April 10, 2020, https://tass.ru/armiya-i-opk/8207635.
[29] Roman Kretsul, Bogdan Stepovoy and Alexey Ramm, "In the sea battle: Russian helicopter carriers will become floating headquarters," *Izvestiya* (in Russian), July 24, 2020, https://iz.ru/1039189/roman-kretcul-bogdan-stepovoi-aleksei-ramm/v-morskoi-boi-rossiiskie-vertoletonostcy-stanut-plavuchimi-shtabami.
[30] "Russia itself builds helicopter carriers: about the characteristics and prospects of domestic LHD," *Voennoe Obozreniye* (in Russian), October 15, 2020, https://topwar.ru/176051-rossija-sama-stroit-vertoletonoscy-kakie-onibudut-dlja-chego-oni-nuzhny-i-chto-ot-nih-ozhidajut.html.

Arsenal of Empire | 273

amphibious assault forces in the Arctic.[29] However, the use of LHDs in northern latitudes will be limited because these warships are not built with steel alloys designed for operations in difficult ice conditions. Moreover, Moscow would need at least four such ships in the Arctic Ocean (one at sea, one in reserve under immediate readiness, the third in a state of combat-readiness recovery after repair and a fourth that would inevitably undergo long-term repair and modernization), as well as an outfit of escort forces.

The Black Sea and the Eastern Mediterranean as operational zones for LHDs look more preferable due to the proximity of Russian warm-water naval bases as well as the possibility of being covered by coastal air-defense systems (S-400, S-300 and coastal-based fighters). It is also important to note that the LHD is designed as an operational-level command-and-control (C2) center, and since Russia lost its missile cruiser *Moskva* to a Ukrainian missile attack on April 14, 2022, there is no warship in the Black Sea Fleet that can currently perform the functions of the fleet's C2 management center. Finally, it is worth considering the technical aspect: modern-day Russian shipyards have heretofore never built a warship with a displacement of more than 5,000 tons. This means that it is likely the new LHDs will require technical fine-tuning and maintenance near the construction site even after their commissioning.

Further support for such plans comes from the fact that, in 2014, Russia considered the Sevastopol or Novorossiysk ports as the possible home bases for the French Mistrals[31]; and Moscow now appears to be modernizing its naval bases in Novorossiysk[32] and

---

[31] "Russia wants to deploy Mistral helicopter carrier in Sevastopol," *Glavred* (in Russian), May 30, 2014, https://glavred.info/world/281065-rossiya-hochet-razmestit-vertoletonoscy-mistral-v-sevastopole.html.

[32] "Modernization of the main base of the Black Sea Fleet in Sevastopol is planned to start in 2019," *Bez Formata* (in Russian), January 11, 2019, https://sevastopol.bezformata.com/listnews/modernizatciyu-osnovnoj-bazi-chf-v-sevastopole/60308231/.

Tartus (Syria)[33] for the purpose of accommodating and providing for the deployment of these types of large warships. Moreover, Russia began modernizing the Black Sea Fleet's main base in Sevastopol in 2019. Finally, as a sign of its strategic significance, only the Black Sea Fleet, from among the four Russian fleets, received the above-mentioned Russian federal resources specifically for this type of naval base modernization. Thus, it is a near guarantee that at least one of the amphibious assault helicopter carriers currently under construction will join the Russian Black Sea fleet, which would dramatically alter the naval balance of power in the Black Sea and beyond.

LHDs are unique in naval warfare because they have an unparalleled capability to carry out surprise, *blitzkrieg* amphibious missions. At the same time, they can operate beyond the reach of coastal artillery and even some missile systems. In the Black Sea or the Mediterranean, those capabilities can significantly change the regional balance of forces by giving Russia more military options than it has had until now. Namely, Russian naval forces will be able to jointly operate their LHDs in combined arms operations with other naval assets and the Russian air force, permitting highly maneuverable amphibious assault operations from the air and sea against a potential adversary. Generally, such operations can include:

- The rapid seizure of a coastal foothold along with two to three strategically important state objects (ports, hydro-electric dams, nuclear power plants, etc.) by an amphibious battalion tactical group. This unit would hold the territory for up to a couple days, until the main amphibious forces land.
- The deployment of several air and sea amphibious echelons (up to three to four airborne/marine brigades) together with landing ships and military transport aircraft.

---

[33] "Russia begins modernization of its naval base in Tartus," *Vzglyad* (in Russian), March 11, 2017, https://vz.ru/news/2017/3/11/861450.html.

- The deployment of amphibious forces with live-fire support, jointly using a combination of combat aviation and naval forces.
- The extension of C2 management and control of different combat operations (amphibious and airborne, strike, anti-submarine and others).

Russian LHDs should not be seen primarily as defensive assets. They were designed to conduct active offensive amphibious operations.

Missile Corvettes and Patrol Ships

Russian Defense Minister Sergei Shoigu, in 2017, defined multi-role frigates as the main class of Russian warships.[34] However, it is revealing that, after this statement was made, Moscow had not placed any new frigates in the Black Sea, even though the Black Sea Fleet is significantly ahead of the Northern, Baltic and Pacific fleets in terms of the number of new ships being deployed and laid at its shipyards. In fact, the VMF leadership has decided to focus not on frigates, but on corvette building—such as the Project 22800 Karakurt-class missile corvettes equipped with long-range Kalibr missiles as well as the Project 22160 small patrol ships (OPV class). These vessels were the main platforms ordered by Moscow for the Black Sea Fleet since 2014. According to Russian General Staff plans, the Karakurt-class corvettes, together with already-deployed Project 21631 (Buyan-M) missile corvettes, would form a powerful mobile naval strike force in the Black Sea region and beyond.[35]

---

[34] "Shoigu: The Navy basis will be frigates like 'Admiral Gorshkov,'" *Voennoe Obozreniye* (in Russian), April 21, 2017, https://topwar.ru/114050-shoygu-osnovoy-flota-stanut-fregaty-podobnye-admiralu-gorshkovu.html.

[35] Anton Novoderezhkin, "Modernization of the Black Sea Fleet of the Russian Federation has alarmed the West," *Voennoe Obozreniye* (in Russian), March 6, 2018, https://topwar.ru/137336-modernizaciya-chernomorskogo-flota-rf-obespokoila-zapad.html.

276 | BLACK SEA BATTLEGROUND

Russia's Naval Dilemma: Diesel Engines Versus Gas Turbines?

Undoubtedly, Moscow's long-term naval construction plan prior to 2014 was based on the presupposition that Ukrainian gas turbine supplies would continue into the next decade. But after the invasion and annexation of Crimea, this critical supply was interrupted and indefinitely postponed, causing Russian strategic planners to postpone the Kremlin's frigate-building program. It is worth noting that since Soviet times, gas turbine engines for Moscow's warships were produced in Mykolaiv (Ukraine),[36] while diesel engines were built in St. Petersburg (Russia).[37] Mykolaiv's turbines were installed on all large Soviet and Russian warships (frigates, destroyers, cruisers), and the diesel engines from St. Petersburg plants were designated in particular for smaller vessels (corvettes, missile and torpedo boats, as well as diesel submarines).

After 2014, Ukraine ceased the supply of gas turbines to Russia,[38] which consequently froze the construction of large warships in the Russian Federation—first and foremost virtually all of its frigate program. In other words, the Russian navy since 2014 has had to become a corvette-centric, diesel navy, and any great power ambitions to build a blue water fleet were held hostage to the loss of Ukrainian gas turbine engines. This fact partially helps explain why Ukraine matters so much to Russian imperial planning for Putin's *"Reconquista."*

Russian diesel engines are built according to the "monoblock star" (aviation scheme) design and are viewed largely as insufficient and highly unreliable for Russia's requirements. For this reason, in the first decade of the 21st century, Moscow primarily bought German diesel engines for its corvettes, but the supply of these

---

[36] For background on this firm see: https://zmturbines.com/.
[37] For background on this firm see: http://www.zvezda.spb.ru/index.php/o-predpriyatii.
[38] "Ukroboronprom finally froze arms supplies to Russia", *Zerkalo Nedeli* (in Russian), March 29, 2014, https://zn.ua/UKRAINE/ukroboronprom-nakonec-to-zamorozil-postavki-oruzhiya-v-rossiyu-142213 .html.

crucial components was also halted after the occupation of Crimea, due to Western sanctions.[39] Moscow instead tried to replace the German engines with Chinese ones but has faced problem with the latter's low reliability. Due to this experience, all newly built Russian corvettes are now using Russian diesel engines.[40]

The Rise of the Project 22800 Karakurt Class and the Kalibr Cruise Missile

In light of Russia's gas-versus-diesel engine dilemma, Moscow opted for a construction program in Crimean shipyards to give the Russian navy greater punch and striking power in the northwestern part of the Black Sea, where its short-term military objectives lay. Namely, Moscow decided it needed greater striking power against Ukraine's coastal defenses in the Sea of Azov and to guard Crimean sea flanks near the occupied peninsula's isthmus to block the smaller Ukrainian Navy in its bases and provide freedom of movement for Russian forces in the northwestern part of the Black Sea. In such conditions, Romanian naval bases and forces may be at risk as well. Moscow's defense orders for a dozen corvettes (eight Project 22800 Karakurt-class corvettes equipped with Kalibr long-range cruise missiles and four Project 22160 OPV-class patrol ships) for the Russian Black Sea Fleet were placed at the Crimean shipyards in Kerch and Theodosia in 2016–2019. It is worth noting that there were plans to equip the Project 22160 OPVs with modular container weapons, including Kalibr cruise missiles and/or Oniks (SS-N-25 Switchblade) anti-ship missiles. Such a modular system was tested in the Northern Fleet, onboard the OPV vessel *Vasiliy*

---

[39] "Germany and China deprived Russia of missile ships", *Novosti VPK* (in Russian), February 7, 2018, https://vpk.name/news/206004 germaniya i kitai lishili rossiyu rak etnyh korablei.html.

[40] "The Navy refused to remotorize "Karakurt"", *Voenno-Promyshlenniy Kur`er VPK* (in Russian), https://vpk-news.ru/news/45537; "Non-perpetual motion engine: how industry and the Navy are looking for a way out of the diesel crisis", *Flot Prom* (in Russian), August 8, 2018, https://flotprom.ru/2018/%D0%9E%D0%B1%D0%BE%D1%80%D0 %BE%D0%BD%D0%BA%D0%B0348/.

Bykov, in August 2020, but no such modules have been deployed to the Black Sea up to now.[41]

Once the entire corvette program is implemented, the total missile salvo of the Russian Black Sea Fleet will be doubled compared to just before the launch of the 2022 full-scale war against Ukraine. It will be increased to 124 Kalibr missiles with a range 1,500–2,000 kilometers against coastal targets and up to 76 anti-ship missiles with a range of 80–300 kilometers against naval targets. The formation of this offensive naval group of forces is driven by Moscow's desire to build a multi-directional system for projecting military power across three frontiers: 1) Ukraine's littoral waters in the northwestern part of the Black Sea and in the Sea of Azov; 2) a possible confrontation with the North Atlantic Treaty Organization (NATO) in the Black Sea basin; and 3) in the Eastern Mediterranean, where the Russian naval task force has maintained a constant presence since 2010.[42]

An assessment of Russian Black Sea Fleet naval exercises and operational deployments in recent years indicates the likely main tasks and areas of operation for Russia's corvette-class warships in various theaters. In the Black Sea and Sea of Azov: [43]

- During peace-time conditions, to maintain a naval presence, sea control and sea denial capabilities in the

---

[41] Roman Kretsul and Alexei Ramm, "Container with an eye: Navy combat modules will be tested before the end of the summer," *Izvestiya* (in Russian), July 22, 2020, https://iz.ru/1038280/roman-kretcul-aleksei-ramm/konteiner-s-pritcelom-boevye-moduli-vmf-protestiruiut-do-kontca-leta.

[42] "Admiral Essen" on the tail of 'Florida,'" *Rossiyskaya Gazeta* (in Russian), January 28, 2020, https://rg.ru/2020/01/28/rossijskij-flot-provel-rotaciiu-korablej-v-sredizemnom-more.html.

[43] Irina Kuteleva-Kovalenko, "Russia conducted exercises in the Black Sea with the participation of a missile ship and coastal missile complexes Bal," *Novoye Vremya* (in Russian), February 19, 2019, https://nv.ua/world/countries/rf-provela-ucheniya-v-chernom-more-s-uchastiem-raketnogo-korablya-i-beregovyh-kompleksov-bal-50006869.html.

northwestern part of the Black Sea and in the Kerch Strait maritime zone, where these Russian naval ships may carry out periodic combat duty in a state high-degree readiness for missile strikes.[44]

- In the event of a renewed local armed conflict, to actively participate in naval strike operations as part of a group of multifunctional strike forces involving the Black Sea Fleet to bolster Russian A2/AD bubbles[45] in and around Crimea. This would include two of its mobile components (one of these bubbles is centered on the seized Ukrainian offshore natural gas platforms, which Moscow captured in 2014 and which extends between the Tarkhankut peninsula and Serpent Island; the other is near the approaches to the Kerch Strait).

- When a local armed conflict develops into a regional war, to take part in the fight for domination in the northwestern, central and eastern parts of the Black Sea by launching missile strikes on designated coastal and maritime targets, blockading other Black Sea littoral countries' naval assets, as well as preventing non–Black Sea countries' warships from gaining access to the Black Sea via the Turkish Straits.

---

[44] "The Kavkaz exercises showed who the master in the Black Sea is," *Rossiyskaya Gazeta* (in Russian), September 22, 2016, https://rg.ru/2016/09/22/reg-ufo/glavnye-fakty-o-strategicheskih-ucheniiah-kavkaz-2016.html; "Small missile ships 'Uglich' and 'Great Ustyug' entered the Sea of Azov," *Kubanskiye Novosty* (in Russian), October 21, 2019, https://kubnews.ru/obshchestvo/2019/10/21/malye-raketnye-korabli-uglich-i-velikiy-ustyug-voshli-v-azovskoe-more/.
[45] Glen E. Howard and Matthew Czekaj, eds., *Russia's Military Strategy and Doctrine*, The Jamestown Foundation, Washington, DC, April 2019, https://jamestown.org/product/russias-military-strategy-and-doctrine/.

280 | BLACK SEA BATTLEGROUND

In the Mediterranean:[46]

- During peacetime, to engage in combat duty from Tartus (Syria), in a designated level of readiness; moreover, to put to sea and to carry out missile strike exercises.
- In the event of a local armed conflict in the Middle East and North Africa, to deploy on combat patrols and take part in stand-off firing positions in the Black Sea, the Caspian Sea as well as in the Eastern Mediterranean, carrying out missile strikes on coastal/maritime targets as part of Moscow's support for Russian-backed authoritarian regimes.

Thus, taking into account the capabilities of Russian corvettes laid at Crimean shipyards, Moscow is forming a serious group of naval strike forces capable of a wide range of offensive threat projection missions covering the whole Black Sea region and beyond.

Problems of Implementation for Russian Shipbuilding Projects in Crimean Shipyards

One of the major results of Western and Ukrainian sanctions imposed on Russia after the 2014 annexation of Crimea was the interruption in the transfer and supply of military and dual-use components critical to Russian shipbuilding efforts.[47]

---

[46] "Small missile warships 'Serpukhov' and 'Green Dol' came to the exercises in the Mediterranean Sea," *Military Press Flot* (in Russian), August 15, 2016, https://flot.com/2016/%D0%A7%D0%B5%D1%80%D0%BD%D0%BE%D0%BC%D0%BE%D1%80%D1%81%D0%BA%D0%B8%D0%B9%D0%A4%D0%BB%D0%BE%D1%8237/; Ivan Petrov, "From all calibers. Two more small missile warships joined the Russian Navy grouping in the Mediterranean Sea," *Rossiyskaya Gazeta* (in Russian), June 18, 2018, https://rg.ru/2018/06/18/malye-raketnye-korabli-popolnili-gruppirovku-vmf-v-sredizemnom-more.html.
[47] "How do sanctions work. Military industry of the occupied Crimea," *BlackSeaNews* (in Ukrainian), December 31, 2020, https://www.blackseanews.net/read/171798.

First of all, as referenced earlier, among the biggest challenges for Moscow concerns the propulsion systems needed for the aforementioned amphibious assault helicopter carriers being built at the Zaliv Shipyard in Kerch.[48] The twin LHDs are being fitted with M55R diesel-gas turbine units. The M55Rs were originally developed for Russian frigates but, to date, there are no other propulsion systems available for large Russian warships. Until 2014, gas turbines meant for Russian frigates were supplied from the Ukrainian plant Zorya-Mashproekt, located in Mykolaiv. But since then, following the rupture of Ukraine's military-technical cooperation with Russia, Russian planners were forced to attempt to reestablish domestic gas turbine production. Deadlines for these crucial components' deliveries to the Russian navy were repeatedly postponed—a clear indication of the difficulties the domestic military-industrial complex has had with developing and building this technology. Only in November 2020 did the Russian company ODK-Saturn[49] prove able to manufacture the first gas turbines for the Russian frigate *Admiral Isakov*. Similar engines are expected to be equipped for at least eight more Russian frigates of this type, which Moscow plans to build by 2027.

As noted, frigates were supposed to become the basis for the Russian fleet[35] and are a major priority for the Russian shipbuilding program. Given this and the low rate of gas turbine production,[50] the LHDs being built in Kerch are likely to face serious delays.

At the same time, the Russian navy has a shortage of fast landing boats and attack drones, which are part of the planned arsenal of weaponry that will be deployed on the LHDs. Indeed, Russian industry does not produce any heavy deck-landing helicopter

---

[48] Roman Azanov, "Takeoff from 'Priboy': what will be the Russian helicopter carriers," *TASS* (in Russian), June 30, 2017, https://tass.ru/armiya-i-opk/4374859.
[49] For background on this firm see: https://en.wikipedia.org/wiki/UEC_Saturn.
[50] "'Admirals' waited for the units," *Aviaport* (in Russian), November 27, 2020, https://www.aviaport.ru/news/2020/11/27/659959.html.

282 | BLACK SEA BATTLEGROUND

models, and only a couple dozen Soviet-era Ka-29TB deck transport-landing helicopters are in service in the VMF. A possible candidate to fill this role is the Ka-65 Minoga, but this helicopter is only just now being developed.[51] According to the most optimistic scenario, the first Ka-65s will not be ready earlier than 2025–2026. Moreover, this newly developed system will require lengthy test trials. Consequently, only the Ka-52K reconnaissance-attack deck helicopters and Ka-27 anti-submarine (search and rescue) deck helicopters can be considered for placement on board Russia's first natively built amphibious assault carriers.[52] And without heavy deck helicopters and a shortage of fast landing boats, this LHD pair will initially not be able to carry out amphibious missions in the air and sea domains simultaneously.[53]

Moscow is also experiencing difficulties with building corvettes and OPVs at its Crimean shipyards. In 2019, under the threat of sanctions, the Leningrad Shipyard Pella, owned by J. J. Sietas Shipyard (Germany), stopped the construction of three Karakurt-class missile corvettes at the Theodosian Sea Shipyard and transferred the unfinished hulls to the St. Petersburg region. Commenting on the impact of Western sanctions, Oleg Zachynyaev, the director of the Theodosian facility stated,

---

[51] "Universal amphibious assault ships for the Russian Navy can be equipped with Minoga helicopters," *Novosti VPK* (in Russian), September 30, 2020, https://vpk.name/news/449243 universalnye desantnye korabli dlya vmf rossii mogut osnastit vertoletami minoga.html.

[52] "The source talked about characteristics of the Russian Mistrals," *Center for Analysis of the World Arms Trade* (in Russian), March 4, 2021, https://armstrade.org/includes/periodics/news/2021/0304/101061 888/detail.shtml?fbclid=IwAR3GjAk4lUEEHuTN3xerr a3ee7w7X5OyE xbSo X0VKPojjJCSWV-52mvSzQ.

[53] "What are the prospects for the LHDs building at the Zalyv plant in the occupied Crimea," *Defence Express* (in Ukrainian), March 19, 2021, https://defence-ua.com/weapon and tech/jakimi je perspektivi budivnitstva udk na zavodi zaliv v okupovanomu krimu-3137.html.

Arsenal of Empire | 283

We lose out in state procurements due to logistics and sanctions restrictions, which are associated with the inability to directly purchase various equipment. It is no secret that more than 50 percent of the components and equipment of the vessels and warships under construction are imported production. We have to buy all this using certain schemes, losing out to our partners who make purchases directly. In turn, no one is willing to participate in competitions that we initiate, because they do not want to fall under sanctions for cooperating with Crimean enterprises.[54]

Another case of Western sanctions affecting Russian naval production relates to the Project 22160 Offshore Patrol Vessel, which Moscow originally planned to build using German-made diesel units.[55] However, prior to the imposition of EU sanctions, Russia only managed to import enough diesel units for one OPV— *Vasily Bykov*. The remaining contracted OPVs had to be redesigned to use diesel units manufactured by the Russian Kolomna plant, which caused significant production delays.[56]

Prior to 2014, Crimean shipyards were primarily oriented toward the construction and repair of merchant vessels, as well as tankers, container ships and maritime platforms for the Ukrainian oil and gas sector. To cite one example, commercial projects made up 70 percent of the Zaliv shipyard's annual production capacity before the plant was appropriated by occupying Russian authorities. This shipyard built 3-4 multi-ton merchant ships and

---

[54] Tetiana Guchakova, "How sanctions work. Military industry of the occupied Crimea", *Centr Jurnalistskih Rassledovaniy* (in Ukrainian), December 4, 2020,
https://investigator.org.ua/ua/investigations/230678/.
[55] "Project 22160 patrol ship", *Obyedinennaya Sudostroitelnaya Korporatsyia* (in Russian), https://www.aoosk.ru/products/project-22160/
[56] "Patrol ship of project 22160 "Vasily Bykov" entered the state trials", *Voennoe Obozreniye* (in Russian), October 25, 2018,
https://topwar.ru/148878-patrulnyj-korabl-proekta-22160-vasilij-bykov-vyshel-na-gosispytanija.html.

284 | BLACK SEA BATTLEGROUND

repaired up to 35 various commercial vessels every year.[57] But after the Russian annexation of Crimea in 2014, international commercial contracts were canceled and the facility came under sanctions rom the EU, the US and Ukraine. All Crimean shipyards began to stagnate, leading to outrage among their workforces. This is confirmed by the words of Serhii Aksyonov, the so-called "head of Crimea," who stressed at the end of 2019 that Crimean enterprises on average were working at only 40 percent capacity.[8]

In May 2020, the Zaliv shipyard was paralyzed by a major strike caused by workers' dissatisfaction with falling salaries. Employees participating in the strike stated that "the staff started to leave. The vessels are in an unfinished state. The money has been squandered, and the vessels will not be commissioned."[58] Due to the above-mentioned halt in construction, the deadlines for Russian warship completion at Crimean shipyards have been repeatedly postponed. To date, only two out of five of the Karakurt-class corvettes laid at the Zaliv Shipyard in 2016 have been commissioned and only one OPV, *Pavel Derzhavin*, was built and transferred to the Russian Black Sea fleet in 2020.[59]

Conclusion

In accordance with "The Fundamentals of the State Policy of the Russian Federation in the Field of Naval Activities for the Period up to 2030," the Russian navy bet heavily on its forces being equipped with high-precision long-range missiles, which, for Moscow, would enable a qualitatively new naval objective:

---

[57] "Zalyv increased production," *UNIAN* (in Russian), February 9, 2010, https://www.unian.net/economics/transport/322823-zaliv-uvelichil-proizvodstvo.html.

[58] "Workers prepare for strike at Zalyv plant in Kerch," *Kerch.FM* (in Russian), May 29, 2020, https://kerch.fm/2020/05/29/na-zavode-zaliv-v-kerchi-ljudi-gotovjatsja-k-zabastovke.html.

[59] Vitaliy Timkiv, "The warship 'Pavel Derzhavin' became part of the Black Sea Fleet," *RIA Novosty* (in Russian), November 27, 2020, https://ria.ru/20201127/korabl-1586562871.html.

destroying the enemy's military and economic potential by hitting its forces and vital objects from the sea. At the same time, the buildup of the Black Sea Fleet's operational and combat capabilities—one of Russia's main tasks up to 2030—hinges on the development of an inter-service grouping of forces (troops) on the territory of Crimea as well as ensuring a permanent naval presence in the Mediterranean Sea.[30] Moscow is pursuing this goal by *inter alia* involving the shipbuilding enterprises of occupied Crimea in its rearmament program.

The Russian government's decision to introduce the so-called "curatorship" of Crimean shipyards by other Russian defense industry enterprises, followed by the full acquisition of those facilities by Russian shipbuilding corporations, attests to the level of importance Moscow attaches to its goal of turning Crimea into an unsinkable aircraft carrier. In this scheme, Crimean shipyards execute Moscow's strategy by fulfilling military orders coming from the federal center. In fact, this means a full management of Crimean shipyards according to the former Soviet concept of "big northern brother," which causes justified dissatisfaction within the Crimean shipbuilding labor force.[62]

What is most significant, however, is the impact of sanctions and their restrictions on the industrial capabilities of the Crimean shipyards. All these facilities are under sanctions from Ukraine and the United States, while the Zaliv Shipyard has been targeted by EU sanctions as well. In addition, the US and EU bans on the export/import of military and dual-use goods, technologies and services to/from occupied Crimea have adversely affected the development opportunities for shipbuilding on the peninsula. In light of these conditions, Moscow's increased state military orders to Crimean shipbuilding enterprises do not so much strengthen the Black Sea Fleet as simply keep these confiscated enterprises fiscally afloat. Military orders alone are not sufficient to keep the Crimean shipyards running at full capacity; they used to rely predominantly on international commercial contracts. Unless Moscow can increase these shipyards' production levels or find them new civilian orders, labor unrest or attrition within the workforce may become inevitable.

286 | BLACK SEA BATTLEGROUND

At the same time, it would be wrong to underestimate or discount Moscow's military-industrial efforts in illegally annexed Crimea. Due to the absence of free-market alternatives for the Crimean shipyards, the Kremlin is able to actively exploit their full potential, including access to the warm waters of the Black Sea, crucial to modern-day shipbuilding methods, as well as a robust labor pool. And this intertwining of Moscow's regional military policy with Crimea's industrial sector is driven by the higher-level Russian goal of transforming the peninsula into an outpost for military power projection in the Black Sea region and beyond.

In the final analysis, financing limitations and technological gaps could be the Achilles' heel for Russian efforts to modernize and rearm its navy since both could affect the timing and commissioning schedule for warship construction—already repeatedly postponed. Eventually, Russia will replenish the Black Sea Fleet with a number of missile corvettes and patrol boats being built in its Crimean shipyards, but this is unlikely to occur before the 2025–2027 timeframe.

What should concern the United States and its NATO allies the most when it comes to Russia's naval construction program in Crimea are the two amphibious assault helicopter carriers, or LHDs, being built in Kerch. Moscow will continue the work on these two warships at the Zaliv Shipyard despite the ongoing problems with engine production, labor strikes and a lack of experience with building such large naval vessels at this particular shipyard. Indeed, the Zaliv facility has never built a warship larger than a 4,500-ton frigate. Therefore, the expected commissioning of these vessels may not come before 2028–2029.

However, once completed, the capabilities of these warships will significantly reduce the time it takes for Russian marine infantry to move swiftly and capture vast coastal areas or critical shoreline infrastructure. Based on the current capabilities of the Black Sea Fleet, it could take several days to achieve such an objective at present, but once Moscow puts the LHDs in service, it would reduce the mission time to a matter of hours. In fact, the mere presence of such a warship steaming near the territorial waters of Ukraine, Georgia or even Turkey could add another arrow to the quiver of Putin's coercive diplomacy, which he uses to intimidate regional neighbors.

The sight of one or both Russian amphibious assault ships heading toward the Mediterranean would also raise the threat level beyond the Black Sea. This is why at least one or even two of these warships would likely be deployed outside the Black Sea basin. At the same time, however, LHDs make for tempting potential targets. The Russian helicopter carriers would be quite vulnerable to attacks from the sea and air, and even possibly from Turkish-made attack drones, necessitating escort vessels to provide air defense and ensure their combat resilience.

But once Russia is fully ready to deploy the aforementioned naval strike and assault capabilities, probably no power will be able to challenge Russia in the Black Sea other than the United States and the United Kingdom. The latter two countries' naval presence in the Black Sea would, however, be limited to 21 days, due to the constraints imposed by the 1936 Montreux Convention.

Within the next decade, Moscow will be close to fielding a powerful naval grouping of offensive forces thanks to the direct participation of its seized Crimean shipyards. This will not only strengthen the Kremlin's military power in the Black and Mediterranean seas but also significantly increase Russian naval capabilities by allowing the VMF to conduct high-intensity mobile offensives from the sea and air against ground targets and troops. The addition of these naval assets will permit Moscow to use its expanded military capabilities for coercion and blackmail—as well as to carry out naval blitzkrieg missions to seize coastal territories, ports and islands if needed.

That said, it would be a mistake to think that Kremlin military planners will be happy to limit themselves to solely utilizing occupied Crimea's shipyards. Nearby is the crown jewel of Soviet naval construction—the massive Mykolaiv shipyard, which still retains much of its Soviet-era infrastructure. Topping the Kremlin's list of ambitions are its long-cherished plans to build nuclear-powered warships, including a heavy nuclear aircraft carrier.[60] Ukrainian shipyards located in Mykolaiv played an important role during the Cold War of fulfilling Soviet goals to build such vessels. And Putin sees this area of Ukraine as "historically Russian territory," referred to by the Kremlin leader as "Novorossiya." That is why, on February 24, 2022, a significant number of Russian troops were thrown in the direction of Kherson-Mykolaiv. The Kremlin managed to temporarily occupy districts of the Kherson region and reach the outskirts of Mykolaiv, where fierce attempts by Russian troops to occupy this city and gain access to its shipyards proved unsuccessful. Ukrainian troops are repelling the enemy and, as of early June, the northwesterly Russian advance has stopped.

---

[60] "Russia will build the world's largest aircraft carrier," *Nezavisimoye Voennoye Obozreniye* (in Russian), https://nvo.ng.ru/nvo/2020-01-17/1_1077_main.html.

10.

Turkish Drone Strategy in the Black Sea Region and Beyond

Can Kasapoglu

October 12, 2022

Geopolitically, Turkey is a game-changer. Without Turkey being a member of the North Atlantic Treaty Organization (NATO), the transatlantic Alliance would have had a truly different "mapping" of its surrounding environment. Such a different mapping would, quite negatively, pertain to a broad array of agendas, ranging from anti-ISIS operations to the Black Sea correlation of forces and the ability to pursue crisis management operations beyond NATO's frontiers.

Within only a few years, between 2015 and 2019, Ankara has been transformed from being the main reason behind Russia's anti-access/area denial weapon systems deployments to Syria— including the S-400 strategic surface-to-air missile (SAM) systems—into, strikingly, the one and only NATO nation that procured a Russian strategic weapon in the aftermath of Moscow's 2014 aggression in Crimea. Since then, Turkey has become the primary armed drone seller to the Ukrainian military with a recent combat record in Donbas. This drastic swing is making things much more difficult for analysts and policymakers. The Ukrainian drone strikes in Donbas and Turkish unmanned

290 | BLACK SEA BATTLEGROUND

systems mushrooming in Eastern Europe and the South Caucasus have further complicated Turkish-Russian relations.

The Turkish Armed Forces remain one of the most "dronized" militaries within NATO. In Francis Fukuyama's words, with the lessons learned from the Syrian, Libyan and Karabakh theaters, "it seems Turkey's use of drones is going to change the nature of land power in ways that will undermine existing force structures, in the way that the Dreadnaught obsoleted earlier classes of battleships, or the aircraft carrier made battleships themselves obsolete at the beginning of World War II."[1] More importantly, resembling the Israeli-Arab wars during the Cold War, the Syrian, Libyan and Karabakh fronts have visibly showcased the superiority of Turkish robotic warfare solutions over Soviet- and Russian-manufactured conventional arms.

The Turkish administration does not only sells drones in an off-the-shelf fashion. Instead, Turkey sparks drone warfare ecosystems abroad, cementing its alliances through robotic warfare transactions. Some critical episodes, in this respect, have taken place in Russia's area of strategic interests.

This chapter will first address the leading drivers and visible patterns in Turkish-Russian relations, with a specific focus on the Black Sea. Subsequently, it will analyze the geopolitics of "the Turkish way of drone warfare." Then, the report explains how Turkey's defense transactions in the robotic warfare segment affect Ankara's ties with Moscow. Finally, the work will conclude with its findings.

Turkish-Russian Geopolitical Rivalry and 'Compartmentalization'

Although Turkish-Russian ties can seem complicated and conflicting at first glance, a meaningful pattern has emerged

---

[1] Francis Fukuyama, "Droning On in the Middle East", *American Purpose*, April 5, 2021, https://www.americanpurpose.com/blog/fukuyama/droning-on/

between the two nations. Bilateral relations are shaped by a careful compartmentalization of strategic interests and divergences. This "deliberate dichotomy" clearly manifests itself in various issues, such as on the Libyan, Syrian, Karabakh and Crimean frontiers, on the one hand, and the S-400 procurement, on the other. While the incumbent Turkish government repeatedly condemned Russia's actions in Libya and its illegal annexation of Crimea,[2] the very same administration did not refrain from procuring the S-400, a high-end Russian strategic SAM system that triggered CAATSA (Countering America's Adversaries Through Sanctions Act) sanctions.

The compartmentalization trend between Ankara and the Kremlin, being transactional in nature, favors selective and limited cooperation, alongside "contained confrontation" in which strategic interests remain at odds. The controllable confrontation pattern, from time to time, has been breached by worrisome exceptions, such as the downing of a Russian Su-24 fighter-bomber by Turkish combat air patrols in 2015, or the killing of 36 Turkish troops in the Idlib countryside in 2020. Nevertheless, Turkey and Russia have demonstrated a great capability for rapprochement in their ties. Following the failed coup attempt in Turkey in 2016, for example, Moscow marked the destination for the very first foreign visit of President Recep Tayyip Erdogan.[3]

Primarily, bilateral relations are driven by a high level of economic activity, especially in the energy sector. Russia's most valuable exports are energy related, and Turkey is a major client of Russian natural gas.[4] Although Turkish dependency on Russia

---

[2] Ministry of Foreign Affairs Turkey, Twitter, accessed October 31, 2021, https://twitter.com/TC_Disisleri/status/1440024403115446272
[3] Voice of America, https://www.amerikaninsesi.com/a/erdogan-putin-gorusmesi-oncesinde-rusya-geri-adim-mi-atti/4104625.html, accessed on November 13, 2021.
[4] Robert Hamilton and Anna Mikulska, "Cooperation, Competition and Compartmentalization: Russian-Turkish Relations and Their

decreased after the Trans-Anatolian Natural Gas Pipeline (TANAP) project, Russian natural gas still accounts for an important share of Turkey's gas imports.[5] Russia's position as the prime supplier puts the Kremlin at a point where it can use its energy exports as a tool of leverage against Turkey. However, many experts agree that Turkish-Russian relations are mutually beneficial for broader strategic interests, which would, in fact, not favor Russia playing the energy card recklessly in day-to-day politics.[6]

The Black Sea as a Laboratory for Turkish-Russian 'Compartmentalized' Cooperation

Although Ankara and Moscow cooperate, first and foremost, in the energy sector alongside security and, finally, defense issues, their long-lasting rivalry in the Black Sea and the South Caucasus still stands.[7] Today, any changes in the power dynamics in the

---

Implications For the West", Foreign Policy Research Institute, Black Sea Initiative, April 2021, https://www.fpri.org/wp-content/uploads/2021/04/russian-turkish-relations-bssp.pdf

[5] Gunay Hajiyeva, "Turkey receives largest share of gas supplies from Caspian region", *Caspian News,* October 30, 2020, https://caspiannews.com/news-detail/turkey-receives-largest-share-of-gas-supplies-from-caspian-region-2020-10-30-2/#:~:text=Turkey%20Receives%20Largest%20Share%20of%20Gas%20Supplies%20From%20Caspian%20Region,-By%20Gunay%20Hajiyeva&text=Natural%20gas%20supplied%20from%20the,top%20importers%20to%20the%20country.

[6] Martin Russell, "Russia – Turkey relations: A fine line between competition and cooperation", EPRS – European Parliamentary Research Service", February, 2021, https://www.europarl.europa.eu/RegData/etudes/BRIE/2021/679090/EPRS_BRI(2021)679090_EN.pdf

[7] "Russia and Turkey in the Black Sea and South Causasus", *International Crisis Group,* June 28, 2018, https://d2071andvip0wj.cloudfront.net/250-russia-and-turkey.pdf

Black Sea would inevitably pertain to the wider Turkish-Russian geopolitical calculus[8].

The competition for hegemony in the Black Sea is not new. The Turco-Russian rivalry in the region dates back to imperial times. The Ottoman-Russian wars in the 18th and 19th centuries, particularly the Crimean War (1853–1856), loom large as prominent examples of this long-lasting bonanza.

The Black Sea has been under Russian influence since the 18th century with differing levels of efficiency.[9] Today, although Turkey challenges this hegemony by participating in wide-scale military drills with its NATO allies,[10] the "Kalibr'zation" of the Russian Navy—namely, the introduction of the Kalibr cruise missiles and its long-range conventional strike capability—has turned the tables. In tandem, the Russian Chief of the General Staff Valery Gerasimov claimed that the Russian fleet is now superior to Turkey in the Black Sea and that Russia can "easily strike the Bosphorus straits."[11] He added that this was made possible thanks to the new modernization packages, specifically submarines equipped with Kalibr cruise missiles and the Bastion coastal defense missiles that have boosted Russian military capabilities.

Regarding its policy in the Black Sea, Russia's stance and strategy in the region has remained relatively stable in the post-Soviet era.

---

[8] Giray Derman Saynur. "Analysis – Growing strategic competition in Black Sea and threat of war", *Anadolu Agency*, July 10, 2021, https://www.aa.com.tr/en/analysis/analysis-growing-strategic-competition-in-black-sea-and-threat-of-war/2300473

[9] New Strategy Center & Centro Studi Internazionali. "Militarization of the Black Sea and Eastern Mediterrenean theatres: A new challenge to NATO", 2019. https://www.cesi-italia.org/contents/Analisi/Militarization%20of%20the%20Black%20Sea.pdf

[10] https://www.dailysabah.com/business/energy/turkey-mulls-cooperation-with-us-firms-in-black-sea-gas-extraction

[11] Joshua Kucera. "Russia Claims 'Mastery' Over Turkey in Black Sea", *Eurasianet*, September 25, 2016, https://eurasianet.org/russia-claims-mastery-over-turkey-black-sea

294 | BLACK SEA BATTLEGROUND

The Kremlin, for sure, has high stakes in the basin. It is estimated that, at present, Russia fields approximately 25,000 personnel, 21 pieces of large warships, seven pieces of submarines, 200 support ships and almost 30,000 personnel in the Black Sea.[12]

More importantly, since the Russian intervention in Syria in 2015, the Black Sea—along with the Russian base in Crimea—has offered great outreach into the Mediterranean, turning the basin into a gateway of Russian presence on NATO's south plank.[13]

Following the illegal annexation of Crimea, the Russian Black Sea Fleet has been active in projecting power into the Mediterranean. Taking advantage of free passage through the Turkish straits—in fact, violating the Montreux regime with submarine combat activity back and forth from the Black Sea—Moscow has established a strategic naval route between the Black Sea Fleet and the enhanced naval base in Tartus in western Syria. The strategic route was then extended to Libya in North Africa.

Turkey's policy in the Black Sea is based on a *modus vivendi* and prioritizes a regional cooperation scheme with the other Black Sea countries, rather than solely depending on its Western allies.[14] In fact, this "regional ownership" strategy, has sometimes brought Turkey closer to Moscow's stance when it comes to objecting the outsider—or Western—influence in its north, which

---

[12] Giray Derman Saynur. "Analysis – Growing strategic competition in Black Sea and threat of war", *Anadolu Agency*, July 10, 2021, https://www.aa.com.tr/en/analysis/analysis-growing-strategic-competition-in-black-sea-and-threat-of-war/2300473
[13] Siri Neset, Mustafa Aydin, Evren Balta, Kaan Kutlu Ataç, Hasret Dikici Bilgin and Arne Strand. "Turkey as a regional security actor in the Black Sea, the Mediterrenean and the Levant region", *CMI Chr. Michelsen Institute*, June 2021, https://www.cmi.no/publications/file/7820-turkey-as-a-regional-security-actor-in-the-black-sea-the-mediterranean-and-the-levant-region.pdf
[14] Mitat Çelikpala and Emre Erşen. "Turkey's Black Sea Pradicament: Challenging or Accommodating Russia?", Perceptions, Summer 2018, http://sam.gov.tr/pdf/perceptions/Volume-XXIII/Summer-2018/sf-72-92.pdf

could spark additional tensions with Russia.[15] Thus, so far, Turkey has been a "careful counter-balancer" in the face of the Russian expedition while distancing itself from a hard-liner approach as a NATO ally. Although maritime security is a high priority, Ankara wants to maintain its sober stance and avoid any escalatory pathways in the Black Sea. Turkish Foreign Minister Mevlüt Çavuşoğlu, for example, has repeatedly called for calm in the sea basin, urging Ukraine and Russia to solve their problems through diplomacy.[16] In the meantime, however, Turkey did not refrain from selling drones to Kyiv. Overall, Turkish policy in the Black Sea can be summarized through three frames: being pragmatic, being transactional and keeping loyal to the *status quo.*

Turkey's aforementioned viewpoint produced results too. Over the past two decades, Turkey and Russia found multiple ways to establish a dialogue to discuss their agendas in the Black Sea. The 1992 Black Sea Economic Cooperation (BSEC) was one prominent example of such multilateral mechanisms.[17] At the time, the BSEC improved regional dialogue, especially in the areas of economic relations, energy and trade. Turkey also led the Operation Black Sea Harmony in 2004, which was a joint drill with other riparian countries in the region, including Russia, Ukraine and Romania.[18] While keeping its relations with Russia in check, Turkey also actively takes part in NATO military drills in the Black Sea. As a member of the transatlantic Alliance, Turkey participated in multiple joint maritime drills with other allies, including Greece, Romania, and the US. Led by Bulgaria in July 2021, the five-day

---

[15] Sergiu Celac. "The Regional Ownership Conundrum: The Case of the Organization of the BSEC", 2006.

[16] "Black Sea region must remain tension-free: Turkish FM Çavuşoğlu", *Daily Sabah,* April 23, 2021, https://www.dailysabah.com/politics/diplomacy/black-sea-region-must-remain-tension-free-turkish-fm-cavusoglu

[17] Oktay F. Tanrısever. "Turkey and Russia in the Black Sea Region: Dynamics of Cooperation and Conflict", Black Sea Discussion Paper Series – 2012/1, *EDAM,* https://edam.org.tr/wp-content/uploads/2017/03/bsdp3.pdf

[18] For more information on the operation, see "Operation Black Sea Harmony", https://www.dzkk.tsk.tr/en-US/Harekat/Content/operation-black-sea-harmony

296 | BLACK SEA BATTLEGROUND

maritime drill, Operation Breeze, with 13 NATO Allies looms large in this respect[19]. Until recently, Turkey's balanced approach has appealed to Russia. However, since the Ukrainian Donbas drone strikes mark a critical threshold, Turkey's blossoming defense partnerships, especially with the robotic warfare touch, can upset the carefully managed calculus with Russia.

Geopolitics of Turkish Drone Warfare Assets: Implications for Turkish-Russian 'Compartmentalized Competition'

Current Turkish foreign and security policy is shaped by three main drivers: attaining long-term strategic autonomy in key geopolitical affairs and self-sufficiency in defense technologies, building new partnerships to minimize Turkey's over-dependence on its traditional Western allies and avoiding direct confrontation with Russia. The latter bears significant implications for Turkish military policy,[20] while the first and second drivers can, interestingly, make it harder for Turkey to avoid a collision course with Russia.

Turkey enjoys a fast-growing defense sector. As of the early 2020s, the nation's defense technological and industrial base (DTIB) is well capable of introducing advanced conventional weaponry, such as land warfare platforms, corvettes, smart munitions, as well as electronic warfare and command-and-control assets.

While some critical areas within the Turkish defense industry are dependent on external suppliers, Turkish defense capabilities

---

[19] NATO. "NATO ships exercise in the Black Sea", July 19 2021, https://www.nato.int/cps/en/natohq/news_185879.htm, accessed on October 6, 2021.

[20] Siri Neşet, Mustafa Aydin, Evren Balta, Kaan Kutlu Ataç, Hasret Dikici Bilgin and Arne Strand. "Turkey as a regional security actor in the Black Sea, the Mediterrenean and the Levant region", CMI Chr. Michelsen Institute, June 2021, https://www.cmi.no/publications/file/7820-turkey-as-a-regional-security-actor-in-the-black-sea-the-mediterranean-and-the-levant-region.pdf

have seen a significant improvement in self-sufficiency over the past two decades, witnessing a decrease from some 80 percent of foreign-reliance to around 20 percent.[21] Although this surely marked a critical improvement, whether the crucial components are locally produced or foreign supplied makes a huge difference regarding operational sovereignty—namely, the ability to sustain military operations without outsider contribution.

The uptrend in Turkish military-industrial capabilities with unmanned aerial systems (UAS), in particular the MALE (medium range/long endurance) and tactical classes, has started bringing strategic results with high geopolitical importance, such as in the Second Karabakh War. The critical issue is that these strategic results with geopolitical importance have started to undermine Russia's freedom of movement in its undisputed backyard. To better grasp the ongoing trend, one should first develop a solid understanding of Turkey's drone warfare agenda.

In fact, drone warfare has now turned into the crown jewel for Turkey's military strategic posture. Recently, the Turkish Armed Forces have started receiving the new Akinci UAS. Manufactured by Baykar, the makers of the "Pantsir-hunter" Bayraktar TB-2, the Akinci UAS comes with heavy firepower with 1.5 tons of combat payload and flexible concepts of operations (CONOPS). More importantly, along with other key achievements, such as TUSAS' Aksungur drone[22] with anti-submarine warfare capabilities, STM's Kargu[23] and Alpagu with advanced artificial intelligence

---

[21] "Turkey among top four nations in production of armed drones: Erdoğan", *Hurriyet Daily News,* August 17, 2021, https://www.hurriyetdailynews.com/turkey-among-top-four-nations-in-production-of-armed-drones-erdogan-167153, accessed on October 5, 2021.
[22] TUSAŞ, "Aksungur", https://www.tusas.com/urunler/iha/yuksek-faydali-yuk-kapasitesi/aksungur, accessed on November 15, 2021.
[23] STM, "KARGU", https://www.stm.com.tr/en/kargu-autonomous-tactical-multi-rotor-attack-uav, accessed on November 15, 2021.

298 | BLACK SEA BATTLEGROUND

algorithms, Meteksan and Ares Shipyard-made ULAQ[24] unmanned naval surface combat system, along with newly introduced[25] unmanned ground vehicles, Turkey's defense industry has developed an exponentially growing know-how on robotic warfare solutions.

It is not only the platforms and systems but also the munitions that brought success. Turkish rocket and missile manufacturer Roketsan equipped Turkish drones with MAM-L and MAM-C smart munitions, which boosted target precision by minimizing the margin of error.[26] The MAM-L, in particular, offered versatile solutions against a broad target set through a variety of warhead configurations. MAM-L's tandem charge is designed to destroy land warfare platforms equipped with reactive armor, while the thermobaric variant is particularly effective against targets deployed in closed settings and bunkers. In addition, the high-explosive blast warhead allows for striking troop concentrations and light-armored platforms accurately and effectively.[27]

Turkey's drone warfare success has, subsequently, translated into defense sales and, more importantly, a geopolitical outreach asset. The latter is of significance as an important part of Turkey's drone sales that take place in the Russian hinterland.

---

[24] Can Kasapoğlu, "ANALYSIS - Turkey's robotic warfare efforts set sail to high-seas" *Anadolu Agency*, March 2, 2021, https://www.aa.com.tr/en/analysis/analysis-turkey-s-robotic-warfare-efforts-set-sail-to-high-seas/2161762, accessed on November 15, 2021.

[25] Ayşe Böcüoğlu Bodur, "İHA'larda edinilen tecrübe deniz ve kara araçlarına taşınıyor", *Anadolu Agency,* June 26, 2021, https://www.aa.com.tr/tr/bilim-teknoloji/ihalarda-edinilen-tecrube-deniz-ve-kara-araclarina-tasiniyor/2286832, accessed on November 15, 2021.

[26] The Presidency for Defense Industries Turkey, *Twitter,* accessed October 7, 2021, https://twitter.com/SavunmaSanayii/status/1235547985175556096

[27] Roketsan, "MAM-L", accessed on October 5, 2021 from https://www.roketsan.com.tr/en/product/ mam-l-smart-micro-munition/

Turkish drones are becoming the best available solutions in international weapons markets given their price and combat effectiveness. Following the Azerbaijani achievements in the Second Karabakh War, Turkish UAS manufacturers enjoyed a spike in export clientele. In fact, the Turkish model of drone warfare is becoming quite popular on Russia's doorstep, which further complicates the issue for Moscow.[28]

Ukraine is the most notable example in this respect. In 2019, Kyiv officially signed an agreement to procure Turkish drones.[29] Subsequently, the Ukrainian government made additional requests to purchase more Bayraktar TB-2 UAVs for its navy.[30] Russia reacted to the procurement, voicing concerns about Turkish robotic warfare solutions spreading in its geopolitical surroundings.[31] Following the Ukrainian military's kinetic drone strikes in Donbas, these concerns have turned into a real threat calculus.

Poland is yet another significant market. In light of the lessons learned from the Karabakh War, the Polish strategic community has already highlighted the Turkey-provided UAVs as key enablers of Azerbaijan's success.[32] At the time of writing, Poland

---

[28] Ömer Özkızılcık, "The 'Turkish Model' is resonating in Eastern Europe, and Moscow is worried", TRT World, June 2, 2021, https://www.trtworld.com/opinion/the-turkish-model-is-resonating-in-eastern-europe-and-moscow-is-worried-47191

[29] "Ukraine, Turkey have signed deal for 12 Bayraktar TB2 UAVs, Poroshenko says", Daily Sabah, January 12, 2019, https://www.dailysabah.com/defense/2019/01/12/ukraine-turkey-have-signed-deal-for-12-bayraktar-tb2-uavs-poroshenko-says

[30] "Ukraine considers buying 48 Bayraktar TB2 drones from Turkey", Daily Sabah, October 6, 2020, https://www.dailysabah.com/business/defense/ukraine-considers-buying-48-bayraktar-tb2-drones-from-turkey

[31] "Russia to scrutinize military cooperation with Turkey, if it supplies drones to Ukraine", TASS, April 21, 2021, https://tass.com/politics/1281075

[32] "The Military Dimension of the Conflict over Nagorno-Karabakh", PISM, November 26, 2020,

300 | BLACK SEA BATTLEGROUND

became the first NATO ally to procure the Turkish Bayraktar TB-2s, adding a real transatlantic edge to Turkey's drone sales on the Alliance's Eastern Flank.[33]

The bad news for Russia is that the Baltic allies can follow suit. Notably, Latvia seems to be the next ally opting for Turkey's unmanned systems, opening the gates of the Baltic region to Turkish arms manufacturers.[34] Soon enough, the Kremlin may well witness its Western and Southern military districts surrounded by Turkish drone warfare assets.

Thanks to its drone capabilities, Turkey is now able to neutralize threats at their source, which has made it a pro-active, and in some cases, even preemptive regional actor rather than a defensive-minded one. The drone industry is also offering new routes to establish strategic partnerships, which can further increase Turkey's leverage and bargaining power. On a particular worrying note for Moscow, Turkish drone warfare solutions have attracted international attention due to their efficiency against Soviet-Russian weaponry. Turkish drones also proved themselves to be the true force multipliers in combat in the world's most hostile battlegrounds, including Syria, Libya and Karabakh. In fact, Operation Spring Shield in Idlib, in early 2020, marked the Bayraktar TB-2's biggest moment of glory, hinting at what can follow. Throughout the campaign, Turkey's Bayraktar TB-2 and ANKA-S UAS have inflicted heavy casualties on the Syrian Arab Army, lacking enough sensor-network capabilities. Such was the fate of the Armenian formations in Karabakh soon after.

---

https://pism.pl/publications/The_Military_Dimension_of_the_Conflict_over_NagornoKarabakh

[33] "Poland buys 24 Turkish drones in first for NATO and EU", Daily Sabah, May 24, 2021, https://www.dailysabah.com/business/defense/poland-buys-24-turkish-drones-in-first-for-nato-and-eu

[34] "Latvia hints at becoming second NATO ally to buy Turkish drones", Daily Sabah, June 8, 2021, https://www.dailysabah.com/business/defense/latvia-hints-at-becoming-second-nato-ally-to-buy-turkish-drones

The Second Karabakh War was a milestone in Turkish-Azerbaijani military rapprochement. In essence, the war was fought between two strategic paradigms: the Armenian belligerent's Sovietic, 20th-century warfare against Azerbaijan's modern, high-tech military strategy. The latter triumphed, proving the importance of technological supremacy and flexible CONOPS in modern warfare. During the Karabakh War, Baku successfully used high-end defense technology, particularly Turkish and Israeli drones, at a high-operational tempo. Azerbaijan followed a networked approach to optimize its drone capabilities, by integrating them with friendly sensors and land units. The swift targeting of the enemy's air defense systems quickly changed the balance of power right at the outset of the war, while the networked approach allowed for enhanced coordination and communication between UAVs and land-based-fire-support units. In a way, Azerbaijan closely mirrored Turkey's strategy against the Syrian Arab Army in Operation Spring Shield, as Turkish drones fast-attacked the Syrian mobile (SAM) systems (including Russian Pantsirs) right at the beginning of the conflict.[35] In full resemblance, the Azerbaijani military used drones—mainly the Bayraktar TB-2 and the Israeli Harpo/Harmy kamikaze drones/loitering munitions—to destroy air defense during the Second Karabakh War. Within a week, the Azerbaijani Armed Forces had destroyed a total of 60 SAM systems, which mimicked the Turkish hunt for the Syrian Pantsirs during Operation Spring Shield[36].

Along with the Karabakh War, Turkish drones' entry into the Ukrainian defense market also raised brows in Russia—as

---

[35] Joseph Trevithick and Thomas Newdick, "Everything we Know About the Fighting that has Erupted Between Armenia and Azerbaijan," *The Drive*, September 28, 2020, accessed October 5, 2021, https://www.thedrive.com/the-war-zone/36777/everything-we-knowabout-the-fighting-that-has-erupted-between-armenia-and-azerbaijan

[36] Azerbaijani Ministry of Defense, *Twitter*, accessed October 12, 2021, https://twitter.com/wwwmodgovaz?ref_src=twsrc%5Egoogle%7Ctwcamp%5Eserp%7Ctwgr%5Eauthor

302 | BLACK SEA BATTLEGROUND

Turkish robotic warfare solutions can strengthen Kyiv's hand vis-à-vis the Russian invasion.[37]

Probably for the first time in recent history, a nation's defense body asked for a specific weapon via Twitter during an ongoing war.[38] This happened between Ukraine and Turkey, showcasing a special relationship in the Black Sea. In this regard, the potential synergy that Turkish-Ukrainian strategic ties could bring is another area of concern for the Russians. Turkey and Ukraine have previously worked together on various defense-related issues. They currently cooperate in critical segments of the defense industry, such as on jet engines, and have penned remarkable partnership agreements such as the Joint Ukrainian-Turkish Commission on Defense Industrial Cooperation.

In the past few years, both countries have also started some joint initiatives in drone production. In return for a generous technology transfer and affordable military solutions, Ukraine makes crucial contributions to the Turkish defense industry. Notably, Turkey's latest high-end combat drone Akinci (Raider)'s Type C will be equipped with Ivachenko-Progress Ukrainian AI-450T turboprop engines. Both countries have taken steps to co-produce the Turkish armed drone Akinci, a project that they allegedly consider amongst their top priorities[39].

The Turco-Ukrainian strategic partnership also manifests itself in the Black Sea. Recently, Baykar and the state's military-technical conglomerate's member, Ukroboronprom, signed a joint venture

---

[37] Yuri Lapaiev. "The Akinci Strike Drone and Ukrainian-Turkish Defense Cooperation", *Jamestown Foundation,* February 12, 2020. https://jamestown.org/program/the-akinci-strike-drone-and-ukrainian-turkish-defense-cooperation/, accessed October 2, 2021.
[38] Ministry of Defense of Ukraine, *Twitter,* accessed June 25, 2022, https://twitter.com/defenceu/status/1534747114294726656?s=24&t=4GBdXml-5lsDVaR-cpW-gQ
[39] Yuri Lapaiev. "The Akinci Drone and Ukrainian-Turkish Defense Cooperation", *Jamestown Foundation*, February 12, 2020, https://jamestown.org/program/the-akinci-strike-drone-and-ukrainian-turkish-defense-cooperation/, accessed October 2, 2021.

Turkish Drone Strategy in the Black Sea and Beyond | 303

deal—namely, the Black Sea Shield program.[40] The move was significant, as it opened up new avenues for cooperation, such as the co-production of aerospace engines and joint production of missile technologies.[41] In fact, the program already has had positive implications, as some Turkish defense companies are currently exploring outsourcing parts of their production or establishing joint production lines with Ukraine. Some leading Turkish defense conglomerates, such as Aselsan, are expanding their portfolios to cover the Ukrainian market. The company signed lucrative deals with local firms to produce active protection systems and state-of-the-art military communication items in local production facilities set in Kyiv.[42]

Turkey's key projects benefit from this improving relationship. Ukrainian sources claim that the countries are in negotiations for a co-produced unmanned fighter jet (MIUS) that would provide an indigenous solution that can complement Turkey's unmanned aerial capabilities. Baykar will chief the unmanned aircraft's production, which will use Ukrainian-manufactured engines[43].

In the ongoing war, Turkish TB-2s have already scored significant gains against Russian ground and naval units. Especially in urban settings, the Ukrainian military masterfully used its drones to strike the Kremlin's critical kinetic targets, such as overstretched supply and logistics routes. In the maritime warfare segment, Kyiv benefited from the Turkish drones to successfully identify

---

[40] Yuri Lapaiev. "The Akinci Strike Drone and Ukrainian-Turkish Defense Cooperation", *Jamestown Foundation*, February 12, 2020. https://jamestown.org/program/the-akinci-strike-drone-and-ukrainian-turkish-defense-cooperation/, accessed October 2, 2021.
[41] Yuri Lapaiev. "The Akinci Strike Drone and Ukrainian-Turkish Defense Cooperation", *Jamestown Foundation*, February 12, 2020. https://jamestown.org/program/the-akinci-strike-drone-and-ukrainian-turkish-defense-cooperation/, accessed on 2 October 2021.
[42] Göksel Yıldırım, "ASELSAN'dan ihracat rekoru". *Anadolu Agency*, December 20, 2019, https://www.aa.com.tr/tr/ekonomi/aselsandan-ihracat-rekoru/1679027, accessed October 2, 2021.
[43] *Ukrainian Defense Review*, January – March 2020, https://issuu.com/ukrainian_defense_review/docs/udr1_magazine_issuu/s/10208333

and strike some of Russia's most significant naval assets, including the *Moskva* missile cruiser, the flagship of the Russian Black Sea Fleet. Using its drones as critical ISTAR assets and using UAVs to assist strikes and ground unit movements, Ukraine's adoption of the "Turkish way" of drone warfare has reminded the international military community about the importance of network-centric warfare.

The Limits of Compartmentalization

While it acts carefully to avoid antagonizing the incumbent *siloviki* rule, the Turkish administration well knows that the drone transfers are now a powerful deterrent against Russia in the Black Sea. In fact, the Bayraktar TB2's successful use by Azerbaijan in the Second Karabakh War was an eye-opener for Russian defense planners. This is especially relevant for the "area of privileged interests"—or near abroad—an area that Russian analysts define as the post-Soviet land mass that constitute Russia's immediate "sphere of influence."[44] Notably, Turkey's ability to change the military balance of power in the Armenian-Azerbaijani conflict through drone warfare transfers marks a stress test for the future of Russia's hegemony in its once undisputed backyard.[45] In a way, Turkey's drone capabilities provided the Erdogan government with drastically increased leverage and bargaining power against the Kremlin, especially on NATO's eastern flank and in the Caucasus[46].

---

[44] Nicholas Velazquez. "Rise of a 'Drone Superpower?' Turkish Drones Upending Russia's Near Abroad", *Geopolitical Monitor,* February 9, 2021, https://www.geopoliticalmonitor.com/turkish-drones/

[45] Nicholas Velazquez. "Rise of a 'Drone Superpower?' Turkish Drones Upending Russia's Near Abroad", *Geopolitical Monitor,* February 9, 2021, https://www.geopoliticalmonitor.com/turkish-drones/

[46] Omer Ozkizilcik. "The Turkish model is resonating in Eastern Europe, and Moscow is worried", *TRT World,* June 2, 2021, https://www.trtworld.com/opinion/the-turkish-model-is-resonating-in-eastern-europe-and-moscow-is-worried-47191, accessed October 5, 2021.

The Turco-Ukrainian deal on the Bayraktar TB-2 marks a textbook example of the aforementioned leverage boost trend. Apart from the Ukrainian army, who has already used Turkey-manufactured drones in Donbas, the Ukrainian Navy's plans reflect the pronounced geopolitical dimension of Turkey's drone sales. Ukrainian Navy Chief of Staff Admiral Oleksiy Neizhpapa announced that the drones will also be used in the Black Sea and in the Sea of Azov.[47] While the use of Turkish UASs against Russian satellites and client entities, such as the Syrian Arab Army or the Armenian occupation regime in Karabakh, is one thing, boosting Ukraine's drone warfare definitely marks a whole different chapter.

By forging new strategic partnerships with its drone-export clientele, Turkey places itself as a rising regional power in southeastern Europe. In fact, some experts argue that Turkish foreign policy has been successful in building a new geo-strategic axis by forming alliances with Western-leaning post-Soviet and former Warsaw Pact nations, with significant outreach to the GUAM group (Azerbaijan, Ukraine, Georgia and Moldova).[48] This axis is important in energy- and security-related agendas vis-à-vis the Russian Federation. Turkey recently agreed to rely more on gas supply from Azerbaijan, which bothered Russia, as the TANAP pipeline enables Azerbaijan to become a major gas exporter to the European energy market, which threatens Russia's hegemony.[49]

---

[47] Tayfun Ozberk. "Turkey delivers first armed drone to Ukrainian Navy, much to Russia's ire", *Defense News,* July 26, 2021, https://www.defensenews.com/unmanned/2021/07/26/turkey-delivers-first-armed-drone-to-ukraine-much-to-russias-ire/

[48] Taras Kuzio. "Turkey Forges a New Geo-Strategic Axis from Azerbaijan to Ukraine", *RUSI,* November 18, 2020, https://rusi.org/explore-our-research/publications/commentary/turkey-forges-new-geo-strategic-axis-azerbaijan-ukraine

[49] Rauf Mammadov. "Azerbaijan's Gas Reaches Europe", *Jamestown Foundation,* January 19, 2021, https://jamestown.org/program/azerbaijans-gas-reaches-europe/

306 | BLACK SEA BATTLEGROUND

The second-dimension rests on Turkish regional policy, which is characterized by forming strong, strategic alliances in a contested region that Russia wants to see under its undisputed authority. In doing so, Turkey not only emphasizes its presence and status in the South Caucasus, but it also builds key partnerships of special geostrategic value that serve its interests in the Black Sea. For example, Turkey is one of the actors rebuilding the Ukrainian Navy with MILGEM-class corvettes and drone warfare weaponry.[50] Rebuilding the Ukrainian Navy, for starters, goes well beyond a defense transaction deal. It is rather a counter-balancing move against Russian dominance in the Black Sea.

Conclusion

Despite its ongoing divergence with the West, when it comes to the post-Soviet space, Turkey is NATO. In a hypothetical scenario in which Turkey closely aligns with Russia, the Turkish-Ukrainian partnership would inevitably come to an end. In tandem, Georgia would feel increased pressure with no geographic opening to the West. Besides, Azerbaijan's natural geopolitical ally will no longer have a transatlantic security bridge. But above all, the Black Sea dynamics would be forever changed, should Turkey opt out of the transatlantic Alliance. As US General Ben Hodges, former commander of the US Army Europe, puts in perspective, "Russia's concerns [in the Black Sea] are aggressive, but also defensive. It fears growing Western and, in particular, Turkish influence in the Black Sea region, which could turn the Black Sea into a 'NATO lake.'"[51]

To date, Turkey has had to cautiously balance its cooperation and competition patterns with Russia. This sober and carefully calculated foreign policy understanding has long manifested itself in various Turkish administrations' stances on the Montreux Convention. With its drone warfare edge seeing historic success and its export clientele growing in Russia's strategic hinterland,

---

[50] "Migrem Class Multimission Corvettes", *Naval Technology*, https://www.naval-technology.com/projects/milgem_class_corvett/
[51] Ben Hodges, *The Black Sea or a Black Hole?*, CEPA, 2021. p.3.

interestingly, Turkey's *marge de manoeuvre* in pursuing its traditional Russia policy may have hit a critical threshold.

While Azerbaijan and the Turkish military targeted Russian clients before, the Ukrainian drone strikes in Donbas mark a whole different story. From now on, it remains to be seen how the Turkish administration will fine-tune its compartmentalized cooperation and competition patterns with Russia.

Author Biographies

Dr. John C. K. Daly is a Eurasian foreign affairs and defense policy expert for The Jamestown Foundation and a non-resident fellow at the Central Asia-Caucasus Institute in Washington, DC.

Lt. Col. (ret.) Glen Grant served 37 years in the British Army in a wide variety of postings and jobs. He was the first advisor to the Ukrainian Ministry of Defense when the war started in 2014, at Ukrainian ministerial request. Since then, Lt. Col. Grant has worked in Ukraine as a defense contractor for the United States and as a project manager in the Ukrainian Ministry of Defense on a UK project in defense housing, in which he was both a member of the Reform Office and on the General Staff reform committees and working groups. He has been a defense analyst with the Ukrainian Institute for the Future and now is the operations director in the new World Trade Center Kyiv. He keeps close daily contact with serving and former military, military nongovernmental organizations and volunteers who support the front-line forces. He publishes regularly about Ukraine, the Black Sea and Baltic regions with the *Kyiv Post* and Baltic Security Foundation. He has additionally worked as an SME for the United States in 11 other Central and Eastern European countries since 2010, giving him an in-depth view of how the US conducts the defense reform business.

Alla Hurska is an associate expert at the International Center for Policy Studies (Kyiv) and a research assistant at the University of Alberta. Hurska's research at the University of Alberta concerns geo-economic and geopolitical issues in the post-Soviet area, including the Arctic region and the geopolitics of gas and oil. She is also interested in the role of Russian propaganda campaigns in influencing public opinion and decision-making in the post-Soviet countries. Her articles and expert comments have been solicited by international think tanks, research institutions and news outlets, including *Diplomaatia* (Estonia), ICPS (Ukraine), *Kyiv Post* (Ukraine) and, in Spain, CIDOB, Autonomous University of Barcelona, *El Periódico de Catalunya*, and *El Confidencial*.

Author Biographies | 309

Ihor Kabanenko is a retired admiral with the Ukrainian Navy. From 1983 to 1990, he served in the Soviet Navy in various positions up to commander of the ship and chief of staff of the Missile Ships Division. Since 1993, he has served in the Ukrainian Armed Forces. He was appointed to the positions of chief of operations and chief of staff of the Ukrainian Navy, the military representative of Ukraine to NATO, chief of operations of the Ukrainian Armed Forces, and the first deputy chief of defense. He retired in 2013, with the rank of admiral. From May to August 2014, Admiral Kabanenko served as the Ukrainian deputy Minister of Defense, and from August to October 2014—as Deputy minister of fefense of Ukraine for European Integration. Currently, he is the president of UA.RPA (Ukrainian Advanced Research Project Agency), which focuses on high-tech solutions and products for defense.

Dr. Can Kasapoglu is a defense analyst. Dr. Kasapoglu holds an MSci degree from the Turkish Military Academy and a PhD from the Turkish War College. He was an Eisenhower fellow at the NATO Defense College in Rome and a visiting scholar at the NATO Cooperative Cyber Defense Center of Excellence in Tallinn. Currently, Dr. Kasapoglu is the director of the defense and security program at the Istanbul-based think tank, EDAM. He previously held research posts at other reputable think tanks, such as the SWP of Germany, FRS of France and the BESA Center of Israel. His work can be followed on Twitter @EdamDefense.

Dr. Dumitru Minzarari is a lecturer in security studies at the Baltic Defense College. Before this, he was a research associate with the German Institute for International and Security Affairs in Berlin, covering Russia's domestic, foreign and security policies. Dr. Minzarari also had tenures both as a fellow and visiting scholar with the research division of the NATO Defense College in Rome. He received a PhD in political science from the University of Michigan–Ann Arbor and an MA in international affairs from Columbia University in New York. Previously, he worked as the secretary of state (for defense policy and international cooperation) with the Moldovan Ministry of Defense; held expert positions in OSCE field missions in Georgia, Ukraine and

Kyrgyzstan; and worked with a number of think tanks in Eastern Europe.

Col. (ret.) Valeri R. Ratchev is currently a security and defense observer, international consultant and university lecturer. He provides consultancy, feasibility research and professional development training to NATO, OSCE and DCAF projects in Ukraine and several other East European countries. He retired from the army in 2005, after a 34-year career, and moved to the Ministry of Foreign Affairs as the ambassador-at-large of Bulgaria to Iraq. He ended his public service as chief of staff to the Bulgarian defense and foreign affairs ministers (2009–2013).

Capt. (ret.) Andrii Ryzhenko is a former officer in the Ukrainian Navy. He retired from the Ukrainian Armed Forces at the rank of Navy Captain. Capt. Ryzhenko served over 35 years at sea and ashore: aboard surface warships, at Ukrainian Navy headquarters on maritime tactics and PfP exercises, and as a defense and strategic planner. He also worked on Ukrainian Navy transformation to transatlantic standards and on the contribution to NATO-led operations and NATO Response Forces. He served in NATO on partner nation units' evaluation methodology (OCC E&F) at SHAPE (Mons, Belgium), and he developed maritime aspects of the National Security Strategy in Ukraine.

Dr. Sergey Sukhankin is a senior fellow at The Jamestown Foundation and an advisor at Gulf State Analytics (Washington, DC). He received a PhD in contemporary political and social history from the Autonomous University of Barcelona. His areas of interest include Kaliningrad and the Baltic Sea region, Russian information and cyber security, A2/AD and its interpretation in Russia, the Arctic region and the development of Russian private military companies since the outbreak of the Syrian Civil War. He has consulted or briefed with CSIS (Canada), DIA (US), and the European Parliament. His project discussing the activities of Russian PMCs, "War by Other Means," informed the United Nations General Assembly report titled "Use of Mercenaries as a Means of Violating Human Rights and Impeding the Exercise of the Right of Peoples to Self-Determination." He is based in Edmonton, Alberta, Canada.

Todor Tagarev is a professor at the Institute of Information and Communications Technology of the Bulgarian Academy of Sciences and head of the Center for Security and Defense Management. On several occasions, he has moved from academia to government and back and served as minister of defense in Bulgaria's caretaker government, from March to May 2013. Tagarev has significant experience in leading interdisciplinary and international research, most recently focused on cybersecurity and crisis management

George Vişan is an associate researcher at the Romania Energy Center.